Southeast Asia in World History

The
New
Oxford
World
History

Southeast Asia in World History

Craig A. Lockard

OXFORD
UNIVERSITY PRESS

2009

OXFORD

UNIVERSITY PRESS

Oxford University Press, Inc., publishes works that further
Oxford University's objective of excellence
in research, scholarship, and education.

Oxford New York
Auckland Cape Town Dar es Salaam Hong Kong Karachi
Kuala Lumpur Madrid Melbourne Mexico City Nairobi
New Delhi Shanghai Taipei Toronto

With offices in
Argentina Austria Brazil Chile Czech Republic France Greece
Guatemala Hungary Italy Japan Poland Portugal Singapore
South Korea Switzerland Thailand Turkey Ukraine Vietnam

Copyright © 2009 by Oxford University Press, Inc.

Published by Oxford University Press, Inc.
198 Madison Avenue, New York, New York 10016

www.oup.com

Oxford is a registered trademark of Oxford University Press

Library of Congress Cataloging-in-Publication Data
Lockard, Craig A.
Southeast Asia in world history / Craig Lockard.
p. cm. — (New Oxford world history)
Includes index.
ISBN 978-0-19-516075-8; 978-0-19-533811-9 (pbk.)
1. Southeast Asia—History. I. Title.
DS525.L65 2009
959—dc22   2008029792

Printed in the United States of America
on acid-free paper

*Frontispiece: Most Southeast Asians, like these farmers in the Philippines,
planted their rice under water.*
Library of Congress (LC-USZ62-113571)

Contents

Editors' Preface

Green lands and blue waters, lowlands and highlands, peasants and kings, tradition and modernity, continuity and change, and East and West: these are a few of the many analytical constructs that scholars have used to fashion their historical narratives about Southeast Asia. They have resorted to such seemingly contradictory notions to portray and evoke the remarkable historical landscape of that region, a terrain whose richness and variety stems from its role as a crossroads where political, economic, social, religious, and cultural forces emanating from both within and without intersected. Indeed, the experiences of peoples living within the boundaries of the diverse areas of mainland and island Southeast Asia have been shaped by internal dynamics as well as by influences originating from the great civilizations of China and India and, more recently, from Europe and the United States.

Bounded by South Asia on the west, China on the north, and the Pacific Ocean on the east, Southeast Asia today includes eleven countries: Brunei, Cambodia, Indonesia, Laos, Malaysia, Myanmar (Burma), Philippines, Singapore, Thailand, East Timor (Timor Leste), and Vietnam. What binds them together but also sets them apart makes for a rich history that Craig Lockard recounts elegantly and in detail. His account begins with the "ancient roots" of the region when its peoples emerged as "among the world's earliest farmers" and continues with their stories as they became denizens of cultures, societies, and states that were drawn into wider worlds.

This book is part of the New Oxford World History, an innovative series that offers readers an informed, lively, and up-to-date history of the world and its people that represents a significant change from the "old" world history. Only a few years ago, world history generally amounted to a history of the West—Europe and the United States—with small amounts of information from the rest of the world. Some versions of the old world history drew attention to every part of the world *except* Europe and the United States. Readers of that kind of world history could get the impression that somehow the rest of the world was made up of exotic people who had strange customs and spoke difficult languages. Still another kind of "old" world history presented the story of areas or peoples of the world by focusing primarily on the achievements of great civilizations. One learned of great buildings, influential world religions, and mighty rulers but little of ordinary people or more general economic and social patterns. Interactions among the world's peoples were often told from only one perspective.

This series tells world history differently. First, it is comprehensive, covering all countries and regions of the world and investigating the total human experience—even those of so-called peoples without histories living far from the great civilizations. "New" world historians thus share in common an interest in all of human history, even going back millions of years before there were written human records. A few "new" world histories even extend their focus to the entire universe, a "big history" perspective that dramatically shifts the beginning of the story back to the Big Bang. Some see the "new" global framework of world history today as viewing the world from the vantage point of the moon, as one scholar put it. We agree. But we also want to take a close-up view, analyzing and reconstructing the significant experiences of all of humanity.

This is not to say that everything that has happened everywhere and in all time periods can be recovered or is worth knowing, but that there is much to be gained by considering both the separate and interrelated stories of different societies and cultures. Making these connections is still another crucial ingredient of the "new" world history. It emphasizes connectedness and interactions of all kinds—cultural, economic, political, religious, and social—involving peoples, places, and processes. It makes comparisons and finds similarities. Emphasizing both the comparisons and interactions is critical to developing a global framework that can deepen and broaden historical understanding, whether the focus is on a specific country or region or on the whole world.

The rise of the new world history as a discipline comes at an opportune time. The interest in world history in schools and among the general public is vast. We travel to one another's nations, converse and work with people around the world, and are changed by global events. War and peace affect populations worldwide as do economic conditions and the state of our environment, communications, and health and medicine. The New Oxford World History presents local histories in a global context and gives an overview of world events seen through the eyes of ordinary people. This combination of the local and the global further defines the new world history. Understanding the workings of global and local conditions in the past gives us tools for examining our own world and for envisioning the interconnected future that is in the making.

Bonnie G. Smith
Anand A. Yang

Southeast Asia
in World History

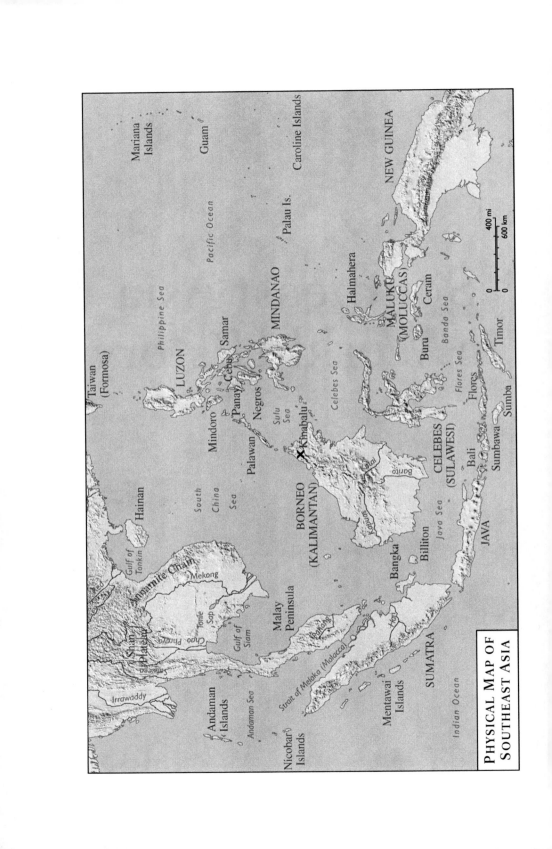

PHYSICAL MAP OF
SOUTHEAST ASIA

Introduction

As the day broke one morning a thousand years ago, the sun's rays drifted westward across the Pacific. Coming to the offshore islands of Asia, the light shone on the spires of countless Buddhist temples, pagodas, and colossal statues of a serene-faced Buddha dotting the hillsides and cities of Japan, Korea, China, Vietnam, Cambodia, and Burma. In Central Java, at Borobodur, the world's largest human-made monument sat on a hilltop amidst the lush green landscape of rice fields stretching to volcanic mountains. This magnificent temple, which had taken decades and thousands of artists and workers to build, was covered with spectacular carvings of the teachings of the Buddha, an Indian sage who lived many centuries earlier and thousands of miles west of Java. Borobodur and other Buddhist temples were some of the most obvious testimonies to the increasing connections between distant societies that eventually resulted in the links and interdependence, often described by the term "globalization," in our contemporary world. The Buddhist temples erected in the first millennium CE as well as the Islamic mosques and Christian churches that were built in Southeast Asia in the middle of the second millennium CE accompanied the spread of traders, ideas, technologies, and adventurers. The increasing connections between distant peoples and cultures meant that the world would never again be the same.

Five centuries ago the first European ships arrived in Southeast Asia, and in the following centuries the region became a major participant in the world economy, providing many valuable resources to Europe and North America. Eleven decades ago the United States became involved in Southeast Asia. This initial U.S. commitment led eventually to a long war in Vietnam that spilled over into Cambodia and Laos—a conflict that touched the lives of millions of Southeast Asians and Americans.

Since the early twentieth century, scholars have debated the identity of Southeast Asia and whether it even constitutes a coherent region comparable to South Asia, the Middle East, or Europe, regions whose diverse peoples share many common traditions. Southeast Asia was described by ancient Indians as the golden peninsula, and by later observers as the crossroads of Asia, the source of fabulous wealth and valuable resources where Chinese, Indian, and Islamic traditions came together. Containing roughly half of the total land area of Europe but about the same size as South Asia (centered on India), Southeast Asia is separated from the rest of Eurasia by significant mountain and water barriers. Southeast Asian peoples developed next door to two great, densely populated societies, China and India, a situation that helped shape their cultures as people and ideas moved across borders. Although some scholars place Vietnam in the East Asian sphere, Burma in South Asia, or the Philippines in the Western Pacific, in this book the term Southeast Asia refers to those lands lying east of modern Bangladesh and India, south of China, north of Australia, and west of Papua New Guinea, and it includes the modern nations of Burma (Myanmar), Thailand, Laos, Cambodia, Vietnam, Malaysia, Singapore, Brunei, Indonesia, East Timor (Timor Leste), and the Philippines.

Southeast Asian peoples were shaped in part by their geography. In 1369 Prince Phu, the son of the Vietnamese emperor, presented a poem to a departing ambassador from China, which concluded, "The Tan Vien mountain is green, the Lo River is blue./May you have a favorable wind as you fly into the land of many-colored clouds."[1] The green lands and blue rivers, lakes, and seas together have nourished the people throughout Southeast Asia for millennia. As one Malay proverb suggests, "where there is water there are fish," a source of livelihood. Water also fostered trade and nourished crops, but too little or too much water could prove devastating. As a result, water also figured strongly in myths, beliefs, and customs throughout the region.

Although historians of Southeast Asia have tried to explain the diverse and distinctive societies and cultural traditions that arose in the region—societies that were very different from those in other parts of the world—they have also necessarily paid attention to the connections with other areas. The encounters of Southeast Asians with peoples from other regions greatly influenced the states, religions, arts, and economies that developed. Like the Japanese, Southeast Asians borrowed ideas from others. Like the Chinese, Indians, and West Africans, they supplied valuable commodities, such as gold and spices, to the world. And like the Arabs, Indians, and Chinese, they transported trade goods around vast oceans. Themes such as borrowing and adaptation, migration and ethnic mixing, the diffusion of religions, maritime trade,

Western expansion and colonialism, and the rise of the global economy linked Southeast Asia to world history.

Today Southeast Asia and its people are closely tied to nations around the globe. As they have done throughout history, Southeast Asians still mix outside influences with their own distinctive traditions. In a Buddhist temple in northern Thailand, for example, a young man kneels to make an offering of flowers and food, wearing a shirt that reads "Property of the Green Bay Packers." Similarly, a group of Muslim schoolgirls visits a historic Hindu temple in Indonesia. From under the hem of one of their long skirts peeks a pair of high-top sneakers.

Southeast Asians have deep roots in the past, but they also participate in the contemporary world. Southeast Asia offers a fascinating blend of tradition and modernity, old and new, where East and West meet and mix, but not without some pain. This convergence of peoples and ideas reflects age-old patterns. In recent decades several million Southeast Asians have settled in the United States, Canada, Australia, and Europe, a continuation of migration patterns that go back centuries.

Most of the modern nations in Southeast Asia came into existence in their present form in the nineteenth and twentieth centuries. Throughout history states rose and fell and the boundaries between them regularly fluctuated. Five hundred years ago, nobody would have recognized names such as Malaysia, Indonesia, or the Philippines. The general frameworks for some nations, including Cambodia and Vietnam, were well established some centuries ago, but current boundaries and national identities for all the Southeast Asian countries were defined by Western colonization between 1500 and 1900. For convenience this book uses modern names, such as Indonesians or Filipinos, to refer to the peoples then living in the regions later defined by modern nations. Sometimes, however, these nations also change names. Until the late 1930s Thailand was known to the outside world as Siam, although many peoples there had called themselves Thai for several centuries. In 1988 the unpopular and repressive military rulers of the country called Burma renamed it Myanmar, a reference to a much older identity. But many foreign observers and Burmese, especially opponents of the military regime, still refer to it as Burma, and for consistency, this book does as well.

CHAPTER I

The Ancient Roots of Southeast Asia to ca. 200 BCE

According to a Malay proverb, "it takes a long time to build a mountain." It also took people a long time to build the foundations for the first complex societies based on farming and cities. The story of Southeast Asians began long ago. Around 2 million years ago, bands of modern humankind's direct ancestor, *Homo erectus* ("upright human"), began migrating out of Africa, carrying with them refined tools, sophisticated hunting skills, a group-oriented social life, and an ability to adapt to new environments. This was the first great migration in human history. Skulls and tools unearthed on Java during the past century suggest that *Homo erectus* may have been widespread in Southeast Asia by 1.5 million years ago and possibly earlier.

The Jakun people of the Malayan mountains believe that all humanity descended from two deities: one male and one female. In the myths and legends of many Southeast Asians their people have always lived in the region or were created there by gods. But the story uncovered by scholars is more complex. The discoveries of bones and tools in Java and Borneo indicate that modern humans, known as *Homo sapiens*, who most scholars believe also originated in Africa, were settling in Southeast Asia at least 40,000 years ago. During the Ice Ages, when ocean levels were lower, the western Indonesian islands were connected by land to the Asian mainland. A few *Homo erectus* populations may have survived in remote areas of Southeast Asia for some millennia, perhaps living alongside more advanced modern humans, but, unable to compete, they eventually died out. Many mysteries about prehistoric life remain, however. In 2004 archaeologists working on the small island of Flores, in Eastern Indonesia, discovered the 18,000-year-old bones of diminutive hominids, 3 to 3⅓ feet tall as adults, sparking a debate as

[handwritten margin notes: "Out of Africa", "to JAVA"]

to where these fossils fit into the human family tree. The Flores people may have been miniature versions of *Homo erectus* or *Homo sapiens* or perhaps constituted some unknown species. Scholars suspect these prehistoric inhabitants may have been wiped out in a volcanic eruption around 12,000 years ago.

Archaeologists may never find remains of the earliest *Homo sapien* arrivals, who probably followed the then existing coastline from South Asia, because this route was probably covered by water when ocean levels rose at the end of the great Ice Age around 10,000 years ago. Scattered around the region are many Stone Age sites, often in natural rock shelters or caves, containing simple tools and pottery. Some are located on Eastern Indonesian islands such as Flores and must have been reached by boat, perhaps something similar to the large rafts made of lashed-together bamboo poles and propelled by paddles that are still used by some island peoples. The hunting or scavenging of wild animals, usually by men, and the gathering of plants and nuts, chiefly by women, were the predominant economic activities for many millennia, and these activities still supply the livelihood for small, reclusive groups in more remote forest and mountain regions, including peoples such as the Penan of Borneo and the Semai of Malaya. People living along the coast or in river estuaries exploited the rich marine habitats, some going to sea to hunt rays, sharks, and dolphins, others catching fish along the shore.

The tropical climate of Southeast Asia, with its alternating annual pattern of rainy seasons and dry seasons, known as a monsoon pattern, also greatly influenced the rhythms of life. "Sky! Let the rain fall down," goes a Vietnamese nursery rhyme. "So there's water to drink, so I can plough my field." For millennia Southeast Asia was known as the "land below the winds" because, except for the Philippines and Vietnam, the region did not experience the summer typhoons (hurricanes) that sometimes devastated China and Japan. Dense rain forests once covered huge expanses of the land. The great rivers that flow through mainland Southeast Asia, such as the Mekong, Red, Chaophraya, Salween, and Irrawaddy, carved out broad, fertile plains and deltas that could support intensive human settlement.

In Southeast Asia it is often said that "the sea unites and the land divides." The topography both helped and hindered communication. The shallow oceans encouraged some peoples to specialize in seafaring, and mastery of the seas linked the peoples of islands such as Sumatra, Java, and Borneo to the mainland and to each other as well as promoted maritime communication with other regions of Asia. Southeast Asia has been a nexus of Asian seagoing trade from ancient times. Control of nearby seas, a source of wealth and means of transport, also fostered wars and piracy. On the other hand, however, the heavily forested interior highlands of the mainland and larger islands complicated but did not prevent overland travel between adjacent areas.

The geography of wide, fertile river valleys separated by forest-covered mountain ranges or plateaus, combined with a maritime environment of widely scattered, often volcanic islands, helped shape cultural diversity, resulting in a wide variety of religions, languages, cultures, and ways of making a living. An Indonesian proverb describes well the complex mosaic of cultures that resulted from geography and history: "different fields, different grasshoppers; different pools, different fish." Geography also produced a cultural contrast between mainland and island realms. Southeast Asia contains some of the world's largest islands, such as Borneo (Kalimantan), Sumatra, and Celebes (Sulawesi) in Indonesia, and Luzon and Mindanao in the Philippines. There are thousands of inhabited smaller islands in both countries. River valleys were more suitable for hunting, gathering, and then agriculture than the often swampy coasts and some of the mountainous islands, fostering denser populations and earlier state building on the mainland.

The transition from hunting and gathering to a food-producing economy based on agriculture and animal domestication was one of the most significant events in human history and may have been generated by an increasingly warmer climate in Eurasia around 10,000 years ago that made growing plants easier. Archaeological discoveries, such as the remains of seeds for peas, beans, water chestnuts, and other edible plants, suggest to some scholars that the people then living in the lands that now comprise Thailand, Vietnam, and Burma were among the world's earliest farmers. Perhaps as early as 8000 BCE, roughly contemporary with the first farmers in Mesopotamia, people in Northern Vietnam may have begun growing food, but farming was not widespread in Southeast Asia until later. Rice was apparently first domesticated in the region that encompasses Northern Southeast Asia, Southern China, and Central China, most probably in the Yangzi River valley, by 7,000 years ago. Southern China and Northern Southeast Asia were closely linked in ancient times and the peoples then living in the Yangzi basin and Southern China were probably more closely related to the modern Thai and Vietnamese than to modern Chinese. The knowledge of rice agriculture may have gradually traveled south along the Red, Mekong, and Irrawaddy rivers, perhaps as people migrated south. By 3000 BCE rice cultivation was becoming more common than before in Southeast

Asia, where the people may have also been pioneers in learning how to cultivate bananas, yams, and taro and to raise chickens and pigs, perhaps even cattle, as domesticated animals, and these remained the major food animals. The wild ancestors of all of these crops and animals are native to the region.

According to an old Malay proverb, "without rice, there is nothing," and, in many societies, people greet each other with the question, "Have you eaten rice yet?" Rock art made by prehistoric people in Thailand reveals the daily life of these people as they shifted from hunting and gathering to farming. The art shows people hunting, fighting with wild buffalo, herding, plowing, dancing, and engaging in ritual ceremonies. These drawings hint that women did more of the farming and pottery making and the men did more of the hunting, and that both were equally involved in ritual activities, suggesting a considerable gender equality. As people became more established in farming, they built villages. Houses situated a few feet above the ground on a platform held up by poles have been common in Southeast Asia for millennia and were probably introduced by early farmers in flood-prone regions, a very practical adaptation to prevailing conditions and the deadly power of rushing water.

The most populous societies developed along the coastal plains or in the river valleys, the regions where wet-rice cultivation was possible. This farming technology provided an ecologically sound, labor-intensive economic mainstay that could be sustained for many generations. There are two main versions of wet-rice farming, both of them relying on water buffalo for plowing fields. In his poem "Grains" the modern Filipino writer Amado Hernandez described the process: "Man and the water buffalo have been companions from the beginning/Industry and strength naturally fuse/the wilderness of thorns is cleared by the far-reaching plow, the fields are tilled/the upturned soil is harrowed."[1] The oldest system in the lowlands relied on annual rains and the flooding that followed. In many places this was replaced by more efficient irrigated systems, in which seeds are planted underwater in a field and with the drainage controlled by gates and dikes. The water holds in nutrients and kills weeds. Hence, the same fields can be used for hundreds of years without fertilizer. Sometimes irrigated rice farming required building terraces on steep mountainsides, an engineering challenge mastered by people from Bali and Java in Indonesia to the Northern Philippines. Wet-rice agriculture represented a highly successful adaptation to the tropical environment and river basin soils.

Centuries ago, the Ifugao farmers living on the Northern Philippine island of Luzon built elaborate terraces that allowed them to control water flow into the fields. Like the Ifugao, many Southeast Asians living in mountainous regions ingeniously learned how to grow wet rice. Library of Congress Lot 11356-8

Rice became the key crop in Southeast Asia, integral to life. Every year for centuries Thai farmers have joined together to mark the beginning of the rice-planting season with a plowing ceremony, invoking divine forces in hopes of a good crop. Wet-rice farming, especially the irrigated version, required some social cooperation for water management, which, in turn, promoted permanent villages and well-integrated communities from ancient times. Wet rice proved productive and stable enough to produce crop surpluses, and this ultimately led to more complex political and social systems. Rulers, bureaucrats, priests, soldiers, craftsmen, teachers, and merchants could be supported by the large majority of the population that remained in agriculture. Since irrigated rice growing also supported the complex societies in China, Korea, Japan, and parts of South Asia, Southeast Asian farming represented a variation on a well-established theme. It was chiefly on the fertile rice-growing plains that the great Southeast Asian kingdoms and empires emerged several thousand years ago.

Probably sometime after 2000 BCE, simple bronze working appeared in Southeast Asia, with the knowledge likely filtering in from China. People used bronze to make useful items such as pots, and evidence from graves hints that women may have been involved in bronze casting alongside men. Unlike in other areas of Eurasia, archaeologists have found rather few bronze weapons, suggesting little organized warfare. Tin mined in Southeast Asia may have been traded to Mesopotamia as early as 2500 BCE, to be used in making bronze there, and fine bronze was being produced in Northeast Thailand by 1500 BCE. The Dong Son culture, which arose in Northern Vietnam by at least 500 BCE and possibly much earlier, is renowned for its huge bronze ceremonial drums that have been found all over Southeast Asia as far south as Java and Bali and in Southern China, indicating complex trading networks. The Dong Son peoples also made beautifully decorated bronze basket-shaped containers, bracelets, necklaces, earrings, and daggers with decorated handles.

Southeast Asians worked iron as early as 500 BCE, several centuries later than in Northern China. They used iron for practical purposes, such as making hoes and spears, but also for decoration, such as making jewelry, including rings and bangles. Iron weapons became more common and many villages were now surrounded by moats, suggesting increased conflict. There were also important local innovations regarding technology. Some people learned how to roll the fibers of the sugar palm together tightly enough to lash together a boat, using various items such as tree resin, bamboo, and water buffalo dung to create caulking. Already some commodities, including marine shells, marble, fine ceramics, copper, and tin, were being exchanged along rivers and coasts over hundreds of miles.

Archaeologists have begun to provide a better picture of these early farmers and metalworkers. For example, Ban Chiang is today a large village shaded by expansive trees, located on the Khorat plateau in northeast Thailand, about an hour's drive from the mighty Mekong River, whose residents grow rice, fish, and raise livestock. But the modern village sits atop the remains of a much more ancient settlement, founded around 2100 BCE, whose inhabitants were also farmers some 4,000 years ago. The ancient people of Ban Chiang and nearby settlements raised chickens, cattle, pigs, and later water buffaloes, had domesticated dogs, and grew rice. Agriculture allowed them to survive the dry season, which lasted some six months a year. Their houses were perched on poles above the ground. Women made beautiful, hand-painted, and durable pottery, some of which has been found intact in archaeological diggings. By 2000 or 1500 BCE Ban Chiang craftsmen also worked metals to make tools and ornaments. No slag heaps have been discovered at the village, suggesting that the metals were smelted elsewhere on the

This dark gray earthenware Ban Chiang pot was incised with decoration around 4,000 years ago. The people of Ban Chiang village in northeast Thailand made some of the finest pottery in the region. Arthur M. Sackler Gallery, Smithsonian Institution, Washington, DC; purchase S1998.122

Khorat plateau and then taken to the village. At first the metalworkers made bronze by mixing copper and tin. Later they made iron. Ancient Ban Chiang's artists, mostly women, fashioned necklaces and bracelets as well as many household items of metal and ivory. Over the past several decades archaeologists have collected many pots, shards, and stone, metal, and woven items as well as human and animal bones in an attempt to reconstruct this ancient society.

In some parts of Southeast Asia centralized farming societies emerged between 1000 and 500 BCE, around 1,500 years after the first Indian cities and 1,000 years after the first Chinese cities and states developed. Larger settlements, like Ban Chiang, offered more occupational options. For example, as burial practices grew more elaborate, many Southeast Asians buried their dead in large pottery jars while others chose great stone slabs or coffins. This provided work for stonemasons, toolmakers, ironworkers, and blacksmiths. Examination of skeletal remains suggests that these ancient Southeast Asians were rather healthy, showing little evidence of infectious disease or violence.

A division between lowlanders and highlanders, each with differing social, economic, political, and cultural systems, produced a situation of cores and fringes. The politically centralized, lowland-dwelling, wet-rice-growing peoples such as the Vietnamese, Khmers, Burmans, Thai, Malays, and Javanese had more material goods and food than the more thinly spread, less technologically oriented, shifting cultivators who dwelled in the highlands and rain forests. These people grew dry rice and, much later, maize (corn) in recurring cycles so as not to abuse and then ruin the marginally fertile highland soils. Shifting cultivation is often called slash-and-burn farming because the land must be cleared of forest growth before the seeds can be spread. These peoples mostly depended on rainfall alone to nurture their crops.

Highlanders like the Rhade in Vietnam, the various Dayak peoples in Borneo, and, in modern times, the Hmong of Laos, who migrated from Southern China, often lived in semi-nomadic communities, moving their villages every few years to new fertile land. These villages tended to be flexible, breaking up and reforming as necessary. Each village usually had a chief, although his power was often limited. Most hill societies had no centralized political authority linking people much beyond the village level, although many identified with a clan spread widely over the region. Some of the highland groups had social orders in which everyone was treated as an equal, while others had more rigid systems of aristocrats and commoners. As long as populations remained small, shifting cultivation could be sustained as a subsistence way of life for many generations. It tended to promote small impermanent settlements and required less social cooperation than wet-rice farming. Most shifting cultivators had to devote their efforts chiefly to farming and other subsistence pursuits such as hunting and fishing. The contacts between hill and lowland peoples varied considerably and included both trade and warfare. Although profoundly differing from them in culture and outlook, the lowland societies attempted to influence or control the highland peoples with mixed success.

The identity of those peoples who pioneered farming and metalworking in Southeast Asia is uncertain, but they probably included the Vietnamese as well as ancestors of the Papuans and Melanesians. Several waves of migrants, probably bringing with them advanced agricultural technologies, may have come into mainland Southeast Asia from China and Tibet sometime before the beginning of the Common Era, perhaps prompting some of the original people to migrate eastward through the islands. Today Melanesians and Papuans dominate Eastern Indonesia, New Guinea, and the Western Pacific islands. The new arrivals probably mixed their cultures and languages with the remaining indigenous inhabitants, and this ethnic merging produced new peoples such as the Khmers (Cambodians), Mons, and Pyu, who later established important states based on wet-rice farming in the Mekong, Chaophraya, and Irrawaddy River basins, respectively. The Khmers were living and farming in Cambodia and Southern Vietnam by at least 2000 BCE. Thanks to the geographical divisions and the continuous immigration of new peoples from the north, Southeast Asia became the most linguistically diverse region in the world. The hundreds of Southeast Asian languages and dialects fall into at least six language families, which are broad groupings of related languages that probably have a common root. Southeast Asian languages belong to such families as the Austronesian (including most of the languages of Indonesia, Malaysia, and the Philippines), Austroasiatic (including Khmer and Vietnamese), Tai (among them, Thai and Lao), and Tibeto-Burman.

Austronesian is a particularly large family of related languages and is closely identified with population movement. Over several millennia peoples speaking Austronesian tongues and possessing advanced agriculture entered Southeast Asia. This migration began around 4000 BCE, when people from Taiwan, who had arrived centuries earlier from China, began moving south by boat into the Philippine Islands. Eventually some Austronesians migrated into Indonesia, replacing or assimilating the earlier hunters and gatherers. They settled Java, Borneo, and Sumatra before 2000 BCE. Some Austronesian speakers also moved to

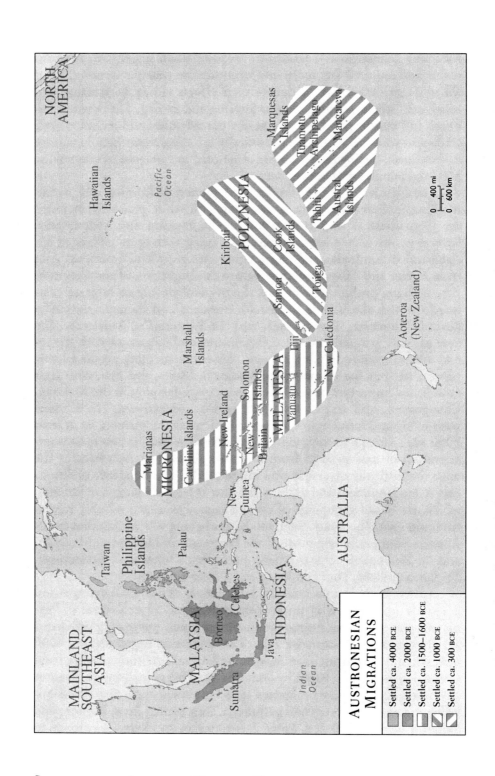

MAINLAND
SOUTHEAST
ASIA

NORTH
AMERICA

Taiwan

Philippine
Islands

Palau'

Hawaiian
Islands

Pacific
Ocean

Marquesas
Islands

Tuamotu
Archipelago

Mangareva

Marianas

MICRONESIA

Caroline Islands

Kiribati

POLYNESIA

Cook
Islands

Tahiti

Austral
Islands

Marshall
Islands

New Ireland

Samoa

Tonga

Sumatra

MALAYSIA

Borneo

Celebes

New
Guinea

New
Britain

Solomon
Islands

MELANESIA

Fiji

New Caledonia

Vanuatu

Java

INDONESIA

AUSTRALIA

Aoteroa
(New Zealand)

Indian
Ocean

0   400 mi
0   600 km

AUSTRONESIAN
MIGRATIONS

	Settled ca. 4000 BCE
	Settled ca. 2000 BCE
	Settled ca. 1500–1600 BCE
	Settled ca. 1000 BCE
	Settled ca. 300 BCE

the Southeast Asian mainland, especially on the Malay Peninsula and along the central coast of Vietnam. By 1000 BCE Austronesian languages were dominant from the Northern Philippines to far Western Indonesia, and few traces of earlier languages remained. These Austronesians brought with them domesticated pigs and dogs, grew rice and millet, used bows and arrows, had looms for weaving, and possessed a knowledge of tattooing, which became a common practice in Austronesian societies. Some early Austronesians built sophisticated ocean-going sailing vessels with multilayered hulls and maneuverable square sails known as balance-lugs. Some had outrigger devices to stabilize the vessel. Oriented to the water, Austronesian culture was, and remains today, full of symbols of the sea and of boats. Many societies buried their dead in boat-shaped coffins. Oral and written literature often reflected maritime themes. A poem from the Makassarese of South Sulawesi imagined the union of a husband and wife as "like two fishing boats/Fishing together the big shiny fish/Tied together for life's voyage."[2]

Seafaring and maritime trade were major forces in the development of Southeast Asian societies, particularly involving Austronesians from Western Indonesia and the Malay Peninsula who learned how to sail by capitalizing on the monsoons. The peoples we know today as Indonesians and Malays were apparently the major seafaring traders and explorers of Eastern Asia before the advent of the Common Era, the counterparts to the Phoenicians in the Mediterranean basin. Skilled navigators who were fearless in confronting the dangers of the open sea, Indonesians traded with India by 500 BCE and China by 400 BCE, and around the beginning of the Common Era, they carried goods between China and India.

The Austronesian maritime migrations that brought new cultures to Southeast Asia had a profound effect on other regions as well. Indonesians carried Southeast Asian foods (especially bananas and rice) and musical instruments to East Africa, where they were adopted by people there. After sojourning along the East African coast, where some may have intermarried with local Africans, most of the migrants apparently settled on the large island of Madagascar sometime between 100 and 700 CE, with other Indonesians apparently joining them. Their descendants account for the majority of that island's population today. Austronesian languages and cultural forms persisted among Madagascar's people in part because trade and contact continued for centuries.

Some of the earliest Southeast Asian peoples, such as the ancestors of the Melanesians, migrated eastward into the Western Pacific islands beginning around 1600 BCE, carrying with them Southeast Asian

A bas relief of a sailing ship with an outrigger and tripod mast, typical of Indonesian ships, was carved into a wall of the great Buddhist temple of Borobodur in Central Java in the eighth century CE. *Indonesians were among the finest ancient mariners, a maritime tradition that continued for centuries.* Werner Forman/Art Resource, NY

domesticated crops such as yams, animals such as pigs and chickens, and farming technology. These adventurous mariners discovered new lands and extended trade networks. A few centuries later, traveling in large double-hulled outrigger canoes and possessing remarkable navigation skills, some Austronesians also sailed from Indonesia into the Pacific, often mixing with the Melanesians, who adopted their languages. Other Austronesians sailed from the Philippines to settle Palau and the Marianas, becoming the Micronesians. By 1000 BCE Austronesian settlers had reached as far east in the Pacific as Fiji, Samoa, and Tonga. In these islands Polynesian culture emerged from Austronesian roots. Fearless and skilled mariners, reading the stars with their eyes and the swells with their backs as they lay down in their canoes, some Polynesians endured the hardships of long sea voyages to reach eventually as far east as Tahiti and the Marquesas Islands, from where, between 400 and 1000 CE, some of their descendants sailed southwest to New Zealand (known to Polynesians as Aotearoa), becoming the ancestors of the Maori, and north to Hawaii.

Today there are some 1,200 different Austronesian languages spoken by more than 350 million people from Madagascar eastward through Indonesia, Malaysia, the Philippines, and Taiwan through the Pacific islands to Easter Island, which is in Eastern Polynesia 2,000 miles off the west coast of South America but more than 3,000 miles east of Samoa. The Austronesian language family was once known as Malayo-Polynesian to indicate its wide reach. The ancient migrations of peoples speaking Indo-European languages from the Caucasus mountain region into Europe, Western Asia, and India, and of Bantu-speaking peoples throughout Central, Eastern, and Southern Africa helped change history, but no premodern peoples migrated over as wide an area as the Austronesians. By 1000 BCE their trade networks stretched for more than 5,000 miles, from Western Indonesia to the Central Pacific, a commercial system unparalleled in the ancient world for its reach. As an example of its scope, obsidian, a glassy, volcanic rock prized for its razor-sharp edges, was mined by Melanesians on the island of New Britain, northeast of New Guinea. From there it was traded as far west as Borneo and as far east as Fiji, some 4,000 miles apart.

With their location at what Chinese travelers described as the "end of the monsoons," the early Malays benefited from a strategic position for maritime commerce. The Straits of Melaka (Malacca) between Sumatra and Malaya had long served as a crossroads through which people, ideas, and trade goods passed. The prevailing wind patterns in the South China Sea and Indian Ocean allowed ships sailing southwest from China and southeast from India to meet in the Straits and on the Malay Peninsula, where they exchanged goods. They sailed back home when the winds reversed. Some Austronesians were already specializing in maritime trade to distant shores using ships with balance-lug sails, which may have been the model for the triangular lateen sails used by Arab mariners. The lateen sail was adopted many centuries later by Western Europeans, helping them sail down the West African coast and across the Atlantic Ocean. A Chinese observer in the third century CE was impressed by large, multimasted Indonesian boats that were more than 50 meters in length and able to carry 600 or 700 people and up to 600 tons of cargo. Using such boats, Austronesians obtained cinnamon grown on the China coast and carried it to India, from where it eventually reached Europe. Cloves grown in Eastern Indonesia have been found in 3,700-year-old Mesopotamian kitchens. Local and imported spices and peppers made Southeast Asian foods hot and spicy, with pungent sauces. The universal appeal of Southeast Asian cooking has led to the spread of Indonesian, Thai, and Vietnamese restaurants around the world beginning in the mid-twentieth century.

The Austronesians, Khmers, Vietnamese, and others established a foundation for the later development of complex societies and states in Southeast Asia based on intensive agriculture, fishing, and international commerce. By around 200 BCE sophisticated societies had developed on both the mainland and in the islands, and the region's population as a whole probably reached at least 2 million. Our knowledge of these peoples is largely based on Indian and Chinese accounts, religious and political inscriptions on stone monuments, and archaeological discoveries. The Greek geographer Claudius Ptolemy in the second century CE wrote about the "golden peninsula" and its trading cities and products. By that time small coastal trading states based on lively port cities had emerged in the Malay Peninsula and Sumatra. This area had long enjoyed an international reputation as a source of gold, tin, and exotic forest products.

Some societies developed around inland agriculture rather than coastal trade, although they were often linked by rivers and caravan trade to other societies. At the same time as the Greeks were establishing states along the northern shores of the Mediterranean, a few small bronze-using states emerged on the mainland between 1000 and 500 BCE, based on wet-rice farming and metalworking. The Vietnamese created the first known Southeast Asian states between 1000 and 800 BCE and believed in a god that, according to their myths, "creates the elephants [and] the grass, is omnipresent, and has [all-seeing] eyes."[3] One of these early states was Van Lang in Northern Vietnam. The hereditary Van Lang kings ruled through a landed aristocracy that controlled vast estates worked by peasants. During the third century BCE the earliest cities with monumental architecture appeared, such as Co Loa Thanh in Vietnam. Here, near present-day Hanoi, a ruler employed many workers to build a huge citadel, surrounded by concentric walls. The outer wall was five miles long and some ten yards wide, allowing for chariot traffic on the top of the rampart.

Cities became more common as centers for trade and government. One of the earliest, later known as Beitkhano (named for the Hindu god Vishnu), was built in Burma by the Pyu people probably during the first or second century BCE. The city walls encircled a settlement several miles in circumference, and one entered the city through 12 wooden gates protected by guardhouses. Many of the city's houses were built of brick, and silver coins are commonly found in the ruins. By the beginning of the Common Era sophisticated societies with pronounced social classes emerged in the river valleys among peoples like the Khmers and engaged in maritime trade.

Distinctive religious views were also taking shape. From earliest times many Burmese believed in *nats*, spirits who were everywhere, in the house, forest, water, and air. Staying in the good graces of these spirits, some benevolent and some malevolent, helped ensure bountiful harvests, addressed problems of daily life, and kept the cosmic order in balance. Initially all Southeast Asians believed in some form of spirit worship, or animism. Animism involved communicating with ancestors and spiritual forces such as the *nats* based in the natural world. Most animist societies had shamans, specialists in communicating with supernatural forces. Shamans were often women, and as a result, women held a high status in many animist societies. The Javanese believed in a pantheon of gods and goddesses and a cosmology as complex as that of the classical Greeks. Eventually religions coming from outside Southeast Asia, such as Hinduism, Buddhism, Islam, and Christianity, replaced, incorporated, or coexisted with animism and local gods in the most populous regions. But these outside religions were slow to penetrate into remote forests, mountains, and islands, where animism remained predominant until the nineteenth century.

Societies developed around coastal trade.
Inland agriculture (rice)
Straits of Melaka b/ Sumatra & Malaya
— Trade networks, cities emerge
Van Lang in N. Viet (Co Loa Thanh)
Burma w/ city of Beikthano built by Pyu

So cities w/ social classes, distinctive religions,
ethnic diversity

CHAPTER 2

Southeast Asians in the Classical World, ca. 200 BCE–800 CE

Historians cannot be certain when the first sailing ships from India and China began making regular visits to the lands of Southeast Asia, but around 2,000 years ago tales of such expeditions were becoming common in India, offering information about strange and exotic lands such as *Yavadvipa*, an island said to be awash in silver and gold. The *Ramayana* ("Story of Rama"), an ornate Indian epic poem written some 2,500 or more years ago, but probably revised several times by the first century CE, mentions this island. Another ancient Indian book, the *Vayu Parana*, describes it as "full of varieties of flowers and fruits. . . . There are . . . towns where live men and women in happiness. . . . [It is full] of mines of precious stones and gold, besides sandalwood. . . . It is a veritable paradise."[1] Scholars debate whether *Yavadvipa* refers to Java, Sumatra, or perhaps Borneo. The Indian adventurers reaching the region were chiefly merchants in search of wealth, and commerce fills their stories. Meanwhile Chinese sources from the late first century BCE record encounters with Southeast Asian traders carrying goods around the region and relate that an early emperor of the Han dynasty (206 BCE–220 CE) dispatched agents—known as the "Interpreters of the Yellow Door"—from Northern Vietnam to the east coast of India in search of pearls and various other exotic products. The Chinese, Indians, and Southeast Asians built a vast maritime trade network stretching from the Red Sea to the South China Sea, and Southeast Asian connections to the wider world increased rapidly after 200 BCE.

Just prior to the Common Era, China and India began exercising a strong influence in Southeast Asia. In the second century BCE the Han dynasty of China built a huge empire in East and Central Asia and conquered the already well-organized society of Vietnam, imposing a colonial rule that endured for a millennium and spread many Chinese customs and ideas. Chinese influence also reached into other societies as Chinese traders regularly visited many other Southeast Asian states over the centuries. Some of these Chinese established permanent communities in trading cities and maintained networks linking the region with Southern Chinese ports. Historians often compare the South China and Java Seas to the Mediterranean, a center of maritime commerce, as ships regularly connected the trading ports of the islands and mainland. Between the fourth and sixth centuries the overland trading routes between China and the West along the Silk Road were closed off by unsettled conditions when various tribal groups contended for control of Central Asia, increasing the importance of the oceanic connection through Southeast Asia.

Despite the region's longstanding trade connections to China, India exercised more cultural influence on Southeast Asia, except in Vietnam. Traders and priests began casting off from ports in Eastern India, swept by summer winds across the Bay of Bengal to Burma, the Malay Peninsula, and the Straits of Melaka. In 414 the Chinese Buddhist pilgrim Faxian, who had spent years in India, decided to return to China by sea. He traveled on a large Indian merchant ship, carrying some 200 passengers, from Sri Lanka to Sumatra and, in his account of the journey, reported on the dangers at sea: "The sea is infested with pirates, to meet whom is death. The expanse of ocean is boundless, east and west are not distinguishable. [In a typhoon] they had no place where they could cast their stone anchor and stop."[2] Some Indians settled in mainland and island states, where they married into or became advisors to influential families. At the same time, Southeast Asian sailors were also visiting India and returning with new ideas about religion and government. During the era of the Gupta Empire (320–550 CE) Northern India was enjoying its golden age and was perhaps then the world's most developed society in mathematics, medicine, astronomy, chemistry, technology, and political organization. Gupta India provided a natural model for Southeast Asians.

The process by which Indian ideas spread into and influenced many Southeast Asians is often termed "Indianization." Between around 100–1000 CE, Indian ideas mixed with local ones and a mutual sharing took place, and so some historians prefer the term *convergence* to describe the pattern. For a millennium Southeast Asian peoples such as the Khmers in the Mekong basin, the Mons in Central Thailand, the Chams along the central coast of Vietnam, and the Javanese on the fertile island of Java were connected to India by economic and cultural exchanges. As a result, some Southeast Asians took part in the general intellectual, political, and economic trends of the Afro-Eurasian world more intensely than many of the peoples of Europe between 500 and 1400 CE. Just as the Phoenicians spread their alphabet around the Mediterranean basin in ancient times, writing systems such as North Indian Sanskrit and South Indian Pallava were adapted to Southeast Asian spoken languages, and by 500 CE writing was common around the region for political and religious leaders.

Indian influence was particularly strong in religion, and Hinduism and Buddhism were readily adopted among the upper classes. The eclectic and flexible religion known today as Hinduism had been taking shape in India since the second millennium BCE, incorporating the beliefs of various traditions in the subcontinent. The Hinduism that flourished in Southeast Asia emphasized reincarnation, the accumulation of a balance sheet weighing the consequences of an individual's actions through the procession of lives (*karma*), the impermanent nature of reality, ritual practices, hereditary social classes (called in India the caste system by later observers), and the powerful role of the priestly caste, known as *brahmans*.

Buddhism emerged in India around 2,500 years ago as a reaction against the power of Hindu priests. The founder of the Buddhist religion was Siddhartha Gautama (563–483 BCE), born a prince of a small North Indian kingdom. Siddhartha led a privileged, carefree, and self-indulgent life, then was shocked when he ventured from his palace and encountered the disease, sorrows, and miseries experienced by average people. Siddhartha abandoned his royal life to search for truth as a wandering holy man. For several years he lived in the forest meditating and fasting. Eventually Siddhartha believed he understood the cosmic truths about existence and morality. Thereafter his followers called Siddhartha the Buddha ("The Enlightened One").

Eventually, around 2,000 years ago, Buddhism divided in India into several rival schools, the most significant of which were Mahayana and Theravada. The two forms differed substantially in theology and organization but also had many similarities. Both schools accepted the basic tenets preached by the Buddha. They believed that this life is one of suffering, which results from desiring what one does not have and clinging to what one already has for fear of losing it. One must stop all desire by following the Noble Eightfold Path of correct behavior and thought, which includes having, for example, positive views, intent, speech, and actions. Following these guidelines means leading a good life that does no harm to others. To Buddhists, the world is in a constant state of flux. When mortals try to stop the flow of events, they suffer. Buddha also urged his followers to avoid taking animal life if possible, and as a result, many became vegetarians. Along with following the path of non-violence, moderation, and love for all creatures, Buddhists were encouraged to live morally and to consider the needs of others. For example, men were urged to treat women with respect. Buddhists, like Hindus, believe that the individual soul progresses through a series of lives. But the goal for Buddhists was *nirvana* (literally, "the blowing out"), a kind of everlasting peace or end of suffering achieved through perfection of wisdom and compassion. Mahayana Buddhism, which was the more influential school in Southeast Asia for a millennium, places an emphasis on meditation and the intercession of Buddhist *bodhisattva* ("saints") to assist believers on the road to nirvana.

The Theravada (or "Teachings of the Elders") school, known to its Mahayana rivals as Hinayana ("Lesser Vehicle"), seems to have been closer to Buddha's original vision. To its followers, Buddha was not a god but rather a human teacher. The universe was a temporary place, in continuous change, with no supreme being or immortal soul. Because gods could not help or hinder humans, believers could take refuge only in the ever wise and compassionate Buddha, his teachings, and the community of monks who maintained them. Theravadans emphasized acquiring merit through devotion and meditation but also through good works, such as feeding monks or supporting a temple. But, to Theravadans, pursuing enlightenment and acquiring merit were the responsibility of the individual believer. And, for males, the only sure way to dramatically improve the chances of ending rebirth and reaching nirvana was by becoming a monk and following strict monastic rules, abandoning the temptations and responsibilities of normal life. Although all men were expected to spend some portion of their lives as monks, usually two years as a youth, a much smaller number made a long-term commitment.

The influence of Mahayana Buddhism in some Southeast Asian societies during this era was reported by a Chinese Buddhist pilgrim, Yijing, who stopped off in Sumatra in 688 CE after some two decades of travel in India and Ceylon. An ordained monk, Yijing had been visiting Buddhist sites and studying the religion in India. In the Sumatran city he called Bhoga, probably today's Palembang, he wrote:

> Many kings and chieftains admire and believe in Buddhism, and their hearts are set on accumulating good actions. In the fortified city of

Bhoga Buddhist priests number more than 1,000, whose minds are bent on learning good practices. They investigate and study all the subjects that exist just as in India; the rules and ceremonies are not at all different. If a Chinese priest wishes to go to the West [India] in order to hear lectures and read the original [Buddhist writings], he had better stay here one or two years and practice the proper rules and then proceed to Central India.[3]

Indian influence was equally strong in the governments of many of the small states emerging in the early Common Era. Early leaders arose in the region because they could convince their followers that they had superior spiritual qualities. Rulers anxious to control growing populations were attracted to the Indian concept of powerful leaders possessing supernatural powers and to an unequal social system in which rulers enjoyed an unchallenged position. Chinese accounts around 600 CE described a king in a state on the Malay Peninsula who "sits on a three-tiered couch, and is dressed in rose-colored cloth, with a chaplet of gold flowers and a necklace of varied jewels. More than a hundred soldiers mount guard. Several hundred brahmans sit in rows facing each other."[4]

This sculpture of Agni, the Hindu god of fire, was fashioned in the tenth century by the Chams, who lived along the coast of what is today Central and Southern Vietnam. The Chams were one of the earliest Southeast Asian peoples to adopt Indian religions, Hinduism, and Mahayana Buddhism. Photo by Craig A. Lockard

The Hindu idea of karma suggested that the rich and powerful had earned their status because of their achievements in previous lives. The imported religions of both Hinduism and Buddhism developed a complex relationship with the local animism, and many Southeast Asians blended them together rather than following one exclusively.

Governments were organized around temples or trade centers. Hence, the Mon people, who increasingly adopted Buddhism, established several states in the Chaophraya basin of what is today. Thailand and, several centuries later, in Southern Burma. The new states that emerged in these centuries did not have fixed boundaries. Rather they were fluctuating zones of influence flowing out from a central court, headed by a king and his officials, which attempted to dominate economic resources and people in outlying areas through a combination of diplomacy and military might. Using a multipurpose Hindu-Buddhist concept, early inscriptions on stone pillars and buildings refer to these political units as *mandala*, which can mean a circle, with the country a replica of the cosmos, and the monarch, just like the Hindu gods, at the center. These kings often styled themselves as "wheel-turners" possessing spiritual power, intangible and mysterious, rather than just as purveyors of military force. These early kings excelled in pomp and circumstance, with elaborate coronations and court rituals, but they also wanted to be recognized as role models and teachers. The fifth-century rulers of Kutai in Eastern Borneo commissioned stone pillars with inscriptions praising their careers. But most kings ruled uneasily over troublesome local chieftains seeking to extend their own power.

Perhaps the first important Indianized Southeast Asian state was   *Funan* Funan, which was founded in the first century CE and flourished into the sixth century. According to legends, an Indian brahman, Kautilya, sailed to Funan with a magic bow, defeated and then married the queen, a daughter of the king of the cobras, and founded a new royal line. Whether the king ruled a large area or the state was instead a federation of trading cities remains unclear. Whatever the truth of an Indian founder, Khmers probably dominated the government and society of Funan, which was centered in the fertile Mekong delta of what is today Southern Vietnam and Eastern Cambodia. There may also have been Mon people in the country as well as numerous Austronesians, who probably dominated Funan's maritime commerce, living in Funan's cities. The Funanese were in regular contact with China, valued literacy, and linked their cities with canals, which may have been used for irrigation, aquaculture, drainage, or transportation. Probably based on the reports of Kang Tai, a third-century Chinese emissary, Chinese records revealed that the king "gave three or four audiences [each day]. Foreigners and subjects offered him presents of bananas, sugar cane, turtles, and birds. . . . The king, when he travels rides an elephant. So do his concubines."[5] For amusements the Funanese enjoyed cockfights and hog fights. The Chinese envoy Kang Tai described Funan's "walled cities, palaces and houses" occupied by people who ate with silver utensils and paid their taxes with "gold, silver, pearls and perfumes."[6] He was impressed with the many history books that were produced and the well-kept archives. Engraved gold plaques show women playing harps.

With its access to major land and sea trade routes, Funan was part of several large trading networks. Roman coins and trade goods such as glassware and ceramics from as far away as Arabia, Persia, Central Asia, and perhaps East Africa have been found in its ruins, but these may have come east by way of India. Merchants from various countries, including India and China, lived in the major port city, Oc Eo. Funan's people skillfully manufactured jewelry, pottery, and other trade goods, and they also exported forest products such as ivory.

Another predominantly Khmer kingdom or grouping of city-states, called Zhenla by the Chinese, seems to have emerged inland in the Mekong River basin around the fifth century CE and gradually outshone, and perhaps even conquered, Funan. Zhenla played a dominant regional role until the seventh century when it was destroyed during a civil war. Zhenla kings were powerful. One promised punishment to those "who seize carts, boats, slaves, cattle, buffaloes or contest the king's orders."[7] A fertile and strategic location, a vigorous and adaptive society, powerful kings, and a knack for political organization made the Khmer-speaking peoples the major power and most influential society of mainland Southeast Asia for many centuries.

The Cham people, who lived along the coast of Central and Southern Vietnam, were also among the first to establish Indianized states. Champa was a large state or, some historians believe, the collective name for several states, linked by kingship and marital alliances, which dated from the second century CE. The Chams, who spoke an Austronesian language, became renowned as sailors and merchants, with Cham traders even based in China, Funan, and Java. Like many other maritime peoples, during trade downturns they resorted to piracy. They also earned enemies by trying to control the increasingly dynamic coastal commerce between China and Southeast Asia. A Cham inscription from 774 tells of a raid they suffered at the hands of a seagoing people, possibly Malays or Javanese, who were "ferocious, pitiless men, whose food was more horrible than corpses."[8]

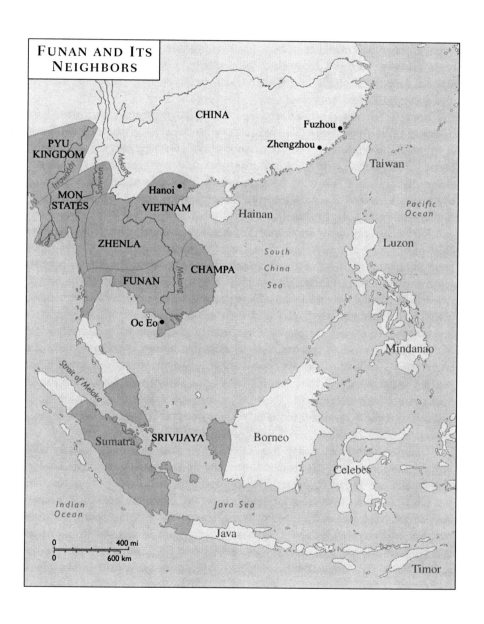

FUNAN AND ITS NEIGHBORS

CHINA

Fuzhou

Zhengzhou

Taiwan

PYU KINGDOM

Irrawaddy

Salween

Mekong

MON STATES

Hanoi

VIETNAM

Hainan

Pacific Ocean

ZHENLA

Luzon

CHAMPA

South China Sea

FUNAN

Mekong

Oc Eo

Mindanao

Strait of Melaka

Sumatra

SRIVIJAYA

Borneo

Celebes

Indian Ocean

Java Sea

Java

400 mi

0

600 km

0

Timor

Chams exported timber and wood products and fashioned elaborate woven cloth. Their society was matrilineal, tracing kinship through the female line, and also had elements of matriarchy. Cham kings, for example, were chosen because of their kinship to a senior woman, and royal women had considerable political influence. Both men and women were allowed to have more than one spouse. Hinduism was especially strong, and the Chams, like the Indians, believed the cow to be sacred and practiced yoga exercises.

VIETNAM Because of their power and resources, the Chams came into frequent conflict with the Vietnamese, who were continually pushing southward, forcing the Chams to shift their own settlements down the coast. Eventually by 1471 the Vietnamese had conquered all the Cham states, assimilating many of their people. Today only scattered remnants of the once powerful Cham people, most of them now Muslims, remain in Vietnam and Cambodia.

Vietnam was also an important society even during the long period of Chinese colonial rule, but it was very different from the Indianized kingdoms. China was a centralized and powerful society, whose conquest of its southern neighbor in 111 BCE ended the independent evolution of one of the earliest Southeast Asian kingdoms. There was already a relatively dense Vietnamese population in the Red River valley, the heart of a Chinese colony mostly confined to what is today Northern Vietnam. A census in 2 CE recorded a Vietnamese population of around 1 million. Initially the Chinese ruled through appointed governors, mostly local leaders whose main obligation was collecting taxes and tribute, but eventually, after facing armed opposition, the Chinese tightened their domination and governed directly by sending in Chinese rulers.

Chinese policy was to assimilate the Vietnamese and instill Chinese values, customs, and institutions, and the changes they generated were significant but failed to destroy Vietnamese identity. Over the centuries the Chinese philosophies of Confucianism and Daoism, and the Chinese version of Mahayana Buddhism, were gradually adopted by most Vietnamese, although never as strongly as among the Chinese. Confucianism is a philosophy of social relations, developed by Confucius, who lived 2,500 years ago. He emphasized social obligations and the hierarchical nature of a society of superiors and inferiors. Confucianism placed a heavy emphasis on people interacting with people rather than with gods, and offered a framework of ethics, paternalistic government, a strong family system, hard work, thrift, self-sacrifice for the good of the family, and courtesy to others so as to avoid conflict. Hence Confucian societies have tended to emphasize the group and a view of history emphasizing links between past, present, and future. Daoism was an ancient Chinese philosophy emphasizing mysticism and living in harmony with nature. Chinese Buddhism offered the hope of an afterlife and a power greater than humanity. The Chinese referred to the three traditions as the three ways of thought and turned them into an eclectic, tolerant mix, complementary ways to the same goal: happiness. According to one old story, Confucius, the Buddha, and Laozi (the legendary founder of Daoism) were seen walking and talking together before crossing a bridge into the mist. But then one much larger figure could be seen emerging from the mist, the blend of the three ways. China's patriarchal family system, written language, and ideas about government also sank deep roots. But Chinese ideas were blended with Vietnamese traditions, such as the worship of spirits and ancestors.

Although the Vietnamese adopted enough of Chinese culture to sometimes be misleadingly labeled by modern scholars "the smaller dragon," they sustained a hatred of Chinese rule and resisted cultural assimilation for a thousand years, a display of national pride and determination practically unparalleled in world history. The survival of the Vietnamese identity, language, and many customs such as ancestor worship during a millennium of colonialism by the strongest power in eastern Eurasia was remarkable. Perhaps the Vietnamese avoided cultural and national extinction because they already had several centuries of statehood behind them when the Chinese colonized. A sense of Vietnamese nationhood may have aided resistance to assimilation. It reflected a love of independence and a collective identity that reached right down to the villages. Foreign conquerors found that they had to do more than defeat or co-opt the rulers. They also had to conquer each village, one by one. The Vietnamese were formidable in resisting enemies collectively. For more than 2,000 years the continuing question for the Vietnamese has been how they could benefit from Chinese culture without becoming Chinese themselves.

A memorial erected by the Chinese reflected the Vietnamese tendency to rebel that often provoked harsh Chinese retaliation: "At every stream, cave, marketplace, everywhere there is stubbornness. Repression is necessary."[9] The rebels often fought for decades against hopeless odds. The Chinese colonial period was punctuated by many revolts, all of them well remembered today in Vietnam as moments of patriotism.

A few of the major anti-Chinese rebellions in Vietnamese history were led by heroic women, such as the Trung Sisters in 39 CE, although it is hard to separate myth from fact in their story. According to legend, the sisters were daughters of prominent landed aristocrats living near Hanoi. The oldest sister, Trung Trac, had married a member of another landed family. He protested an increase in taxes by colonial authorities, for which he was apparently executed. The spirited and courageous sisters then sparked a rebellion that rapidly spread throughout Vietnam and involved both the upper class and the peasantry. With local Chinese officials in retreat, her followers declared Trung Trac queen of a newly independent country. The sisters ruled for two years. Their policies included an abolition of taxes. But the sisters also sought to restore the pre-Chinese order and protect their local autonomy, which the Han government was trying to erode. The revolt was apparently supported by the common people, who disliked the authoritarian Chinese rule.

However, Chinese leaders could not allow this valuable component of their large empire to secede and so dispatched their most able general and his army to destroy the rebellion. As the fighting and repression intensified, most of the sisters' upper-class supporters abandoned the cause. Eventually their remaining forces were defeated in 41 CE, and the sisters either committed suicide or were captured and executed. They became enshrined in images of brave and beautiful, sword-bearing women mounted on elephants, leading their troops into battle. Over the centuries they became symbols of patriotism and opposition to foreign rule. Even after 2,000 years, the Vietnamese today honor their martyrdom with annual ceremonies at cult shrines dedicated to their memory.

Their revolt had failed, but the Trung Sisters established a model for later rebels, as China intensified its direct control and launched a more deliberate assimilation policy. Another anticolonial leader, the 23-year-old Lady Trieu (Trieu Thi Trinh) in the third century CE, demonstrated her ambitious commitment. When advised to marry rather than fight, she replied in words that still stir the Vietnamese: "I want to ride the storm, tread the dangerous waves, win back the fatherland and destroy the yoke of slavery. I don't want to bow down my head working as a simple housewife."[10] Her actual story may have been embellished by myth, and later male Vietnamese writers and scholars probably described her as almost superhuman—bewitching, nine feet tall, with a voice like a temple bell—to separate her from the actual flesh-and-blood women most of them believed to be inferior to men in this patriarchal society. Modern feminist historians have argued that women such as the Trung Sisters and Lady Trieu are most often remembered as heroic only when they excel in stereotypically masculine pursuits such as war and government. Lady Trieu seems an almost modern figure in her mix of patriotic and social defiance. But there was a human cost for such resistance. Phung Khac Khoan, a sixteenth-century Buddhist poet, described the results of chronic rebellion and warfare: "War, no end to it, people scattered in all directions. How can a man keep his mind off it? The winds dark, the rains violent year after year, laying waste the land, over and over."[11] The Vietnamese qualities of patience, determination, and sense of a larger national community eventually generated a successful struggle for independence in the tenth century.

While rice agriculture was fundamental to states like Vietnam, various Indianized states capitalized on growing maritime trade to became trade hubs linking East and South Asia. Between the seventh and thirteenth centuries, many of the small trading states in the Straits of Melaka region probably came under the loose control of Srivijaya (the Sanskrit term for "Great Victory"), an empire based on the river port of Palembang (Faxian's Bhoga) in Southeastern Sumatra and a fierce rival of the aggressive trading kingdoms in Southern India, particularly the Cholas. Srivijaya used its gold, a natural resource in that part of Sumatra, to cement alliances, most importantly with the powerful Buddhist state ruled by the Sailendra dynasty in Central Java, a highly productive rice-growing region. Srivijaya's system was not centralized but rather a federation of trading ports held together by a naval force that exercised considerable power over the region's international commerce. The empire maintained close trade relations with powerful China.

Early Southeast Asian cities were cosmopolitan and offered refined living. Chinese visitors reported around 800 that, in the capital of the Pyu kingdom in Burma, the men wore gold ornaments and jewels on their hats, while the women wore gold and silver ornaments as well as pearls in their hair. The women dressed in blue skirts and gauze silk scarves and carried fans. The Tibeto-Burman-speaking Pyus were also described by Chinese visitors as fond of music and dancing, modest, decent, peaceful, and courteous, greeting each other by grasping an arm with their hand and bowing. Their laws were humane and prisons unknown.

Although cities and trade were important for the economic development of the region, most Southeast Asians were peasants, subsistence farmers working small plots on which they grew just enough food to supply local needs and pay taxes. They lived in villages that were largely self-sufficient, and they emphasized kinship ties and a spirit of cooperation. Instead of private land ownership, land was owned either by families or, more commonly, by the ruler, who allowed successive generations of peasants to use the land as long as taxes were paid. Religious or harvest festivals provided periodic diversion from work. Itinerant traders also made occasional visits to villages. Before modern times migration from district to district was not uncommon to escape warfare or hardship, but many people rarely traveled more than a few miles from their home village. Life was hardly static but their lives were mostly governed by the endless cycle of crop planting and harvesting, birth and death, rainy and dry seasons. Too much rain or too little could ruin their crops. The farther from the royal capital they lived, the less peasant families were likely to know about the state they inhabited.

For both city and rural folk, the family became the key social institution and most cultures emphasized close cooperation among family members. Family gatherings reflected the often intense emotional attachment people felt for their relatives. Unlike in China or India, where people traced their descent through the father's family (known as a patrilineal pattern) and older men held most of the power at all levels (known as patriarchy), Southeast Asians (with exceptions, such as the Vietnamese) developed flexible notions of family, emphasizing a large number of both paternal and maternal kin. This system, known as bilateral kinship, is similar to the customs in the modern Western nations. As with the Chams, however, some matrilineal systems tracing descent through the mother's family existed, and senior women generally held a distinguished place in family affairs. Before modern times, women in Southeast Asia also generally enjoyed a higher status and played a more active public role, including doing most of the buying and selling in local markets, than was true for women in China, India, the Middle East, and Europe. In many societies wives owned property jointly with their husbands and also had the right to initiate divorce. Women often endowed religious facilities. Sometimes women even became rulers, but this meant overcoming some gender biases about strength and power. For example, in Java the ceremonial sword, known as a *kris*, wielded by royalty and warriors was a symbol of male virility. The major religions and philosophies that became dominant in the region—Hinduism, Buddhism, Islam, Confucianism, and Christianity—treated women as inferior to men socially and spiritually to varying degrees, although Buddhism was the least patriarchal. Nonetheless, few Southeast Asian societies cloistered women or devalued their contributions to their families and villages.

Even in these early centuries, Southeast Asians were open to the outside world. A third-century CE Chinese account described a kingdom on the Malay Peninsula that was a commercial hub between East and West, "so that daily there are unnumerable [*sic*] people there. Precious goods and rare merchandise—there is nothing which is not there."[12]

Some Southeast Asians benefited from the growth of seagoing trade between China and Western Eurasia, and most of the larger Southeast Asian states were multiethnic in their population, including foreign merchants in temporary or permanent residence. Seafaring Malay and Indian traders were common in Funan, often sojourning for months at a time. Many people specialized in interregional commerce, but wet-rice agriculture was the base for prosperity. Indeed, Funan's prominence was chiefly due to its highly productive farming. The enduring social and cultural traditions forged in Southeast Asia between 500 BCE and 800 CE, influenced by China or India but demonstrating many unique characteristics, provided the frameworks for later societies that established even closer ties to the wider world.

CHAPTER 3

The Kingdoms of the Golden Age, ca. 800–1400

A round 900 an Arab trader named Abu Dulaf arrived at the port of Kalah on Malaya's west coast. He wrote in his travel accounts that the city was "very great, with strong walls, numerous gardens and abundant springs. I found there a tin-mine such as does not exist in any other part of the world."[1] Arab traders had begun visiting Southeast Asian ports in the seventh century in search of tin and agricultural products to sell all over the Eastern Hemisphere. Kalah is even mentioned in one of the major works of Arab literature, *The Thousand and One Nights*, as "a great empire bordering on India, in which there are mines of tin, groves of bamboo and excellent camphor [for perfumes]."[2] The green lands and blue waters were attracting the world's attention, with the sea becoming a link rather than a barrier. Nor were the blue waters that Abu Dulaf traveled significant only to coastal states, because most Southeast Asians benefited from maritime trade and also depended on the muddy rivers for survival. Before modern times most inland trade was carried out along rivers, in fact. The era from around 800 to 1400 can be viewed, as it has been by many Southeast Asians, as a "Golden Age" in politics, economic prosperity, and cultural development.

On Sumba, an island in Eastern Indonesia, the Kodi people have a song about imported valuables: "Brought across the wide seas, to fall at our feet and be grasped by our hands, the stalk of foreign banana now sits at our ancestral hearth."[3] From earliest times Southeast Asians blended outside influences with local creativity. Traditionally China and India provided political, religious, and cultural ideas, although the impact of these varied greatly from society to society. Later, the Middle East, Western Europe, and the United States provided some other models, in the latter two cases imposed in part by military force. But despite centuries of borrowing and sometimes foreign conquest, Southeast Asians were never passive beneficiaries and rarely became carbon copies of the cultures influencing them. Like the Japanese and Europeans, they took ideas that they wanted from outsiders and adapted them to their own use, creating in the process a distinctive synthesis. For example, the Hindu temples on the Indonesian island of Bali look little like those built in Burma centuries ago, and neither resemble most Hindu temples in India. Furthermore, the Golden Age states were built on the foundations of earlier states such as Funan and Srivijaya.

Southeast Asians also showed a tendency to blend seemingly incompatible elements into a cultural unity. Animism was often incorporated into or coexisted quite easily with Hinduism, Buddhism, Confucianism, and other imported religions. There was a widespread pattern, as in East Asia, for religions to be inclusive and eclectic, a mix of influences. Even Christianity and Islam, which tend to demand exclusive allegiance, have incorporated local customs such as animist spirits and village healers in Southeast Asia. Some outside influences became superficial glosses overlaying strong indigenous values while others penetrated more deeply. Many local traditions had a resilience that allowed them to survive the centuries of borrowing and change.

India had a strong influence on Southeast Asia until the fourteenth century, and many Southeast Asian states made selective use of Indian models in shaping their politics and culture. Rulers and their courts adopted Mahayana Buddhism and Hinduism, although animism remained influential among the peasantry. Hindu priests (brahmans) became advisers on ritual in the courts, presiding over coronations and serving as scribes, clerks, astrologers, and in other offices. Indian sculpture and architecture provided artistic models. Hindu Indian epics like the *Ramayana*, with their kings, gods, and demons, became deeply imbedded in various cultures. The *Ramayana* told of the wanderings of the hero, Rama, and his faithful wife, Sita. The *Ramayana* conveyed insights into the character and endless intrigues of North Indian court life, which, judging from the epic's enduring popularity in Southeast Asia, may have resembled Southeast Asian courts.

Buddhism also spread more widely during this era. By 1000 CE the Buddhist world stretched from the Indian subcontinent and Sri Lanka (Ceylon) eastward to Japan and included much of Southeast Asia. In most places Buddhism existed alongside, rather than replacing, earlier religions. One of the two main Buddhist schools, Mahayana, became entrenched in China, Japan, Korea, Vietnam, Mongolia, Tibet, and parts of Central Asia. Over the centuries the other main school, Theravada, expanded first to Sri Lanka and then to mainland Southeast Asia, where it first became strong among the Mon and Burman people. When the Golden Age kingdoms waned, Theravada Buddhism helped reshape cultures, societies, and worldviews with notions of moderation, social equality, and individualism.

Indianized rulers declared themselves god-kings (*devaraja*), reincarnated Buddhas, or Shivas (the Hindu god of fertility, life, and death) worthy of cult worship. By maintaining order in this world, they ensured cosmic harmony. In theory these god-kings were absolute rulers, but their power faded with distance from the capital cities. Kings enjoyed enormous prestige but also faced continuous threats from rivals, who sometimes succeeded in acquiring the throne. Warfare was no less frequent and deadly than in other areas of the world as rulers sought more land and labor to supply revenues, and as one Malay proverb put it, "when elephants fight, the ant between them is killed."

Whatever the power and stability of their rulers, most states depended to some degree on the waters of blue, whether oceans or rivers, for their prosperity and survival. From early in the Common Era a complex maritime trading system gradually emerged that linked the Eastern Mediterranean, Middle East, East African coast, Persia, and South Asia with the societies of East and Southeast Asia. This system particularly benefited maritime states such as Srivijaya in Eastern Sumatra, which maintained its influence as the dominant power in the Straits of Melaka and a major hub of China-India trade well into the 1200s. A Chinese visitor reported in the early twelfth century that "merchants from distant places congregate there [and] the country is very prosperous."[4] Srivijaya was also a major center of Buddhist observance and study, with thousands of Buddhist monks and students from other countries. Srivijaya became a Buddhist version of Islamic Cairo or Christian Paris, as an international center of religious learning. However, destructive conflicts with the Cholas and several Javan kingdoms reduced Srivijayan power and the increasing competition from Chinese trading ships undermined Malay shipping. By the fourteenth century Srivijaya had lost much of its glory.

The states alongside the Straits of Melaka, such as Srivijaya and Kalah, or directly facing the Java and South China Seas depended more heavily on maritime trade than farming, although most could not have flourished without their food-producing hinterlands. Inland states such as Angkor and Pagan, while not ignoring trade, were based largely on rice agriculture. New drought-resistant, early-ripening rice seeds exported from Champa during the ninth and tenth centuries were productive enough to sustain large centralized states. Champa rice allowed China to double the land under cultivation. Some successful peoples, including the Burmans, Siamese (Thai), and Vietnamese, used irrigated rice technology, which may have helped them supplant rain- and flood-based wet-rice farmers like those of the Chams, Mons, and Pyu. Meanwhile, maritime trading states used the open frontier of the sea to compensate for a swampy location unsuitable for intensive agriculture, such as that found in coastal Malaya and Sumatra.

Political leaders used the imported religions to buttress their power. A Javanese historical chronicle recounts the divine origins of King Angrok, who founded the state of Singosari in Eastern Java in 1222. The main Hindu god, Brahma, announced to the other gods: "Know that I have a son who was born a human being; he shall make the land of Java firm and strong."[5] By the fourteenth century the Javanese had composed verse chronicles and prose narratives about the course and meaning of their history. These writings reflected the privileged classes that produced them and often focused on legitimizing rulers while upholding moral and religious values. In the Golden Age kingdoms there was a clear social and political distinction between what anthropologists have termed the "great tradition" of the courts, based on the royal governments and capital cities, and the "little traditions" of the villages which persisted for many centuries. Literature such as poetry, philosophical speculations, and historical chronicles became an important aspect of "great tradition" culture and expression.

Despite the split between city and rural life, the continuous migration and mixing of peoples were important for all areas of Southeast Asia. Following in the footsteps of earlier arrivals from the north came peoples such as the Burmans from Tibet into Burma in the ninth century and the Tai from China into Thailand and Laos in the seventh to thirteenth centuries. Their success may have had as much to do with creative adaptation to the ecology and assimilating the values of local cultures as to military prowess or cultural values. Their irrigated rice technology, however, may have been superior to that of many indigenous peoples. Ethnic and cultural frameworks were seldom rigid. Just as they blended diverse influences into coherent cultures, Southeast Asians throughout their history redefined social, cultural, and ethnic identities. This resulted in part from the fluctuating nature of state power and the persistence of migration into the region, and there was a tendency for some fringe peoples to be incorporated into the emerging ethnic majorities. This process closely resembled the migrations and assimilation of various "barbarian" peoples in Western Europe such as Vandals, Visigoths, and Franks between 200–800 CE, which undermined Roman civilization. The Khmers, Burmans, Vietnamese, Siamese, and Malays assimilated many of the peoples they dominated politically.

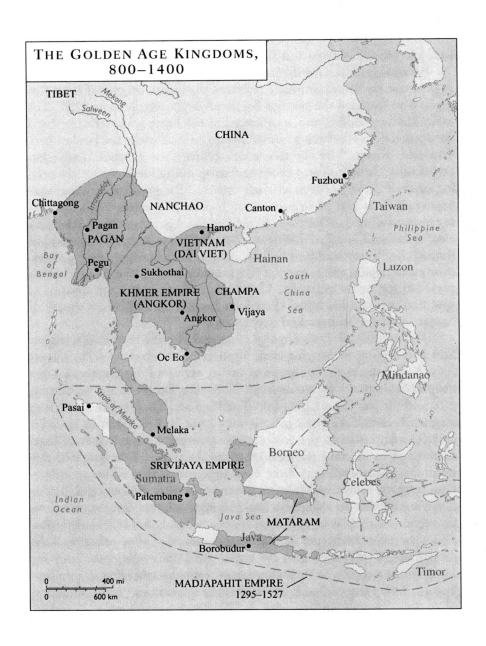

THE GOLDEN AGE KINGDOMS, 800–1400

TIBET

CHINA

Mekong

Salween

Irrawaddy

Chittagong

NANCHAO

Fuzhou

Canton

Taiwan

Pagan

PAGAN

Hanoi

VIETNAM
(DAI VIET)

Hainan

Philippine
Sea

Bay
of
Bengal

Pegu

Sukhothai

South

China

Sea

Luzon

KHMER EMPIRE
(ANGKOR)

CHAMPA

Angkor

Vijaya

Oc Eo

Mindanao

Strait of Melaka

Pasai

Melaka

Borneo

Celebes

SRIVIJAYA EMPIRE

Sumatra

Indian
Ocean

Palembang

Java Sea

MATARAM

Borobudur

Java

Timor

0   400 mi

0   600 km

MADJAPAHIT EMPIRE
1295–1527

The largest and most powerful Golden Age state was the Khmer kingdom of Angkor in Cambodia, established by King Jayavarman II in 802. The name Angkor derives from the Sanskrit term for "holy city," and Jayavarman considered himself a reincarnation of Shiva, the Hindu god of destruction and fertility. Jayavarman himself had lived many years at a Hindu court in Java before returning to Cambodia, indicating the widespread contacts among Southeast Asian states. His successors consolidated the kingdom and conquered Dvaravati, a heavily Indianized and largely Buddhist Mon state in central Thailand. One of the greatest Angkor kings, Jayavarman VII (who ruled from 1181 to 1219) was a devout Buddhist who boasted of his compassion for his people. He expanded the empire, commissioned important artworks, built roads and sturdy stone walls, and sponsored the construction of monuments and temples. His main legacy was the Bayon temple, which featured towers with large carved faces, probably of the egocentric king himself.

Angkor's kings bragged about their achievements, and royal engravers gushed as they described on a monument King Yasovarman I in the late ninth century: "In all the sciences and in all the sports, in dancing, singing, and all the rest, he was as clever as if he had been the first inventor of them."[6] Angkor flourished for half a millennium. At its height in the twelfth and thirteenth centuries, the kingdom was a loosely integrated empire controlling much of present-day Cambodia, Laos, Thailand, and Southern Vietnam. Angkor carried on an active trade with China, with many resident Chinese merchants. Zhou Daguan, a Chinese ambassador in Angkor in 1296, left vivid descriptions of the society and its leaders. In a report back home, he outlined the system of justice presided over by the king: "Disputes of the people, however insignificant, always go to the king. Each day the king holds two audiences for affairs of state. Those of the functionaries or the people who wish to see the king, sit on the ground to wait for him."[7]

Zhou Daguan also observed a spectacular royal procession of the Angkor king, Indravarman, in 1296:

> When the king goes out, troops are at the head of the escort; then come flags, banners and music. Palace women, numbering from three to five hundred, wearing flowered cloth, with flowers in their hair, hold candles in their hands, and form a troupe. Even in broad daylight, the candles are lighted. Then come other palace women, carrying lances and shields, the king's private guards, and carts drawn by goats and horses, all in gold, come next. Ministers and princes are mounted on elephants, and in front of them one can see, from afar, their innumerable

red umbrellas. After them come the wives and concubines of the king, in palanquins, carriages, on horseback and on elephants. They have more than one hundred parasols, flecked with gold. Behind them comes the sovereign, standing on an elephant, holding his sacred sword in his hand. The elephant's tusks are encased in gold.[8]

The well-financed Angkor government supported substantial public services including hospitals, schools, and libraries. The Khmer wrote on stone, palm leaf, and hides, but only the stone inscriptions have survived the ravages of time and a tropical climate. Some kings were noted as avid patrons of knowledge and the arts. One wrote that having drunk the nectar of knowledge, the king gives it to others to drink. Theater, art, and dance reflected Hindu values and stories. But military abilities were also highly prized, and the Khmers acquired and maintained their substantial empire by a skillful combination of warfare, diplomacy, and pragmatism. Nonetheless, only the most powerful and ruthless kings wielded unchallenged power over regional governors, who usually had considerable autonomy. The government mixed political and religious power, and priestly families held a privileged position and led a cult to worship the god-kings. By the twelfth century the bustling capital city, Angkor Thom, and its immediate environs had perhaps as many as 1 million people, much larger than any medieval European city but comparable to all but the largest Chinese and Arab cities of that era. This was clearly one of the major urban complexes in the preindustrial world. The magnificent temples still standing today and a remarkable water-control network testify to prosperity and organization.

Many stone temple mountains were built by thousands of conscripted workers as sanctuaries and mausoleums, designed to represent the Hindu conception of the cosmos. At their center was a replica of Mt. Meru, where Hindus believe that the gods dwell. These temples also provided vivid and concrete symbols of a monarch's earthly power. The temple complex Angkor Wat was the largest religious complex in the premodern world, built by some 70,000 workers in the twelfth century, and surrounded by a four-mile-long moat, dwarfing the magnificent European cathedrals and grand mosques of Baghdad or Cairo. The reliefs carved into stone at Angkor Wat and other temples provided glimpses of daily life, showing fishing boats, midwives attending a childbirth, festival jugglers and dancers, the crowd at a cockfight, men playing chess, peasants bringing goods to market, and merchant stalls. According to Zhou, women operated most of these retail stalls: "In this country it is the women who are concerned with commerce."[9] Khmer society in this era was matrilineal, and women played a much more important

Angkor Wat, the greatest of the temple complex at Angkor and one of the world's most magnificent buildings, built in the twelfth century during the reign of King Suryavarman II, still inspires Cambodians and amazes visitors. The tallest spire, in the center of the main building, represents Mt. Meru, believed by Hindus to be at the center of the cosmos. Photo by Craig A. Lockard

role in the family, society, and politics than in most other places in the world. Women went out in public as they liked, and Chinese visitors were shocked at their liberated behavior.

Some royal women at Angkor were noted for intellectual activities or service to others. Jayarajadevi, the first wife of King Jayavarman VII, took in hundreds of abandoned girls, training and settling them. After her death the king married Indradevi, a renowned scholar who lectured at a Buddhist monastery and who was acclaimed in a temple inscription as "naturally intelligent . . . very pure . . . the chief teacher of the king."[10] Women dominated the palace staff, and some were even gladiators and warriors. Women were also active in the arts, especially as poets.

In addition to building temples, drafted workers also constructed an extensive hydraulic network of canals and reservoirs for efficient water distribution, demonstrating some of the most advanced civil engineering in the premodern world. With the help of plows pulled by oxen or water buffalo, Khmer farmers brought a moderately fertile region into astonishing productivity. Whether Angkor wet-rice farming was based on rainfall and flooding or on irrigation, or perhaps a combination of both, remains unclear, as does whether this hydraulic system was used primarily for irrigation or for other purposes. Although some scholars are skeptical, according to Chinese visitors, the Khmers may have had the most productive agriculture in history, producing three to four harvests a year, whereas elsewhere in the world only one or two was normal. Only a few premodern peoples, such as the Chinese and Balinese, could even come close to matching Khmer farming capabilities.

The peasants growing this rice were a large component of a Khmer social structure that was quite rigid, with each class fulfilling its appointed role. Below the king and the priests were the trade guilds. Most other people were tied to the soil they plowed, to the temples they served, and to the king's army. In exchange for considerable material security and the protection of a patron to whom they owed allegiance, Khmer commoners tolerated the unequal distribution of wealth. Farmers and soldiers owed substantial labor obligations to the king. Many slaves, often prisoners of war, criminals, or debtors, and various other people lived in some form of temporary or permanent involuntary servitude. Zhou Daguan reported that rich families owned more than a hundred slaves, who did all the work. Even families of tradesmen possessed from ten to twenty slaves per household. Slaves did the most difficult jobs, dredging the irrigation canals, rowing the war boats, working the quarries, and helping build the great temples.

While Angkor enjoyed the most power in Southeast Asia during this era, other states also flourished. West of Angkor, the Indianized state of Pagan was founded by the Burman people, who began migrating into the Irrawaddy River valley from Tibet around 800 CE. In the process, the Burmans gained domination over but also adopted considerable culture from the long-settled, strongly Buddhist Pyu and Mon peoples. In the eleventh century the Burmans established a kingdom with their capital at Pagan, along the Irrawaddy River in Central Burma. Pagan flourished at the expense of earlier peoples, however. Although some historians doubt that a strong Mon state actually existed at that time, the Mon historical chronicles claim that after a Pagan attack, the Mon capital, Thaton, was left "in ruin and silence reigned supreme. In contrast, Pagan shone in glory and in triumph, as if it had become the abode of gods."[11]

At its height in the 1100s, Pagan was one of the architectural wonders of the world, a city filled with temples and shrines to the glory of Buddhism (chiefly the Theravada school) and Hinduism. In 250 years of sustained faith, kings and commoners alike spent their wealth on

This fresco, from the Ananda Temple at Pagan, portrays women going about their daily chores and socializing with their friends. The Burmans of Pagan painted both Buddhist religious images and scenes of daily life in many of their temples. Bridgeman-Giraudon/Art Resource, NY

magnificent religious buildings. Inscriptions on the buildings tell us their motives. One donor claimed that he donated land, cows, and laborers to a monastery in the hope that "the present king, future kings, [my] mother and father, [my] sons and all creatures . . . may benefit equally with me."[12] The legitimacy of the state rested on its relationship to the powerful Buddhist monkhood. But the monkhood and royal families competed for control of resources such as land and labor, and the state gradually lost valuable sources of wealth such as farms to the monkhood.

As in Angkor, women occupied an important status in Pagan, serving as village heads, royal officials, scribes, bankers, artisans, and Buddhist nuns and scholars. Occasionally an influential queen gained power. Indeed, in Burmese legend, the thirteenth century Queen Pwa Saw was among the greatest of the Pagan leaders, helping to rally the country in a time of invasion and instability. Much of what we know about her life comes from a chronicle of the country's history compiled by Burmese scholars in the nineteenth century, and modern historians are divided on whether it contains more myth than fact. Whatever the accuracy, in their traditions the Burmese remember Queen Pwa Saw as witty, wise, and beautiful, exercising political influence for 40 years during one of their most difficult periods.

Her life reveals how capable royal women could exercise power behind the throne, even under the most strong-willed of kings. The girl who would become queen is thought to have been born to a prosperous peasant family around 1237. King Uzana, a playboy, found her attractive and took her back to Pagan as one of his many wives, making her a deputy queen. A short time later, Uzana died in an accident while hunting wild elephants. With her husband's death, Pwa Saw was thrown into the scheming and rivalries of the royal court as various factions maneuvered for power. She and her court allies convinced officials to support one of Uzana's sons, Narathihapade, as king and make Pwa Saw chief queen. But the young king proved arrogant, quick-tempered, and ruthless, alienating many at court. While the economy declined, the king boasted, with much exaggeration, that he had 3,000 concubines and was "the commander of 36 million soldiers, [and] the swallower of 300 dishes of curry daily."[13] His zeal to build an expensive Buddhist pagoda fostered the proverb that "the pagoda is finished and the great country ruined." Pwa Saw remained loyal but lost respect for the king.

Pwa Saw skillfully survived the king's paranoid suspicions and the constant intrigues of the court nobles, attendants, and other queens. Because the king trusted the widely revered queen, she could often overrule his destructive tendencies and talk him into making wiser state decisions. She also convinced the erratic king to appoint capable officials. But she had to keep her wits about her. Increasingly paranoid, Narathihapade executed any perceived enemies. In the 1270s, anxious to prove himself a great leader, he rejected her advice to meet Mongol demands for tribute and avoid conflict and instead escalated tensions, leading to war and the temporary Mongol occupation of Pagan. Even as the Pagan state declined, Pwa Saw asserted a benevolent influence. For instance, in 1271 she donated some of her lands and properties to a Buddhist temple, expressing hope that in future existences she would "have long life, be free from illness, have a good appearance, melodic of voice, be loved and respected by all men and gods, [and] be fully equipped with faith, wisdom, nobility."[14] In 1287 the mad king was murdered by one of his sons and Queen Saw and surviving ministers selected a new king, Kyawswar, another son of Narathihapade.

In the Indianized states on Java, the adaptation of outside influences produced a unique religious and political blend often termed *Hindu-Javanese*. In Hindu-Javanese thinking, the earthly order mirrored and embodied the supernatural one and people must avoid disharmony and change at all cost. The purpose of the god-king was to prevent such deterioration by maintaining order in a turbulent human society and thereby harmonizing with the cosmic balance. Kings boasted of their success in such matters. In 1365 a court poet extolled King Hayam Wuruk of Madjapahit: "He is praised like the moon in autumn, since he fills all the world with joy. His retinue, treasures, chariots, elephants, horses are (immeasurable) like the sea. The land of Java is becoming more and more famous for its blessed state throughout the world."[15] Madjapahit, the largest Javanese kingdom, was formed in 1292 and reached its peak in the mid-1300s under Prime Minister Gajah Mada, when it controlled Eastern Java and Bali and, according to Javanese chronicles, some sort of larger empire embracing much of present-day Indonesia and Malaya. The army commander and his 30,000 solders were paid in gold, suggesting that Madjapahit had a standing army.

Although women sometime ruled Javanese kingdoms, men usually dominated government at all levels. Kings bragged of their womanizing. The court chronicles described Hayam Wuruk as "without cares . . . he indulges in all pleasures. All beautiful maidens . . . are selected for him, as many as possible, and of those who are captured in foreign countries the prettiest girls are brought into his harem."[16] Court life was full of pageantry and celebration, and the women of the royal harems and their many female attendants were advised to be grateful, as one contemporary male poet noted: "the women's quarters seemed to radiate a shimmering light/It was as if the amazing beauty emanated from heaven."[17] Well-bred women were expected to stay in their secluded quarters and not venture outside the palace.

Trading ships, including some from China, called at ports on Java's north coast, and a thirteenth-century Chinese official, probably basing his account on the reports of such traders, provides a vivid account of political and economic life in a West Javan kingdom:

> The king wears his hair in a knot, on his head is a golden bell; he wears a silken robe and leather shoes. His throne is a square seat, and his officers at their daily audience bow three times when withdrawing. When he goes forth he rides an elephant, or is carried in a chair followed by a company of from 500 to 700 armed soldiers. When any one of the people see the king, he squats down until [the king] has passed by. . . . The [government does] not inflict corporal punishment

and imprisonment on criminals; they are fined an amount in gold varying according to the gravity of the crime. . . . [The country] produces rice, hemp, millet, beans, but no wheat. Ploughing is done with buffaloes. They also pay attention to the raising of silkworms and the weaving of the silk; they have various colored brocaded silks, cotton, and damasked cotton gauzes. They cast coins in an alloy of copper, silver, white copper, and tin. Foreign merchants use gold and silver in trading. There is a vast store of pepper and the [Chinese] merchant ships, in view of the profit they derive from that trade, are in the habit of smuggling out of China copper cash for bartering purposes.[18]

As the Chinese report illustrates, the Javanese developed a complex etiquette for regulating the relations between those of different status, confirming the rigid social order. Like Angkor, Java's capital and palaces were built to imitate the Hindu cosmic order. Hindu-Buddhist influences were most pronounced in the many temple complexes, such as Borobodur. This massive 400-foot-wide terraced stone temple mountain, built in the ninth century from more than 2 million stone blocks, represented Javanese ideas of the Buddhist cosmos as a series of concentric circles, while also symbolizing the wealth of the ruler.

Many of the temples built in Java before the coming of Islam reflected Hindu or Buddhist influences. Perhaps the greatest example of Buddhist monumental architecture was the huge temple mountain of Borobudur, in Central Java, which houses many statues and images of the Buddha. Photo by Craig A. Lockard

Hindu-Buddhist values were also reflected in stories and other arts, such as the shadow puppet play (*wayang kulit*), which was popular by the twelfth century with people of all ages. Using leather puppets illuminated by an oil lamp behind a cloth screen, the wayang puppeteers wove engaging stories about a world of gods, demons, princes, and clowns. Many of the stories were based on Hindu epics such as the *Ramayana* but with local content as well. The puppeteer, at once storyteller and philosopher, gave life to the characters and developed the stories to teach manners and morals, usually with much humor, poking fun at local notables and even sometimes national leaders. Versions of the *wayang kulit* also became popular in Balinese, Malay, and Siamese cultures.

The Javanese courts may have been splendid, but most people lived in villages, where life was substantially different from that in the royal capital. The village headmen linked village and court. Much of the village work on canals and other public works was planned and carried out on a communal basis, establishing a tradition of local democracy and mutual self-help. Each village had a meeting hall, as a Madjapahit poet noted: "And in the shelter of the banyan tree stood the hall . . . always the scene of many deliberations."[19] The villagers' main link with the central government was through paying taxes and undertaking labor as ordered. Peasants identified more with their village community than with distant kings in their palaces, but Javanese culture encouraged compliance with official demands.

Not all Golden Age kingdoms reflected Indian cultural influences. Vietnam remained more a part of the Chinese cultural world than the Indian in this era. In 939 CE, however, China was in turmoil with the collapse of the once-great Tang dynasty, and a rebellion finally succeeded in pushing the Chinese out of Vietnam. The new Vietnamese state, then called Dai Viet, began to play a more aggressive role in Southeast Asia, and it wisely maintained many Chinese political structures and philosophies. Vietnam even became a vassal state, sending regular tribute missions to maintain Chinese goodwill. But these concessions did not discourage Chinese forces from occasionally attempting a reconquest. The permanent Chinese threat forced the Vietnamese to become masters at marshalling military forces to resist foreign invasions. A unique sense of common identity, perhaps even of nationhood, greatly aided Vietnamese survival in a dangerous regional environment over the centuries. When the country was at peace, literature, poetry, and theater, among other art forms, flourished. The fourteenth-century poet Tran Thanh-tong celebrated the beauty of a favorite destination in Vietnam: "In the morning the mountains. Clouds. Night, the moon-lit bay—Suddenly, the charm of this place: My [writing] brush shapes multitudes at its tip."[20]

Most of the great kingdoms in Southeast Asia came to an end between 1250 and 1450, but the changes were generally gradual. The southward expansion of the Vietnamese displaced the Cham states and dispersed the population. Angkor declined due to a combination of causes: military expansion overstretched resources. Increased temple building resulted in higher tax levies and more forced labor, which prompted rebellions. The irrigation system may also have broken down. Outside forces also contributed to Angkor's collapse. For centuries various groups from Southwest China speaking closely related tongues of the Tai language family had made the arduous, sometimes dangerous journey across rugged mountains into the Khmer Empire. The Tai brought with them their water buffalo, pigs, dogs, and baskets full of their possessions. Some Tai fought as mercenary soldiers for Angkor and other states. By the 1200s some Tai were setting up states in the middle Mekong valley and Northern Thailand. These were the ancestors of the Siamese (Thai) and Lao peoples. Tai speakers later known as Shan also settled in Burma's eastern highlands. As they moved south, the Tais conquered or absorbed the local peoples, and by the 1400s the Tai had repeatedly sacked Angkor and seized much of the empire's territory. The Khmer rulers abandoned the Angkor capital in 1431, and the grand palaces and temples were gradually engulfed by the jungle. The expanding Vietnamese and Siamese states periodically controlled or dominated the demoralized remnants of the once splendid Angkor society. Yet, even today, the image and spirit of a long-abandoned Angkor continues to inspire the Khmer people and promote cultural pride.

The Mongols also invaded territory in Southeast Asia. During the thirteenth century, horseback-riding Mongol warriors with a fearsome reputation and advanced weapons had expanded out of their impoverished Central Asian grasslands to conquer the greatest land empire in history, stretching from China and Korea to Eastern Europe. Interested in adding Southeast Asia to their possessions, they attacked Pagan in 1287, after the Burman king Narathihapade rashly refused to recognize Mongol overlordship. Unused to the tropical heat, however, Mongol forces soon withdrew to China. Historians debate the degree of damage inflicted by the Mongols. Pagan was already in decline and the Mongol attack hastened the eventual political collapse, beginning a long competition for power among various groups in Burma, including Burmans, Mons, and Shan. Various Tai speakers, including the Shan, dominated the north. The Mons established a state at Pegu on the southern coast in 1281, profiting from foreign trade. Burmans and Shans built a kingdom, the successor to Pagan, centered at Ava (also known as Inwa) in Central Burma in the early fourteenth century. Another Burman state, Toungoo, emerged further south, at Prome, in the 1500s, vying with Ava, Pegu, and the Shans for power in Burma, resulting in long-term conflict until the 1800s.

The Mongols also found frustration elsewhere in Southeast Asia. Between 1281 and 1285 they were defeated off the Vietnamese coast by a joint but temporary Vietnamese-Cham military alliance, although the ill-fated Mongol land and sea invasion inflicted terrible damage on Vietnam's capital, Hanoi. A Vietnamese general, Tran Hung Dao, inspired the resistance fighters by having his soldiers tattoo "Kill the Mongols" on their right arms. A Mongol naval expedition to Java using Chinese ships also proved a costly failure, the Javanese defenders forcing the Mongols back to their ships. The discouraged Mongols soon sailed home. Southeast Asians were among the few peoples to successfully resist Mongol conquest and power, a tribute to their skill and might, although their distance from the Eurasian heartland and the weakness of Mongol naval power also played a role.

In contrast to military invasions, new religions peacefully swept over Southeast Asia. By early in the second millennium, Theravada Buddhism and Islam were filtering into Southeast Asia. Theravada Buddhism, sometimes termed "the southern school," had been present for several centuries but, except among the Burmans and the Mons, was generally less influential than the Mahayana Buddhism patronized by Indianized kings. In the late twelfth century some pagan leaders adopted a revitalized version from Sri Lanka (Ceylon). Mon traders and monks helped to spread the faith to other societies. Theravada Buddhism provided a revolutionary challenge to the rigid political orders of the Indianized kingdoms. Theravada Buddhism offered a message of egalitarianism, pacifism, and individual worth that proved highly attractive to peasants weary of war, public labor projects, and tyrannical kings. Furthermore, this was a tolerant religion able to incorporate the animism of the peasant villages. It was already an important influence in Pagan by the eleventh century. By the 1300s most of the Burman, Khmer, Siamese, and Lao peasants had adopted Theravada Buddhism as well and blended it with animism, while the upper classes mixed the new faith with the older Hindu–Mahayana Buddhist traditions.

The other outside religion, Islam, spread widely from the fourteenth through seventeenth centuries, coming from the Middle East by way of

India. Islam arose in central Arabia at the beginning of the seventh century, when Muhammad ibn Abdullah, a merchant in Mecca, founded the faith based on what he and his followers believed to be revelations to him from God. These messages were recorded in the *Qu'ran* ("recitation"), which became Islam's most holy book; to believers, it is the inspired word of God. Muhammad's followers considered him to be the last of God's prophets, and the faith also incorporated some Jewish and Christian traditions such as Kosher meal preparation and belief in angels and an afterlife.

Islam means "submission to God's will." Muslims ("those who submit to God's will") had clear duties known as the "five pillars." These included, first, the profession of faith: "there is no God but Allah and Muhammad is his messenger (or prophet)." Muhammad was not considered divine but rather a teacher chosen by God to spread the truth of a monotheistic God who is eternal, all powerful, all knowing, and all merciful. Second were the formal prayers performed five times daily. The third pillar required giving assistance to the poor and disadvantaged. Fourth was the fast (*Ramadan*). For one month each year, Muslims must abstain from eating, drinking, or fornicating during daylight hours, to demonstrate sacrifice for their faith and understand the experiences of the poor and hungry. But this was done with lively gatherings of families and friends before sunrise and after sunset. Finally, if possible, at least once in their lives, believers should make a pilgrimage (the *haj*) to the holy city of Mecca for spiritual activities, worshiping with other believers from around the world.

Islam's tenets also gave Muslims a social and political framework and a sense of community in the wider brotherhood of believers. The idea of unity in the oneness of God was applied to the human family. To ensure moral behavior within the community, Islam regulated how people lived together, offering a legal code and rules addressing daily life. But many Muslims adopted a more mystical version of the faith known as Sufism, which stressed a religion of the heart rather than rigid theology and legal restrictions. Arab and Indian Sufis were active in spreading the faith to Southeast Asia. The division between the more orthodox believers and the Sufi mystics was, however, less significant than that between the Sunni and Shia, the result of a bitter dispute among Muslims over the leadership of the community after Muhammad's death. The great majority of Muslims, including most Arabs, were Sunni and this branch also became dominant in India and Southeast Asia.

Islam spread rapidly from Western Asia westward to North Africa and eastward to Central Asia and India, fostering an Islamic age in the Eastern Hemisphere. The new religion emphasized the equality of believers, which challenged the power of the ruling classes, and a theology that appealed to peasants and merchants in the coastal regions of the Malay Peninsula, Sumatra, Java, and some of the other islands. By embracing Islam, rulers hoped to attract Muslim Arab, Persian, and Indian merchants. Some people adopted Islam in a largely orthodox form, while others mixed it with animism, Hinduism, or Buddhism. The adaptable, mystical Sufi ideas fostered conversion by promoting an emotional approach rather than dogmatic theology, and Sufism meshed well with the mysticism that had been long present in places like Java. The result was that, during the next several centuries, many Southeast Asians were drawn into the wider world of Islam.

CHAPTER 4

New Cultures and Connections, ca. 1300–1750

In 1468 Sultan Mansur, the ruler of the Malaysian state of Melaka, wrote a letter to the king of the Ryukyu Islands, just south of Japan, extolling the benefits of trade relations: "We have learned that to master the blue oceans people must engage in commerce and trade. All the lands within the seas are united in one body. Life has never been so affluent in preceding generations as it is today."[1] The collapse of the Golden Age kingdoms proved a prelude to a dynamic new era in which many societies, among them Melaka, became increasingly involved with world trade and the larger Eurasian realm. Theravada Buddhism and Islam spread widely throughout Southeast Asia, and new cultures emerged. New states and empires were founded on the legacies of older ones. Most Southeast Asians lived within one of three broad social and cultural spheres that had developed by the fifteenth century: the Theravada Buddhist, the Vietnamese, and the Malayo-Muslim or Indonesian. All these peoples flourished into the 1700s.

Theravada Buddhist states rose and fell in what is today Burma, Thailand, Cambodia, and Laos, but a shared religion did not eliminate political and ethnic conflict among rival peoples. Between 1539 and 1555 the Burman state of Toungoo conquered much of Northern and Southern Burma, including Pegu. During the sixteenth century ambitious Toungoo kings invaded the Thai and Lao states in quest of regional supremacy, temporarily annexing some of Northern Thailand, sacking cities, and carrying home much wealth. Under King Bayinnaung, who ruled from 1551 to 1581 from Pegu, Toungoo was the strongest state in mainland Southeast Asia although it had no sea power. However, the Siamese Thai and Lao states regained their independence in the late sixteenth century, and Toungoo maintained a shaky hold on its other

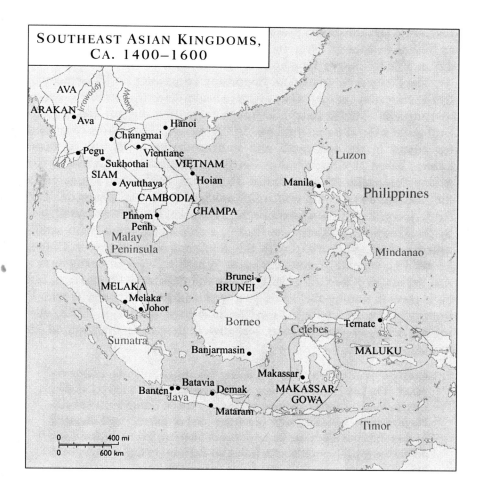

SOUTHEAST ASIAN KINGDOMS,
CA. 1400–1600

territories against Burmese rivals. Eventually Toungoo kings relocated their capital to Ava, located in a rich rice-growing region, and solidified their position as Burma's dominant power. Although located well inland, Ava was connected to maritime trade and also had a flourishing overland commerce with China.

By the mid-1700s Toungoo was weakening, suffering from poor leadership and internal dissension, and in 1752 southern rebels captured Ava. This allowed Alaungp'aya, a charismatic Burman village headman, to gather an army and seize power, forming the Ava-based Konbaung dynasty in 1752. By 1757 his forces controlled much of Central and Southern Burma, and in 1760 the king led an invasion of the Siamese state of Ayutthaya, during which he was fatally wounded. His successors struggled to capture and hold Northern and Western Burma as well as to contain Mon and Shan unrest. Not until the early 1800s did an able Konbaung king build a strong, stable state.

The Siamese were also an important Theravada Buddhist people. By the sixteenth century some Siamese began referring to their states as *mueang thai* (Thai country), although the nation did not adopt Thailand as its official name until the 1930s. Several Thai states competed for power in the thirteenth and fourteenth centuries, among them Lanna, based at Chiangmai in Northern Thailand, and Ligor in the Malay Peninsula. Another major Thai state, Sukhothai, appeared in the 1200s and eventually controlled much of the central plains of Thailand. According to Siamese tradition, Sukhothai's glory was established by Ramkamhaeng (Rama the Brave), a shrewd diplomat who established a close relationship with the dominant regional power, China, by sending regular tribute missions. Whether Ramkamhaeng was a real person or a mythological figure is still debated by historians, but he is revered among the Thais as a wise and popular ruler. A temple inscription traditionally believed to have been written in 1292, during his reign, praises the king, although it may have exaggerated his merits.

> During the life of King Ramkamhaeng this city of Sukhothai has prospered. The Lord of the country levies no tolls on his subjects as they travel along the roads, driving cattle to go trade, riding horses to sell. He is never in collusion with practicers [*sic*] of thievery and deceit. If he sees someone else's wealth he does not interfere. He accords aid and assistance to whomever comes riding an elephant to find him, requesting his protection for their country. If he captures some enemy soldiers he neither kills them nor beats them. In the (palace) doorway a bell is suspended; if an inhabitant of the kingdom has any complaint or any matter irritates his stomach and torments his mind, and he desires to expose it to the king it is not difficult: he has only to ring the bell that the king has hung there. Every time King Ramkamhaeng hears the sound of the bell he questions the complainant on his case and settles it in an equitable fashion.[2]

Whatever its accuracy, the inscription reveals the expectations for a Siamese king and the values admired in this Buddhist society. But Ramkamhaeng's claims to a special moral quality may also have helped Sukhothai kings to undercut the power and influence of rival Thai states, making Sukhothai central to the official Thai version of history.

Under Ramkamhaeng's pragmatic leadership, Siam adopted the Indian-influenced Khmer writing system. Indeed, Khmer influence permeated Siamese literature, art, and government. The king consolidated his power at the expense of rival lords and nearby states, making Theravada Buddhism the state religion and, as the inscription suggests, establishing laws that were highly humane by world standards at that time. The adoption of Theravada Buddhism won the support of the Mon people, who were still numerous in Central Thailand in those years. Over time most of the Mon were assimilated into Thai and Burman society, and today they are a small ethnic minority in Thailand and Burma.

By 1350 Sukhothai had been eclipsed by several neighboring states. Lan Xang—known as the kingdom of a million elephants and the white parasol, the symbol of Tai kingship—united many Lao people on both sides of the Mekong in what is today parts of Northeast Thailand and Western Laos, with its capital first at Luang Prabang and then Vientiane. Lan Xang survived for three-and-a-half centuries, occasionally repulsing invasions by Siamese and Burmans. A rival state dominated by the Siamese emerged in the plains of Southern Thailand, with its capital at Ayutthaya, just north of present-day Bangkok. Ayutthaya was involved in maritime trade and developed a regional empire, extending influence into Cambodia, Malaya, and some of the Lao states. Ayutthaya competed with the Burmans, Vietnamese, and Lan Xang for regional dominance, occasionally leading to war. Its greatest rivalry was with the Toungoo state, and indeed, in the 1560s, a Burmese army ravaged Ayutthaya, carrying back to Burma thousands of Siamese prisoners and their families. Burmese historical chronicles listed the occupations of these Siamese captives, and the variety of jobs indicates the sophistication of Ayutthaya's society: actor, actress, architect, artist, blacksmith, carpenter, coiffeur, cook, coppersmith, goldsmith, lacquerware maker, painter, perfume maker, silversmith, stone carver, wood carver, and veterinarian.

Ayutthaya eventually recovered from Burma's invasion, however, and flourished. The capital was open to merchants and creative people from all over Eurasia, and it was ringed by settlements for various foreign residents, including Malays, Chams, Chinese, Japanese, Indians, Arabs, and Persians, making it a vibrant crossroads of exchange and influence. Some 20,000 Chinese lived in the kingdom by the early 1700s, and one wrote that "Siam is really friendly to the Chinese."[3] Although most foreigners were merchants, some Japanese and Chinese were doctors and several Persians served as government officials. One king, Narai (1656–1688), used some of his revenues to promote literature and art, often with a Buddhist emphasis, in the process fostering a cultural renaissance. Because Theravada Buddhist monks sponsored many village schools, Buddhist societies such as Siam had some of the highest literacy rates in the preindustrial world. The high numbers of readers provided an audience for writers, some of whom focused on religious themes while others addressed more earthly affairs.

One of the finest Siamese poets of Narai's era was Sri Mahosot, whose work established new forms of expression and emphasized

A visiting French diplomat portrayed King Narai, a seventeenth-century ruler of Ayutthaya, riding out of his palace on an elephant as his ministers prostrate themselves before him. Most Southeast Asian kings surrounded themselves with pomp and ceremony. Bibliothèque Nationale, Paris, Estampes Od. 59

mood, often a cheerful one, as in his long poem, "Verses on Verses," which described the courtship rituals of young people along the riverside during the evening hours:

O beautiful night, bright sky! Excited voices on the riverbank.
Couples closely embraced they stare at each other.
One can see their teasing play and the beat of their hearts.
They stroll into the center all at the same time and snap their fingers, waving their clothes and whistling a song . . .
The handsome lovers stroll, all calling at the same time.
The women listen uneasily in expectation, in sweetness and seductive beauty.
There is smiling, touching, singing in chorus, looking eye to eye.
Walking to and fro, delightedly, the women let their eyes roam, they hope . . .
Outward they are proud, but their thought bent on love.
There is excitement, craving and longing forever.[4]

Another long war with the Burmese in the 1760s ended in Ayutthaya's defeat, and looting left the once splendid city in ruins. A Thai chronicle described the aftermath: "Some wandered about, starving, searching for food. They were bereft of their families, their children, and wives, and stripped of their possessions and tools. They found only the leaves of trees and grass to eat."[5] In 1778 Taksin, a general who was the son of a Chinese immigrant, expelled the Burmese forces and established a new Siamese state downriver from Ayutthaya, at Bangkok, which soon became the dominant state in Thailand and gradually absorbed its rivals. In 1781 Taksin himself was ousted by Rama I, also of part-Chinese ancestry, who formed the Chakri dynasty, which still sits on Thailand's throne today.

The Siamese society and culture had many similarities to those of other Theravada Buddhist peoples, such as the Khmer, Burmans, and especially the Lao, who lived on both sides of the Mekong River from Cambodia north almost to China. The Siamese kings continued to be viewed as semidivine reincarnated Buddhas, and they lived in splendor and majesty, advised by brahman priests in ceremonial and magical practices. A bureaucracy administered a centralized government, but royal power lessened as distance to the capital increased. The fierce competition of rivals for the throne on the death of a king fostered considerable instability. Because kings had many wives and concubines, there were often many men with royal blood who wanted the throne.

Siamese society was composed of a small aristocracy, many commoners including most peasants, and many slaves, most of whom were

By the 1600s several European nations, seeking trade privileges and political influence, were active in Southeast Asia, prompting local leaders to deal with changing realities. Siamese kings generally preferred diplomacy, such as granting an audience to a French ambassador in 1685. Snark/Art Resource, NY

war prisoners or those who became slaves to pay off debts. Male slaves did a variety of jobs from farming and mining to serving as trusted government officials. Slave women often worked as concubines, domestic servants, or entertainers. Despite the egalitarian trappings of Theravada Buddhism, Siamese culture encouraged deference to higher authority and recognition of status differences. Free women enjoyed many rights; they inherited equally with men and could initiate marriage or divorce. They also operated most of the stalls in village or town markets. Women did not enjoy absolute equality, however, and were expected to show their respect for men. They also had fewer rights in law. But visitors from China, India, Europe, and the Middle East were often shocked at the relative freedom of Siamese women. Ibn Muhammad Ibrahim, a Persian diplomat in late seventeenth-century Ayutthaya, wrote, "It is common for women to engage in buying and selling in the markets and even to undertake physical labor, and they do not cover themselves with modesty. Thus you can see the women paddling to the surrounding villages where they successfully earn their daily bread with no assistance from the men."[6] In contrast to the extended families of China and India, most Siamese lived in small nuclear families. And although Theravada peoples encouraged cooperation and mutual obligations within the family and village, they also maintained a sense of individualism.

In 1636 a Dutch trader, Joost Schouten, wrote an account of Siam that stressed the tolerance of Buddhists for other faiths, a contrast to the zealous proselytizing of Christians and Muslims in that era. He observed that they did not condemn any "opinions, but believe that all, though of differing tenets, living virtuously, may be saved, all services which are performed with zeal being acceptable to the great God. And the Christians [and Muslims] are both permitted the free exercise of their religions."[7] Siamese were also tolerant of those less devout, because an individual's spiritual state was his own responsibility. Most Siamese desired to build up a stock of merit to help them progress toward nirvana. In many ways, Siamese society reflected Theravada values, which emphasized gentleness and meditation. In order to escape from the endless round of life, death, and rebirth, believers were expected to devote themselves to attaining merit through commitment to the monastic life or generous deeds. Women could not become monks, although some became nuns. Laypeople could gain merit by supporting the monks. A Dutch visitor in 1619 marveled at their generous treatment: "[The monk's] food, clothing and needs are supplied very finely, richly and abundantly by all, both great and small."[8] Buddhist monks played an important role in local affairs as teachers and advisers on social and religious life.

At the village level, peasants moved easily between supporting their local Buddhist temple and appealing to the animistic spirits of the village and fields. Many rituals were designed to keep the spirits happy. Buddhism dealt with remote ends but did little to shield people from the crises of daily life. Because the faith offered no gods to worship, many turned to astrology, omens, and spirits to resolve personal problems, and to shamans, most of them women, to communicate with the spirits. In one of their rituals, peasants hung food from a post in their fields before plowing, an offering to the land spirits. The monks tolerated these practices, and many of these ideas are still common among the Theravada Buddhist peoples.

Vietnam, where Chinese influence was much greater than in Siam, offered a striking contrast to Theravada society. The Chinese believed in a supernatural or moral force that governed the universe. Western

Christian visitors later translated this concept, somewhat inaccurately, as "heaven." Like China, Vietnam had an imperial system in which the emperor was considered a "son of heaven," not an Angkor-style god-king but an intermediary between the earthly and supernatural realms. The emperors claimed divine support as long as conditions were tolerable for the people, what the Chinese called the "mandate of heaven." Vietnam was a tightly organized state, governed through a bureaucracy staffed by scholar-administrators (*mandarins*) chosen by civil service examinations designed to recruit men of talent and education. The emperor and his officials adopted Confucianism as the ruling ideology, although whether most Vietnamese had a deep knowledge of Confucian doctrines in this period remains subject to debate among historians. Just as successive Chinese governments wanted neighboring countries to become their vassals, Vietnam also sought to influence or control the peoples of the highlands as well as the neighboring Cham, Khmer, and Lao states.

The influence of China was less powerful among the peasant majority than it was among the rulers of Vietnam. In the villages, religion was an eclectic blend of the Mahayana Buddhism, Confucianism, and Daoism adopted from China, combined with the ancient spirit and ancestor worship. Considerable village autonomy and solidarity existed, summarized in the folk saying that "the authority of the emperor ends at the village gate." Yet the central government also had influence through the local mandarins. Despite the high status of mandarin families, peasants had to be respected. An old Vietnamese proverb advised that "the scholar precedes the peasant, but when the rice runs out, it's the peasant who precedes the scholar." Although individual families owned much of the land, the village also owned land that could be farmed by landless peasants. The social and political system provided security, but peasants could be mobilized for rebellions or to resist another Chinese invasion. The Vietnamese had a social system much like China's, in which older men held both family and village power, and a Vietnamese proverb observed that "a husband is one who commands wives." But women did most of the buying and selling of food and crafts at the local markets, and their influence increased with age, especially if they had sons.

Vietnam had an ancient tradition of folk poetry. The authors of most of these poems are unknown, and many of the verses were based on work chants, love songs, lullabies, ballads, riddles, and sayings. They dealt with the universal themes of love, marriage, religion, work, and nature, often with humor and realism. One anonymous poem,

"The Cherished Daughter," reveals a women's desperation. She wants her parents to arrange a marriage for her but they keep reducing their expectations in a system in which the bridegroom's family reimbursed the bride's family with gifts.

> Mother, I am eighteen this year and still without a husband.
> What, Mother, is your plan?
> The magpie brought two matchmakers and you threw them the challenge:
> not less than five full silver pieces, five thousand areca nuts, five fat pigs, and five suits of clothes.
> Mother, I am twenty-three this year and still without a husband.
> What, Mother, is your plan?
> The magpie brought two matchmakers and you threw them the challenge:
> not less than three silver pieces, three thousand areca nuts, three fat pigs, and three suits of clothes.
> Mother, I am thirty-two this year and still without a husband.
> What, Mother darling, is your plan?
> The magpie brought two matchmakers and you threw them the challenge:
> not less than one silver piece, one thousand areca nuts, one fat dog this time, and one suit of clothes.
> Mother, I am forty-three this year.
> Still without a husband.
> Mother, look, Mother, will you please just give me away?[9]

Beginning in the tenth century some Vietnamese began to leave the overcrowded northern river valleys to migrate southward along the coast in a process, often peaceful but sometimes accompanied by military forces, that took many centuries. By the 1400s imperial forces overran most of Champa, opening the central coast to settlement. By the 1500s settlers were pushing south toward the Khmer-dominated Mekong River delta.

Vietnamese society retained some of its essential characteristics as it colonized the south because whole families and sometimes even villages moved together. At the same time religious beliefs, dietary habits, and temperament gradually diverged between northerners and southern migrants. The Vietnamese who moved south changed as they encountered not only diverse new cultures and customs, including Khmer Theravada Buddhism and Cham Hinduism, but also a more tropical climate and fertile land. In particular the Mekong River delta provided a rich and uncrowded environment. The Southern Vietnamese never abandoned the cooperative values and religious traditions of the north, but they gradually modified them into a less group-oriented pattern. Furthermore, the central and southern dialects gradually came to differ from those in Northern Vietnam, and Theravada Buddhism influenced Southern Vietnamese religion. As the migrating Vietnamese encountered local peoples, they either absorbed them, pushed them out, or subdued them, ending their political independence. Given the new geographical reality of two heavily populated river deltas in the far north and deep south linked by a thin coastal thread bordering heavily forested highlands, Vietnamese described their country as being like two rice baskets at the opposite end of their carrying pole.

The Vietnamese could never ignore, however, the constant threat from China, their powerful neighbor to the north, which sporadically sent in military forces. During one such Chinese incursion in the twelfth century, the resistance leader Tran Hung Dao rallied his forces by appealing to their sense of nationalism: "The [Chinese] invaders and we are enemies who cannot live under the same sky. If you do not care to wash away the stain of humiliation . . . [and instead] raise your empty hands in capitulation . . . shame shall descend on you for thousands of generations. How will you be able to face heaven and Earth?"[10] In 1407 China, under the Ming dynasty, invaded and conquered Vietnam in an attempt to restore its colonial mission and destroy Vietnamese identity. The Chinese used forced labor and high taxes to exploit Vietnam's mines, forests, farms, and marine fisheries for China's benefit. While his country endured harsh repression, the rebel Le Loi, a landlord's son and a mandarin, organized a resistance movement that struggled tenaciously for the next two decades, finally expelling the Chinese in 1428. Le became emperor and founder of a new Le dynasty, which remained in power until 1780. His efforts to launch social and economic reforms to help the common people, as well as his struggle against Chinese domination, made him one of the national heroes of Vietnam's long struggle for independence. As Le Loi told his people in his proclamation of victory: "Over the centuries, we have been sometimes strong, sometimes weak; but never yet have we been lacking in heroes. Of that let our history be the proof."[11] To strengthen the state, the new rulers also adopted the successful Chinese political and cultural models, such as Confucianism, even more enthusiastically than in previous centuries. Yet unity proved elusive. Rival northern and southern states emerged in the sixteenth century.

While the Theravada Buddhist and Vietnamese traditions were found on the mainland, the Malayo-Muslim traditions arose largely on the Malay Peninsula and the Indonesian Archipelago, where various states had emerged, most of them closely tied to international commerce. By the year 1000 maritime trade had become more important in the Eastern Hemisphere's economic life. Both the Chinese and Arabs proved particularly skillful in seagoing technology and were active in Southeast Asian trade. The trade between China and various Southeast Asian states around the South China Sea continued to grow, and China remained the major market for Southeast Asian goods in these centuries. However, this trade became part of a much larger commercial exchange as the Indian Ocean routes between Southeast Asia and the Middle East became the heart of the most extensive maritime trade network in the world between 1000 and 1500. This system linked China, Japan, Vietnam, Champa, Cambodia, and Siam in the east through Malaya and Indonesia to coastal Burma, India, and Sri Lanka (Ceylon), and then extended westward to Persia, Arabia, Egypt, the East African coast as far south as Mozambique, and through the Red Sea and Persian Gulf to the Eastern and Central Mediterranean.

Over these trade routes the spices of Indonesia and East Africa, the gold and tin of Malaya, the sugar of the Philippines, the textiles, sugar and cotton of India, the cinnamon and ivory of Ceylon, the gold of Zimbabwe in Southeast Africa, the coffee of Arabia, the carpets of Persia, the silver of Japan, and the silks, porcelain, and tea of China traveled to distant markets. Many of these products reached Europe, sparking interest there in reaching the eastern sources of the riches. Pepper from Java as well as cloves and nutmeg from the small, volcanic Maluku (Moluccan) Islands of Northeast Indonesia were worth fortunes on international markets. Indonesian spices, in fact, became important to the European diet. During the long cold North European winter, farm animals died or were killed for meat, and spices hid the bad taste of the decomposing meat, making it easier for people to eat and survive these harsh months. An English book from the early 1400s reported the popularity of Javan pepper in Europe: "Pepper is black and has a good smack, And every man doth it buy."[12]

As in the Mediterranean, no state dominated the trading routes through the Indian Ocean. The dynamism of commerce depended primarily on port cities like Hormuz on the Persian coast, Kilwa in Tanzania, Cambay in Northwest India, Calicut on India's southwest coast, Melaka in Malaya, and Quanzhou in China. These trading ports became vibrant centers of international commerce and culture with multinational populations. Various states around the Indian Ocean and South China Sea were also closely linked to and benefited from maritime trade. The waters of blue were becoming increasingly significant for Southeast Asians as sources of profit and as a method of communication with a wider world.

Appreciation for open sea lanes and trade was well expressed in 1615 by the ruler of Gowa, a state in Southern Sulawesi, whose Bugis people were renowned seafaring traders. In a letter to Dutch officials who sought a trade monopoly, he wrote: "God has made the earth and the seas, has divided the earth among mankind, and given the sea in common. It is a thing unheard of that anyone should be forbidden to sail the seas."[13] Southeast Asia became an essential intermediary in the Indian Ocean trade network, which enhanced the value of regional ports like Melaka, Ayutthaya, Pegu in Burma's Irrawaddy delta, and Banten in West Java. Malays and Javanese, especially, played active roles in the seagoing trade. For centuries some Indonesians had even visited the northern coast of Australia, a continent then unknown to Europe, to obtain items such as ornamental shells and pearls. The growing trade throughout the region attracted merchants from afar. For example, in 1650 the inland capital city of Arakan, a coastal kingdom in Western Burma, attracted so many traders from the Middle East, Central Asia, Africa, and India that an observer could write that "from diverse lands, diverse peoples, having heard of the wealth of [Arakan], come under its King's shadow."[14]

Some historians refer to an "age of commerce" in Southeast Asia between 1400 and 1650, in which increased trade with China and across the Indian Ocean, marked by increased demand for Southeast Asian commodities, encouraged the growth of cities and political changes. In the archipelago ports, merchants became a more powerful group in local politics. A new type of maritime trading state emerged to handle the increased amounts of products being obtained and transported. Revenue from trade became more significant than agricultural taxes in many states. This transformation in the maritime economy fostered more commercial prosperity than ever before as well as cultures more open to the outside world. Trade was not the only expanding activity, however. Agricultural improvements brought new crops and varieties of rice, which spurred population growth and migration. These changes, in turn, fostered more centralized states, some large and many small ones.

Trade networks also fostered the expansion of Islam, which became dominant in the Middle East, Central Asia, and parts of Southern Europe by 800 and continued to spread. By the 1300s Islam had a large following in parts of West Africa, India, China, and the East African coast, and merchants and sailors carried it into Southeast Asia along the maritime trade routes. *Dar al-Islam* ("The House of Islam") eventually linked societies as far apart as Morocco and Indonesia with a common faith and trade connections. Commercial people were attracted to a religion that sanctioned the accumulation of wealth to afford the pilgrimage to Mecca and help the needy, and preached cooperation among believers. Muslim merchants, especially Arabs, Persians, and Indians, who had been visiting and settling in the ports of China and Southeast Asia since the seventh century, now became even more prominent traders in the region. Some Arabs claimed descent from the prophet Muhammad, giving them high status in Muslim communities as political and religious leaders. Members of this prestigious group and their descendants were often accorded a special title, such as *sharif* or *tuanku* ("your highness"), and they remain influential today in Malaysia and Indonesia.

In the 1300s the great Moroccan traveler Ibn Battuta spent 30 years touring the length of Darul Islam, reaching as far east as Southeast Asia and the coastal ports of China. Ibn Battuta was a pilgrim, judge, scholar, Sufi mystic, ambassador, and connoisseur of fine foods and elegant architecture. His writings about his remarkable journeys provide valuable and often unique eyewitness accounts of many societies. He reported visiting the North Sumatran port of Samudra where he was treated with great deference by the Muslim ruler, who enjoyed discussing points of law with legal scholars and took a keen interest in hearing the Moroccan's stories of his travels. Ibn Battuta's experiences showed that Islamic culture was a globalizing force, dominating huge sections of Africa and Eurasia.

Islam became a major influence in Southeast Asia in part because of its close connection to interregional trade. In the late thirteenth century, the Achehnese of Northern Sumatra, who dominated Samudra, were among the first Southeast Asians to embrace Islam and became known for their devotion to the faith. In the 1400s some Hindu-Buddhist rulers of coastal states in the Malay Peninsula and Indonesian islands became anxious to attract the Muslim Arab and Indian traders. Impressed by the global reach of Islam, they abandoned their earlier religions and adopted Islam, converting themselves into sultans, rulers who promoted Islamic laws and customs.

The spread of Islam coincided with the rise of the great port of Melaka (Malacca), on the southwest coast of Malaya facing the Straits of Melaka. This city replaced Srivijaya as the region's political and economic power as well as the crossroads of Asian commerce. In the early 1400s the Hindu ruler, Parameswara, adopted Islam and transformed himself into Sultan Megat Iskander Shah. The sultans became,

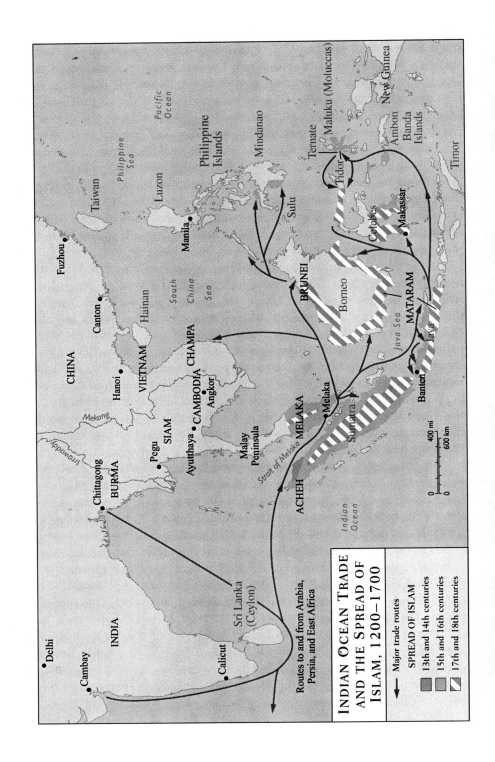

INDIAN OCEAN TRADE
AND THE SPREAD OF
ISLAM, 1200–1700

Major trade routes

SPREAD OF ISLAM

13th and 14th centuries

15th and 16th centuries

17th and 18th centuries

in Malay tradition, the deputies of God. In typically Southeast Asian fashion, the Melakans blended Islamic faith and culture with the older Hindu-Buddhist and animist beliefs for some generations and many were somewhat lax in their practice. Parameswara's motivation was probably as much political and commercial as spiritual. Melaka became the main base for the spread of Islam in the archipelago.

Melaka's historical significance, however, is based primarily on its crucial role in international trade. Chinese records reported that in 1405 "the ruler of Melaka . . . sent envoys to pay tribute. An edict was promulgated appointing . . . [the ruler] king; [the envoys] were provided with seals and . . . suits of colored silks."[15] Thanks to this alliance, the Melakan kings made their port a way station for the series of grand Chinese voyages to the Western Indian Ocean led by Admiral Zheng He (Cheng Ho), who called there several times between 1409 and 1431. These sea voyages, unmatched in world history to that point, involved dozens of huge ships and thousands of sailors, and they reached East Africa and the Persian Gulf. In exchange for Melaka's service as a naval base, the Ming emperor supported the young state in regional disputes. Soon merchants from around Asia traveled to Melaka, rapidly transforming the port into the southeastern hub for the Indian Ocean's maritime trading network.

Melaka became one of the world's major commercial cities, very much a rival to other great trading ports such as Calicut, Cambay, Canton, Hormuz, Aleppo, Alexandria, Genoa, and Venice. An early-fifteenth-century Portuguese visitor wrote that "no trading port as large as Melaka is known, nor any where they deal in such fine and highly prized merchandise."[16] Melaka's rulers and nobles became actively involved in commerce, often operating their own private enterprises and accepting a percentage of a cargo's value as gifts, a pattern that became common among the Muslim trading states. Gradually, Melaka gained domination over much of coastal Malaya and Eastern Sumatra, but the empire was decentralized, with the sultan controlling local leaders rather than ruling directly.

Melaka's key role in world trade was confirmed by Tomé Pires, a Portuguese visitor in 1512, who wrote in his journals that it had "no equal in the world" and praised the importance of Melaka to people and trade as far away as Western Europe: "Melaka is a city that was made for merchandise, fitter than any other in the world. Commerce between different nations for a thousand leagues on every hand must come to Melaka. Whoever is lord of Melaka has his hands on the throat of Venice."[17] Indicative of its international connections, Melaka had a special relationship with the port of Cambay, nearly 3,000 miles away in the Gujarat region of Northwestern India. Every year trading ships from around the Middle East and South Asia would gather at both Cambay and Calicut, on the southwest coast of India, to make the long voyage to Melaka. They carried with them grain, woolens, arms, copperware, textiles, and opium for exchange. Goods from as far north as Korea also reached Melaka.

During the 1400s Melaka was a flourishing trading port attracting merchants from many lands. By the late fifteenth century Melaka's population, which some historians think was as large as 100,000 to 200,000, included 15,000 foreign merchants, some of whom took local wives. The sultan appointed officials, often from the foreign groups themselves, to collect taxes and administer laws. The foreigners included Arabs, Egyptians, Persians, Turks, Armenians, Baghdadi and Indian Jews, Ethiopians, Swahilis from coastal East Africa, Burmese, Vietnamese, Javanese, Filipinos from Luzon, Japanese, Okinawans, Indians (including perhaps 1,000 Gujaratis), and Chinese. The descendants of some of the Chinese and Indians still reside there. Some 84 languages were spoken on the city's streets. There were said to be more ships in the harbor than any port in the world, attracted by stable government and a free trade policy. Perhaps the richest Melaka merchant in the later 1400s, Naina Suradewana, a portly Hindu from Southeast India, started as a moneylender but eventually owned a large fleet that traded with Java and the Maluku Islands. His success was not unusual. Another merchant, Aregimuti Raja, who headed the Luzon Filipino community in Melaka around 1500, owned a local firm that sent trading vessels to Siam, Brunei, China, and Eastern Indonesia.

Melaka's citizens were proud of their central position in Asian trade. As Malay historical chronicles boasted, "From below the wind to above the wind Melaka became famous as a very great city . . . so much so that princes from all countries came to present themselves before Sultan Muhammad Shah, who treated them with due respect bestowing upon them robes of honor of the highest distinction together with rich presents of jewels, gold, and silver."[18] The royal court emphasized ceremony, including titles and elaborate etiquette. According to the historical chronicles, the wedding of Sultan Mansur Shah to a Javanese princess involved feasting for 40 days and nights and enjoying the music of every sort of instrument.

Melaka's past is well known because of both Malay and Portuguese accounts. Although many scholars consider it more a literary than a factual account, *The Malay Annals*, written by court historians in the 1600s from earlier stories, helped to shape the Malay perception of the past. The book portrayed the flowering of Melaka and its leaders, a story known by every Malaysian student. Indeed, the fifteenth-century Golden Age is widely considered by Malays in modern times as their most magnificent era. The *Annals* celebrated great leaders such as Tun Perak, a naval commander who repulsed a Siamese invasion and then served as chief minister to various sultans in the later 1400s. It also told of tragic figures such as Tun Mutahir, a just official and skilled diplomat but so vain that he changed clothes seven times a day in front of a full-length mirror. He incurred the sultan's wrath for betrothing his beautiful daughter to the sultan's rival and was executed for it. These stories were widespread. The Muslim sultanate as a political institution derived largely from the Melakan model as described in the *Malay Annals*. Sultanates all over the Malay Peninsula and Sumatra were linked to Melaka by religion, language, and, often, kinship ties to the Melakkan royal family, creating a permanent respect for the Melaka legacy.

MELAKA

The city's layout was familiar to sailors all over Asia. Located halfway up the narrow and strategic Straits of Melaka, the city flanked both sides of a sluggish river and stretched along a shore backed by defensible hills where the royal palace was situated. The city plan reflected the social structure, with the royal palace walled off from the commercial quarters. Malays lived at the foot of the royal hill while the business district flanked the riverside. Wealthier merchants lived nearby in grand houses. The shops offered textiles from India, books from the Middle East, cloves and nutmeg from Maluku, batiks and carpets from Java, silk and porcelain from China, and sugar from the Philippines. Life for most residents was comfortable. Gold was so plentiful that children played with it. The Melakans enjoyed *sepak raga*, the Malay mix of soccer and volleyball played with the feet and head. The *Malay Annals* report on a particularly talented visiting sultan who enjoyed competing with the royal princes: "[When] the ball came to him [he] would kick it himself for as long as it takes to cook pot after pot of rice and the ball would stay up in the air until he wished to pass it to someone else: such was his skill at the game."[19]

Besides its religious and economic significance, Melaka played a crucial role in the evolution of the Malay ethnic group. The mostly Islamic people of Melaka began calling themselves "Malay" (Melayu) in the fifteenth century. Henceforth, the term applied to those who practiced Islam, spoke a version of the Malay language, and identified themselves as group members. Over time a cultural designation became an ethnic category spread throughout Malaya and parts of Sumatra and Borneo, a region that can be termed the "Malay world." The culture of the Malays is often termed "Malayo-Muslim" because of the centrality of Islam. The Malay language became used widely in trade all over the archipelago, and Malay literary forms—such as the riddle-like, short poem known as *pantun*—found new audiences. Pantuns were often romantic and passionate, featuring such phrases as "of gold be the mat and golden the pillows; but the arms of my love are the pillow for me."[20]

As Islam spread from Melaka, sultanates appeared in many districts and islands, as rulers embraced the new religion for religious, political, and commercial reasons. The king of Mataram, the large state that ruled most of Java, converted to Islam in 1641. Some Islamic states, like Acheh in Northern Sumatra and Brunei in Northwest Borneo, became regional powers. In the Maluku (Moluccan) Islands, the sultanates of Ternate and Tidor, each located on a tiny volcanic island, and a sultanate in the nearby Banda Islands prospered from growing the spices such as cloves, mace, and nutmeg that were greatly prized in Europe. Gradually many of the people in these states, especially those involved in trade, followed the example of their rulers and adopted Islam. As a result, the Malay Peninsula and Indonesian archipelago were joined to the wider Islamic world. Many were attracted particularly to mystical Sufi ideas, which meshed well with their older traditions. Missionaries often used maritime metaphors to present Sufi ideas in ways their local audiences might understand, as in this Malay poem from the 1600s about needing spiritual support in sailing the perilous sea, "where many ships sink/its surges are immensely fierce/. . . If [the seafarer] is not experienced and skilled enough/[His] ship will strand and break into pieces."[21]

The mixing of Islam and maritime trade fostered mobility among many islanders. For example, Hamzah Fansuri, a Sufi poet from Western Sumatra famed for his mystical and romantic writings, lived for a time in Ayutthaya and Baghdad. Fansuri was a follower of an earlier Spanish-born mystic, Ibn al-Arabi, who taught that all reality is one and everything that exists is part of the divine. This approach downplayed ritual and law, instead emphasizing visions, dreams, and achieving ecstasy to know God. Some Muslim travelers shaped politics far from their ancestral homes. In the 1600s Naruddin al-Raniri, from Gujarat in India, studied in Mecca and eventually settled in Acheh, becoming an adviser to the sultan, who, under his influence, promoted more vigorous Islamic practices, such as strict dietary laws and alms-giving. But there also remained many village-based societies, some of them still practicing animism, in more isolated areas such as the Philippine Islands, Central Sulawesi, and the interior of Borneo, with no political authority higher than the level of local chiefs.

Various patterns of Islamic belief and practice, more diverse than elsewhere in the Islamic world, inevitably emerged as Islam was assimilated into far-flung island societies. In some societies, such as Acheh, where four successive women had ruled in the later 1600s, women were by the 1700s prohibited from holding power. Elsewhere, however, women often maintained strong influence, despite the restrictions of Islam. Many Muslim courts in Java and other islands were filled with hundreds, sometimes thousands, of women. Some were wives and concubines, but most were attendants, guards, or textile workers. And women still dominated most of the local markets in the archipelago.

Indeed, in many cases Islam did not displace older customs, and many pre-Islamic political, cultural, and artistic ideas remained influential. On Java, for example, formerly Indianized courts combined Islamic patterns with older Hindu-Buddhist ceremonies and social attitudes. The Southeast Asian version of Hinduism survived only in a few remote societies such as the island of Bali, just east of Java, where the traditional society and culture remained vigorous with an emphasis on arts like dancing, music, shadow plays, and woodcarving. Among the Javanese, the aristocracy also tended to retain many mystical pre-Islamic beliefs. As a result, the aristocratic bureaucrats became obsessed with practicing refined behavior rooted in mystical Hinduism with an Islamic overlay. These aristocrats remained part of a rigid social order in which the sultans, like the Indianized kings before them, remained in their palaces, aloof from common society.

Among the Javanese commoners, two distinct versions of Islam developed during the next few centuries. Many peasants maintained their mystical animist beliefs underneath an Islamic surface, producing a tolerant and accommodating religion. Others, especially merchants, adopted a more orthodox Islamic faith. They followed prescribed Islamic practices, such as daily prayer and Ramadan fasting, and looked toward the Middle East for inspiration. Javanese traditional religion reflected a culture that placed great value on maintaining a tranquil heart by avoiding interpersonal conflict and in which women played an important role in society but, especially for the elite, were also expected to maintain marital fidelity. Although a patriarchal faith, Islam did not entirely transform Javanese family life. Most Javanese retained close ties with both paternal and maternal kin and lived in nuclear families, in contrast to the patrilineal pattern common in Muslim societies outside of Southeast Asia. The Javanese and Malay religious patterns show that Southeast Asians became an integral part of the global Islamic realm but also remained distinctive and creative in forging new cultures.

Influenced by both their Islamic and Hindu-Buddhist backgrounds, the Javanese created many splendid new art forms. By the 1600s *batik*, the highly patterned cloth produced by a wax and dying process, had appeared. Batik arts later spread throughout the world. Many musical or music-related arts also developed, including the *gamelan* orchestras of percussion and wind instruments playing a diverse repertoire. Gongs and drums had reached Indonesia before the Common Era, and by the tenth century the Javanese had added xylophones, fiddles, and flutes while developing unique music scales. Many villages possessed their own ensembles. The ethereal sound of Javanese gamelan music is seemingly formless to Western ears but is, in reality, highly complex. Enthusiasts claimed that gamelan was comparable only to moonlight and flowing water: pure and mysterious like moonlight; always the same and always changing like flowing water. In Java and Bali the *wayang kulit* (shadow play) remained an important artistic medium, accompanied by gamelan music.

Gamelan orchestras, largely composed of percussion and wind instruments, became central to court life in Java and Bali. Like many others, this gamelan ensemble based at an old mosque in Jogakarta still plays a major role in local festivities. Photo: Clare Holt, courtesy of The New York Public Library for the Performing Arts/Jerome Robbins Dance Division

By world standards Southeast Asia was sparsely populated during these centuries, with perhaps 15 to 20 million people by the 1400s, a fifth of them in Vietnam. The population probably grew to between 20 and 25 million by 1600. As elsewhere in the world, wars, famines, or tropical diseases such as malaria could reduce the population substantially, whereas stable conditions fostered rapid increase. Most people lived in the major cities and fertile rice-growing districts. Cities such as Ayutthaya, Melaka, and Hanoi each contained around 100,000 residents, making them as large as the major European cities but small by Chinese standards. The major cities were open to the world and had neighborhoods inhabited by foreign immigrants and sojourners. Chinese, Indian, and Arab merchant communities were common. As was the case during the Golden Age, so was slavery. A Persian observer wrote that in Indonesia, the people "reckon high rank and wealth by the quantity of slaves a person owns."[22] Many Southeast Asians generally enjoyed good health, varied diets, and adequate material resources, certainly in comparison with conditions in Europe, which was engulfed in plague and frequent warfare. Traveler's accounts suggest that around 1600, people in the islands, with access to many herbal remedies, were as long-lived and tall as Europeans and apparently healthier. A Dutch observer reported in 1656 that "the Javanese in general grow very old, the men as well as the women."[23]

A Thai proverb says that "there is rice in the fields and fish in the streams," suggesting that the nearby environment usually provided the essentials for survival. No doubt this was often the case. But peasant life also presented challenges. The dependence on sometimes unreliable seasonal rains meant that poor harvests were always possible and prompted peasants to develop social values that spread the risk and promoted cooperation and mutual assistance. Many of the Southeast Asian languages discourage interpersonal conflict by making it hard to disrespect people and by recognizing status differences, which were stark. A Spanish visitor to Cambodia in the late 1500s described a society divided between "nobles and commoners . . . All the nobles have several wives, the number depending on how rich they are . . . The nobles dress in silk and fine cotton and gauze . . . The [common] people pay the principle [sic] officials, and the king, one tenth of the value of all goods taken from the sea and the land."[24] The Khmer, Javanese, and Thai languages have different words to use in addressing social superiors, equals, and inferiors. Language was one way in which many cultures promoted harmony. Villagers also willingly supported the well-being of their community at the expense of the individual. And fatalism about life's trials was found in all the region's religious traditions, exemplified by the Muslim expression "God wills it."

By 1500 Southeast Asia was a region united by a tropical environment, flourishing commerce, and occasional wars between societies but also divided by diverse states, religions, and cultures. This had long been a region where peoples, ideas, and products met, and this trend has continued into the present. The Venetian traveler Marco Polo passed through the region in 1292 on his way home from a long sojourn in China. His writings praised the wealth and sophistication of Champa, Java, and Sumatra. He wrote of a Burmese temple covered with gold as well as of Java, whose kingdoms are "of unsurpassing wealth, producing all kinds of spices, frequented by a vast amount of shipping. Indeed, the treasure of this island is so great as to be past telling."[25] These reports fostered European interest in these seemingly fabulous lands, and as a result, as the sixteenth century dawned, Southeast Asians faced the new challenge of colonization.

CHAPTER 5

Christians, Spices, and Western Expansion, 1500–1750

In 1509 five unknown but well-armed ships, each with a banner bearing a cross and full of strange, menacing pale-skinned men, lowered anchor off Melaka. The local people were curious about, but also wary of, these Portuguese in their uncomfortable-looking clothes. As the *Malay Annals* recorded: "The Portuguese saw that Melaka was magnificent, and its port was exceedingly crowded. The people gathered around to see what the foreigners looked like, and they were all surprised by their appearance. But these Portuguese are people who know nothing of manners."[1] The fame of Melaka as a treasure trove of Asian luxury goods had reached Europe. For a century the Portuguese had been seeking a sea route to the Orient around Africa. As one of their greatest explorers, Vasco da Gama, put it, they sought "Christians and Spices," meaning allies against Islam and the valuable products of Southeast Asia. The Portuguese voyages inaugurated a new era of European activity in Southeast Asia and eventually led to the colonization of most of the region.

The Portuguese adventurers came from a country with superior military technology and a compelling appetite for wealth but a standard of living that was little, if any, higher than that of Siam, Vietnam, Melaka, or Java. Earlier, in the 1400s, the Portuguese had improved the imported Asian and Islamic naval and military technologies—such as magnetic compasses, lateen sails, and cannons—that had reached Europe over the trade routes, and a century later, they sailed into Southeast Asia with these instruments. The missionary zeal to spread Christianity and the dynamism of capitalism, which was beginning to emerge as medieval feudalism declined, also provided incentives for expansion.

According to the *Malay Annals*, "Around each [Portuguese] there would be a crowd of Malays, some of them twisting his beard, some taking off his hat, some grasping his hand."[2] But the first encounter ended poorly. Portuguese intentions were unclear to the sultan. They did not act like the mostly peaceful Asian merchants who arrived regularly in trading ships, nor did they bring the customary gifts for the sultan and his officials. The Portuguese visitors, ignorant of traditions such as bringing gifts to the sultan, violated local customs, antagonized local officials, and alarmed influential local Indian traders, who feared competition. The Portuguese also considered Sultan Mahmud Shah, who did not welcome them, arrogant and treacherous. Some local merchants, disenchanted with the sultan's growing demands on them, befriended the Portuguese. As tensions rose, fighting between Portuguese sailors and Malay visitors to their ship broke out. After the Melakans arrested

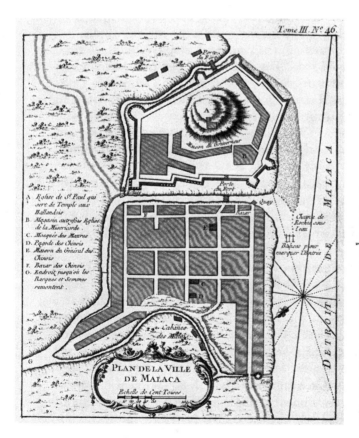

The Portuguese, who conquered the great trading port of Melaka in 1511, added their own flavor, building a fort as well as a Roman Catholic church on a hill overlooking the old Malay and Chinese neighborhoods of the city. But Melaka stagnated under Portuguese and then Dutch rule, losing its position as the region's key commercial entrepôt.

15 to 20 Portuguese sailors shopping in town, the remaining Portuguese force, unprepared to launch a full-scale assault on the heavily defended city, sailed away to India, vowing revenge.

The Portuguese soon returned, making Malaya the first region to be severely disrupted by European power. In 1511 a Portuguese fleet of some 40 ships, mounted with cannon and carrying hundreds of soldiers armed with muskets, captured Melaka. The Portuguese triumphed only after a bloody month-long assault against fierce resistance that resulted in the gutting and looting of the city. According to the *Malay Annals*, "The noise of the [Portuguese] cannon was as the noise of thunder in the heavens and the flashes of fire of their guns were like flashes of lightning in the sky."[3] Admiral Affonso de Albuquerque told his soldiers to "cast the Moors [Muslims] out of this country,"[4] and his men slaughtered much of the population, including the sultan, who led the defense mounted on his elephant. The Portuguese now had a strategic advantage over their European and Malay enemies, as the victorious admiral boasted: "Melaka is the source of all the spices and drugs which the Moors carry every year to [the Middle East]. Cairo and Mecca will be entirely ruined, and Venice will receive no spices unless her merchants go and buy them in Portugal."[5] Melaka became one of Portugal's major outposts in a scattered Asian empire that included ports in Persia, India, Sri Lanka, and China.

Charged by the pope to spread the Catholic faith throughout the world, the Portuguese carried out a crusade against Muslims designed to break Islamic control of the East-West maritime trade. The fanatical Portuguese often forced conversion to Christianity, and their intolerance made both the Portuguese and Spanish missionaries unwelcome in most places. The Portuguese intended to control the maritime trade themselves, mostly using brute force. Although they devoted some 800 ships to the effort and did control some ports, they never completely dominated the Indian Ocean commerce. Asian merchants often outmaneuvered or evaded Portuguese ships, and many Asian states resisted Portuguese demands. Furthermore, Melaka languished under Portuguese control, as fewer merchants chose to endure the higher taxes and Portuguese intolerance of non-Christians. The well-fortified Portuguese also faced constant challenge from various neighboring states such as strongly Islamic Acheh in North Sumatra.

The fall of Melaka shattered the unity of the Malay world. Several strong and dynamic sultanates, including Johor at the tip of the Malay Peninsula and Brunei in Northern Borneo, took over some of Melaka's trading functions, however, and flourished for several centuries. Siam came to control some of the northern sultanates. The population of southernmost Thailand is still heavily Malay Muslim.

The Portuguese conquest of Melaka marked a turning point for Southeast Asia. In the next four centuries traders and colonizers from Spain, Holland, England, France, and finally the United States followed the Portuguese into the region. The Western world had rapidly been transformed and strengthened by expansionism, capitalism, and, later, industrialization. The sixteenth century was an age of discovery for Western adventurers. A Portuguese captain, Ferdinand Magellan, sailing under the Spanish flag, became the first explorer to lead a circumnavigation of the world. Sailing around the southern tip of South America and across the Pacific, he proved that Columbus was correct in believing that Asia could be reached in that direction. The maritime achievement came at a huge cost, however. Magellan's ship barely completed the long voyage across the Pacific, and at one point the crew had to eat rats to survive. Then Magellan was killed in a skirmish with local chiefs in the Philippines in 1521, after claiming the islands for Spain.

Magellan reflected the intolerance of his culture and time, pressuring the Filipinos he encountered to adopt Christianity. According to Antonio Pigafetta, an Italian on the voyage, Magellan ordered the local chief to "burn all the idols, and, instead of them, place a cross, and that everyone should worship it every day on their knees."[6] Despite Magellan's death, his remaining crew continued on to the Maluku or Spice Islands and then finally reached Spain by way of Southern Africa. Today, on the beach at the island of Cebu where Magellan died, a memorial honors Lapulapu, the chief who led the attack, as the first Filipino to repel European aggression.

By the time of Magellan's visit, the Portuguese were already active in the spice-rich Maluku Islands. Some Chinese and Indian merchants were bypassing Portuguese Melaka, however, to obtain spices at other ports, increasing the Portuguese determination to control spice production. In the early 1500s the Portuguese brutally conquered the Maluku Islands, thus gaining near total control of the valuable spice trade to Europe, but they also faced challenges from the Spanish and Dutch. Commenting on Portuguese behavior in Maluku, the Spanish Roman Catholic missionary St. Francis Xavier wrote that their knowledge was limited to conjugating the verb *to steal*, in which they displayed "an amazing capacity for inventing new tenses and participles."[7]

Portuguese traders and adventurers were also active elsewhere in the region. Portuguese mercenary soldiers helped the Toungoo kings to expand their territorial power and invade Ayutthaya. And one Portuguese adventurer, Philip de Brito, even seized power in the Pegu port of Syriam in 1599. But his attempts to impose Christianity alienated the Mon residents, and his attacks on Toungoo resulted in a Burman invasion that killed de Brito and his Portuguese supporters in 1613. The Dutch used military force to take Melaka from the Portugese in 1641, but a small Roman Catholic, Portuguese-speaking community still lives in the city. In Melaka today, Roman Catholic churches, schools, and festivals remain at the heart of Portuguese community life, but the local Portuguese language contains many Malay words, the cuisine has borrowed extensively from Malay and Chinese cooking, and, unlike their merchant, sailor, and soldier ancestors, most men work as fishermen or run small businesses catering to tourists.

First the Portuguese and then the Dutch gained partial control of the Indian Ocean maritime trade by force, altering its character and diminishing its dynamism. By controlling a few Asian ports, such as Melaka, Macao in China, Goa in India, and, for a time, Hormuz in Persia, the Portuguese created what historians term a trading post empire, organized around trade, rather than a true territorial empire. The European monopoly on trade at many ports forced some of the seafaring merchants into piracy to survive. Eventually Europeans affected nearly all Southeast Asia in various ways. Still, states like Siam, Vietnam, Burma, and Acheh were strong enough that it took 400 years of persistent effort for Westerners to gain political and economic control. The several conquests during this era and then the more ambitious Western colonization that followed in the nineteenth century ultimately made Southeast Asia a very different place from what it had been during the Golden Age, although many features of the traditional cultures survived Western domination.

The greatest Western impact before 1750 came in the Philippine Islands. When the first Spanish ships arrived they found these remote islands inhabited by some 1 to 2 million people speaking more than 100 different Austronesian languages and scattered across 7,000 islands, although the great majority lived on Luzon and Mindanao. Muslims occupied the southernmost islands, divided between several rival sultanates, and they were slowly extending their influence northward. The islands had received little cultural influence from India or China. But a few Filipinos were maritime traders who traveled as far as Burma, and Chinese traders had established several outposts in the Philippines, including one at Manila, to obtain gold, sugar, and cotton. The largest non-Muslim political units were villages led by chiefs such as Lapulapu, whose followers had killed Magellan.

The many Philippine societies differed from each other but shared various common traditions. Most were led by nobles and also had both free people and slaves. Most Filipinos were animists, though many also believed in an afterlife and one supreme being. Women enjoyed considerable influence and a high status in many of the societies, producing the textiles, pottery, and rice used as trade goods. They inherited equally with men, owned property, engaged in trade, and occasionally became community leaders. The Spanish were shocked that divorce was common, one official writing that "they used to dissolve these marriages for trifling causes."[8] Although we do not know much about the subject matter, some Filipinos used a simple writing system of 15 characters and carved words into bamboo. A Spanish priest recorded in 1604 that almost all the people, "both men and women, write in this language. There are few who do not write it excellently and correctly."[9] Spanish priests considered the writing to be heretical, however, and destroyed most of the bamboos.

Returning to the region four decades after Magellan's death, the Spanish, who were also conquering vast territories in the Americas, had both commercial and religious motives for colonizing the islands, which they named after their king, Philip II, known in Europe as "the most Catholic of kings." The Spanish also hoped to use the islands as a basis for trade with China and perhaps for conquest of Vietnam, which they naively believed would be an easy task. Given the ethnic divisions and lack of a dominant Philippine state, the militarily superior Spanish had little trouble conquering the islands over a few decades and co-opting many chiefs. But the Spanish never gained complete control over the Muslims in the south, whom they called *Moros* (Moors). Used to considerable autonomy in colonial times, some Muslims in Mindanao and the Sulu Islands still seek separation today from the Christian Philippines. The Spanish established their capital at Manila, a Chinese trading post on a large bay.

Spanning eight decades beginning in 1565, the Spanish imposed many aspects of their culture on the local people, in a process known as *Hispanization*. Some 85 percent of the population adopted Roman Catholicism as a result. Catholic friars accompanied the soldiers into the islands and began the process of conversion, as soon as the first ships landed. The rigidly dogmatic Spaniards considered the Filipino people to be immoral devil worshippers, and the colonial government gave the missionaries special authority over the people and their land. The Spanish crown financed these missionaries' efforts.

The church governed most regions outside of Manila and acquired great wealth. Priests collected taxes and sold the crops grown by parishioners. Several religious orders competed to gain the most converts. They required people to move into towns to better control and evangelize them. Some methods were harsh. In 1842 the colonial government finally forbade friars from whipping their parishioners for not rigorously observing church requirements. There were few schools outside Manila, and what education existed was in church hands and emphasized learning the Roman Catholic catechism. Few Filipinos were allowed to rise in the church hierarchy or in government, however, due in part to Spanish racism. One Spanish observer mocked the Filipino priest as "a caricature of everybody. He is a patchwork of many things and is nothing. He is an enemy of Spain."[10] But Filipinos accepted Christianity on their own terms, incorporating animist traditions, to the disgust of the Spanish. Saints replaced the traditional friendly spirits, and miracles became the new form of magic. Abounding faith in the power of holy water probably derived from ritual bathing in pre-Spanish times.

Inequality between the Spanish and the locals was not limited to government and the church; it also showed up in economic and social patterns. Many Spaniards saw government offices as an opportunity for acquiring wealth and property, fostering widespread corruption, and helping to shape the colonial economy. The China trade remained paramount until the mid-1700s, when Spanish policies more strongly encouraged an emphasis on cash crops for sale on the world market. Much of the land that once grew rice and other food crops became devoted to sugar, hemp, and other valuable crops. Most Filipinos, once masters of the land, now worked as tenants for a few powerful landowning families or the church, almost like serfs in medieval Europe, or on vast plantations. Peasant revolts against local landlords and the Spanish system were not unusual but were put down. The colonial economy created a permanent gap between the extraordinarily rich and the impoverished, resulting in a stunted economic growth dependent on the international market.

The Spanish transported these crops as well as other products, including silk and porcelain imported from China, to Manila. Every year between 1565 and 1815, huge cargo ships known as Manila galleons carried these goods across the Pacific Ocean to Mexico, for distribution in the Americas or for onward shipment to Spain. The Manila galleon trade was highly speculative, and Spanish businessmen bet their fortunes that the galleons would arrive in Mexico safely. But this was a dangerous trip, thanks to storms and pirates. On a crossing in 1604, for example, the *Espiritu Santo* got stuck on a shoal leaving Manila Bay, encountered a terrible storm off California that destroyed much of its rigging, and was struck by lightning that killed three crewmen before limping into Acapulco two months late. Sometimes the galleons never completed their voyages. There could be huge profits but also huge losses. The chance for success, however, fostered a "get rich quick" mentality rather than a long-term strategy to bring prosperity to the islands. The end of Spanish control in much of Latin America in the early 1800s ended the galleon trade and prompted many Spaniards to migrate to the Philippines from the Americas. Their competition with local-born businessmen created tensions, but it also spurred the expansion of export-oriented cash-crop agriculture as the Spaniards sought new sources of profit.

Although the Spanish created a country, they did not build a cohesive society. Regional and ethnic loyalties remained dominant, and the decentralized Spanish government encouraged such regionalism. Stark inequalities also characterized this colonial society. Spaniards controlled the government and church, most lived in Manila in luxury, and few ever learned to speak local languages. In 1603 a Spanish observer described the daily promenade in Manila's main streets of Spaniards

Marriages between Chinese and Filipinos in the Philippines produced a mixed-descent group known as Chinese mestizos, such as this nineteenth-century couple. Like most colonial cities Manila attracted a multiethnic population, including many Chinese. From Jean Mallat de Bassilan, Les Philippines *(Paris, 1846)*

gorgeously adorned in silks. Below the Spaniards were *mestizos*, mixed-descent people who resulted from intermarriage and cohabitation of some Spaniards with Filipinas or Chinese. A few Filipino families who descended from chiefs also enjoyed a high status. Below these groups were the Chinese immigrants, who worked as merchants and crafts-men. A Spanish friar observed in the mid-1600s that although Manila "is small, and the Spaniards are few, nevertheless, they require the services of thousands of Chinese."[11] Some Chinese became rich, but many lived more modestly, especially those who opened small shops in rural towns. Many became Roman Catholic or married Filipinas, forming the basis for a larger, mostly Roman Catholic Chinese mestizo community that gradually gained status. Many of the Philippine political and economic leaders today are of Chinese or Spanish mestizo ancestry. The Spanish needed the Chinese as middlemen but also despised and persecuted them. On occasion, when their resentment of Chinese wealth and concern with their growing numbers became intense, Spanish forces marched into Manila's Chinatown and slaughtered the residents.

Most Filipinos, called *Indios* ("Indies people") by the Spanish, occupied the bottom rung of the social ladder and faced many legal restrictions. It was illegal, for example, for Filipinos to dress in fancy clothes like Spaniards. Filipinos maintained a strong allegiance to their families for support. Women had held a high position in pre-Spanish society, but Spanish culture and church devalued women, imposing restrictions on their activities. For instance, the female priestesses integral to Filipino animism were pushed to the margins of society by male Roman Catholic priests, one of whom described the priestesses as "loathsome creatures, foul, obscene, truly damnable. My task [is] to reduce them to order."[12] A long-lasting contradiction developed between the considerable power of women in family and town life and male-chauvinistic attitudes. Women still controlled family finances, led underground animistic rites, and enjoyed a reputation for self-reliance. One result of this heritage of female power is that today there are many influential women in politics, business, and the professions.

Filipinos used various elements of Spanish culture itself, especially religious festivals, to subtly express opposition to colonialism. The Spanish introduced passion plays (known as *payson*), about the life and death of Jesus, as a way to spread Christian devotion and morality. But some Filipinos wrote their own versions with subtle anticolonial sentiments. These plays became something of a subversive act, with Jesus portrayed as a victim of political oppression. For example, the *Payson Pilapil*, written by an unknown author but based on an eighteenth-century play, presented Jesus as a social activist of humble background, tormented by a corrupt ruling class who had contempt for the common people. The play was popular with rural folk, and one scene portrayed the high priests making the case against Jesus in the Roman court of Pontius Pilate:

> And we gathered here before your excellency, are aristocrats and town chiefs
> so you have no reason to doubt all our accusations [against Jesus].
> We plaintiffs here are gentlemen of rank and wealth.
> He is from Galilee, a man poor and lowly who shelters in other's roofs.
> Furthermore, his father is just a simple carpenter, devoid of fame and wealth,
> living in poverty without property of his own.
> Can he [Jesus] claim to be a gentleman of rank?
> [His disciples] are poor and lowly people without worth on earth,
> ignorant people without any education.
> Another treacherous act of this troublemaker is his plot with the people,
> not to pay taxes to Caesar, such great arrogance!
> We are all men of wealth who obediently follow our exalted king,
> in contrast to that blockhead who talks like a traitor.
> Puts the people in turmoil and turns them into fanatics.
> To be the awaited Messiah, what a preposterous lie![13]

Customs such as these paysons later stimulated movements for change and inspired revolutionaries in the nineteenth century.

Music of all sorts also played a strong role in Philippine life, and this pattern can be traced back centuries, certainly predating the Spanish period. Perhaps the music most identified today as truly Filipino is the *kundiman*—passionate, often sad, and romantic ballads that originated during Spanish colonialism. The emotional nature of the kundiman may have allowed Filipinos to express their love of country while sidestepping Spanish repression of all nationalistic sentiments. But even the classic songs of unrequited love were transformed into revolutionary meanings in the 1800s, through the use of metaphors about enslavement, oppression, and the martyrdom of nationalist heroes. Through the mixing of indigenous, Spanish, and later U.S. influences, the Filipinos developed their unique culture.

The Portuguese and Spanish were the first Europeans to have an impact on Southeast Asia but they were not the last. Portuguese power survived for only a century, and their noneconomic influence never really extended much beyond the small islands and ports they controlled. In Southeast Asia the Spanish were never able to extend their power beyond the Philippines. The major challenge to the Portuguese and Spanish in the 1600s came from the Dutch, who arrived in the region after establishing colonies in South Africa and Sri Lanka. At the end of the 1500s political and economic power in Europe shifted northward from Spain and Portugal to the Netherlands and England, both of which had developed the most dynamic and prosperous capitalist economies in Europe while acquiring advanced naval power. This shift in power was symbolized by the English defeat of the Spanish Armada in 1588 during a Spanish-English war.

Dutch ships had long carried spices from Portugal to Northern Europe, and a few Dutch sailors had even visited the Indies on Portuguese ships. In 1595 the first Dutch fleet visited Maluku and returned to Holland with spices. The architect of the Dutch empire in Indonesia was governor-general Jan Pieterzoon Coen, a former accountant who ruthlessly sought commercial monopoly in the early 1600s. Coen made his trade goals clear while also confirming the vigor of the region's commerce: "Piece goods from Gujerat [sic] we can barter for pepper and gold on the coast of Sumatra . . . cottons from the coast of [India] for pepper in Banten; sandalwood [and] pepper we can barter for Chinese goods . . . we can extract silver from Japan with Chinese goods; piece goods from [India] in exchange for spices . . . one thing leads to another."[14] During the next century the Dutch fought for a share of the maritime trade against Arab, Chinese, Indian, and Indonesian competition, but they had their greatest success against the Portuguese. After many bloody battles, the Dutch dislodged the Portuguese from their outposts and replaced them as the dominant regional European power in Southern Asia. When the Dutch captured Melaka in 1641 from Portugal, the city had become a ghost of its former self. The Dutch tried vainly to revive Melaka as a trade entrepôt but the city never recovered its earlier glory.

During the next several centuries, the Dutch gradually gained control of the Indonesian archipelago, except for the Portuguese-ruled eastern half of the island of Timor in Eastern Indonesia. Like the Portuguese, the Dutch often treated local populations harshly, and they gradually eliminated all competition, often by military force. As Dutch forces attacked and occupied the prosperous trading city of Makassar, in Sulawesi, in 1659, the city's sultan demanded of the Dutch commander: "Do you believe that God has preserved for your trade alone islands which lie so distant from your homeland?"[15] The sultan's secretary, Amin, wrote a long poetic account about the disaster: "Listen, sir, to my advice; never make friends with the Dutch. No country can call itself safe when they are around."[16] The Dutch were ruthless, slaughtering thousands of Indonesians who opposed them as well as repulsing English forces who were arriving in the region. In 1621 the Dutch killed, enslaved, or left to starve the entire population of the spice-producing Banda Islands—some 15,000 people. In 1623 they massacred the residents of an English base on Ambon Island.

But the Dutch were also well-organized, resourceful, and shrewd diplomats, allying themselves with one state against a rival state or against the Portuguese or English. For instance, they cooperated with an ambitious and charismatic Bugis prince, Arung Palakka, to defeat his rival state, Makassar, making Palakka the most powerful chief in Southern Sulawesi. In return, his soldiers aided Dutch forces. Exploiting local conflicts, however, sometimes drew the Dutch into civil wars. Because the Dutch empire in the Indies was built over 300 years, their impact varied widely and they never destroyed all the preconquest commercial networks, such as those of the Chinese and the Bugis. The Dutch sought wealth but, unlike the Portuguese and Spanish, cared little about spreading their culture and religion.

Eventually the Dutch concentrated on Java, a flourishing island with a vibrant culture and mercantile economy. In the 1600s the great trading port of Banten in West Java and Mataram city in Central Java each contained some 800,000 people, and many cities had large, multiethnic populations drawn from throughout Asia. Javan artisans were noted for their fine craftsmanship, and the island's smiths made perhaps the finest steel swords in the world. The commercial prowess of the Javanese, the island's main ethnic group, was renowned. Javanese women were prominent in business alongside the men, and as one English observer noted: "It is usual for a husband to entrust his pecuniary affairs entirely to his wife. The women alone attend the markets, and conduct all the buying and selling."[17]

Requiring a base for exploiting Java, Coen established a settlement at Batavia (now called Jakarta), on the northwest coast, in 1619. Capitalizing on political instability and divisions, the Dutch slowly extended their power across the island, gaining dominance over ports and sultanates. Most of Java was under direct or indirect Dutch control by the end of the 1700s, helped by the Dutch policy of co-opting local rulers and their officials. As one Dutch official wrote: "The Javanese obeys his chiefs. It was only necessary to give them part of the gain—and success was complete."[18] The Dutch concentrated on consolidating and maximizing their gains in Java and Maluku, especially after Batavia became a flourishing trading city. With trade as their major goal, the Dutch left

The pro-Dutch king of Mataram stabs an anti-Dutch rival to death around 1680, coolly observed by Dutch soldiers and officials. The Dutch slowly extended their control throughout Java, marginalizing and co-opting the rulers of the various Javan states. KITLV Leiden 48 M 5

administration to the Dutch East India Company, a joint public-private organization established in 1602. Soon the company shifted in priorities from relying on the export of spices to making Java their primary source of wealth. The Dutch governed some districts through local rulers, and, admiring the activity of Chinese traders who had operated in Java for centuries, invited more Chinese to come in as middlemen.

The burden of economic change fell on the peasantry. Coffee, grown for centuries in Ethiopia and then Arabia, was becoming a more popular commodity in world trade, with a rapidly growing market in Europe and North America. The Dutch introduced coffee planting to Indonesia as an export crop in 1696 and in 1725 began forcing peasants in the West Java highlands, and later in Sumatra, to grow the crop through a system of annual quotas. Between 1726 and 1878 Holland controlled between 50 and 75 percent of the world's coffee trade. The Dutch earned enough profit from coffee to finance much of their industrialization in the 1800s, including building the Dutch national railroad system. And coffee even came to be known in the West as "java."

The Dutch East India Company had great capital and large resources in pursuing profit and seeking a monopoly of Southeast Asian trade, which it believed justified ruthless policies. If the population of a spice island grew restless, Dutch soldiers might kill many and carry off the rest to Batavia, Sri Lanka, or South Africa as slaves. To increase demand and reduce supply, the spice-growing trees and bushes might all be chopped down. Because the company's headquarters in Amsterdam were ten months away by boat, there was little guidance from Holland and few restraints on the company's power. Thanks to company policy, some once-vibrant trading cities, among them Melaka, languished. One Dutch observer regretted that Banten, "once the greatest place of trade in the East . . . has become a home only of wretches."[19] The Javanese merchant class, once major players in the world economy, was slowly displaced by Dutch and Chinese. Some resisted. Shaikh Yusuf, for example, from Gowa in Sulawesi, had studied Islam in Acheh and Arabia and became a spiritual adviser to the sultan of Banten. Enraged by Dutch practices that threatened Islamic morality—such as the toleration of gambling, opium smoking, and cockfighting—in 1683 he led 2,000 followers into a holy war against the Dutch. It failed and he was exiled to South Africa, where he died.

In the developing colonial society, the Dutch occupied the top rung, followed by mixed-descent Eurasians and the local rulers and aristocrats who cooperated. The commercial merchant class was mostly Chinese. Like the Spanish, however, the Dutch feared and occasionally massacred the Chinese. Most Indonesians occupied the lower rungs of society, with many working various occupations as slaves. Slavery had been common in Indonesia for centuries, and the Dutch maintained the practice. Most of the Dutch themselves lived in Batavia, built to resemble a city in Holland. This style, with close-packed, stuffy houses and stagnant canals, was poorly suited to the tropical climate, however. In contrast to Indonesians, who prized personal cleanliness, the puritanical Dutch wore heavy woolen clothes in the tropical heat but bathed only once a week. However, many Dutch soon found Javanese culture seductive, taking local wives, owning slaves, dressing in Javanese clothes, and indulging in the delicious and spicy curries, which became even tastier after the Portuguese introduced chilies from the Americas.

Social and cultural life in the capital was raw. Because few Dutch women came to the Indies, many Dutch men married or cohabitated with Indonesian women, and their Eurasian children often grew up speaking Malay. Batavia fostered a highly mixed, multiethnic society, with many migrants from Bali, Sulawesi, and Sumatra as well as Arabs,

Chinese, and Indians. The majority of Batavians, known as Orang Betawi, were a unique, Malay-speaking blend of Javanese and other peoples. The mostly Protestant Dutch, who recognized religious freedom at home, spent little money on Christian missions. Denied real power, the Javanese rulers and courts turned inward to concentrate on their traditional culture. The royal dances became fantastically fluid, graceful, and stylized. Their *batik* fabrics became more splendid and intricate. The Javanese became even more preoccupied with status. Peasants were encouraged to treat aristocratic officials with even greater awe and respect.

Despite success in Java, Maluku, Melaka, and the Philippines, European imperialists faced numerous thwarted ambitions in Southeast Asia before 1750. Constantine Phaulkon, a Greek-born adventurer

Wearing traditional Sasak garb and armed with traditional spears and shields as well as modern rifles, these local leaders on the Indonesian island of Lombok, photographed in 1865, faced many challenges as the Balinese, Dutch, and native Sasak people contended for political dominance on the island. Whether led by precolonial kings and chiefs or Western colonial rulers, national governments often used local leaders to enforce their policies and collect taxes. KITLV Leiden 3617

who had worked in India and Java for the British East India Company, after some initial personal successes, reflected these setbacks. In 1678 Phaulkon, then 31 years old, moved as a trader to the Siamese capital of Ayutthaya where the king, Narai, was resisting Dutch economic pressure to secure more commercial rights. Narai's reign was turbulent but prosperous and he promoted literature and the arts. He also sent three diplomatic missions to the French court to obtain Western maps and scientific knowledge. Employing foreigners in government was not unusual in Siam. A Persian-born Muslim had recently served as prime minister. Generally Chinese captained and crewed the royal trading ships to China and Japan. After Phaulkon was hired as an interpreter in Siam's treasury department, his British colleagues saw him as an ally in their competition with the Dutch for influence. His accomplishments there soon earned him a promotion to Superintendent of Foreign Trade. Phaulkon himself married into a long-settled Christian Japanese family. But the British fell out with Phaulkon, who was then wooed by French commercial agents. In 1684 the British traders left for India. The talented and charismatic Phaulkon was well liked by King Narai, who, recognizing European ambitions in Southeast Asia, wanted the French as allies to counter the more feared Dutch.

Although now a trusted advisor to Narai, Phaulkon secretly plotted with the French to expand French power in Siam. Meanwhile, French missionaries also arrived in the region, naively hoping to convert the king and then Siam to Roman Catholicism. In response, the Siamese monarch sent a letter back to the French king, arguing that God rejoiced not in religious uniformity but in theological diversities, preferring to be honored by different worships and ceremonies. The large French naval force in Ayutthaya, their demands for territory, endless quarreling among themselves, and obsessive proselytizing finally angered the Buddhist Siamese people. When King Narai fell ill in 1688, anti-French leaders took over the Siamese government, executed Phaulkon as a traitor, and pushed the French out of Siam. For the next few decades the Siamese, who once welcomed foreign influence and interaction, mistrusted the Europeans and refused to grant them any special privileges. But Ayutthaya remained a hub for trade with China and Japan, mostly carried out after 1688 by Chinese.

The French were involved not only in Siam but also in Vietnam beginning in 1615. The French sought trade but also dispatched Roman Catholic missionaries who recruited a small local following. The Vietnamese used the Chinese writing system, and the French missionaries created a romanized Vietnamese alphabet to undercut Confucian and

Chinese influence. In the twentieth century it became the official writing system. But the trading relationships were often disappointing to both parties, and Christian missionaries sometimes earned the hostility of local governments.

Before 1750 Western nations were dominant neither in political nor economic spheres except in a few widely scattered outposts. Vietnam and Ayutthaya were two of the powerful and prosperous states in an Asian region that stretched from Tokugawa Japan in the east to Ottoman Turkey in the west in the 1600s. The Vietnamese, continuing their long expansion down the coast, had annexed the Mekong delta by the late 1600s. The port of Hoian in Central Vietnam became a key hub for China–Japan trade, attracting many Chinese and Japanese traders. However, most of the Japanese left after the Tokugawa Shogunate called them home and banned emigration in the mid-1600s. Around the region European traders still had to compete with Chinese, Arab, and Southeast Asian merchants. Indeed, Chinese, especially from coastal Fujian province in Southeast China, remained the region's main shippers, middlemen, and local merchants and were also harbor masters, tax collectors, and financial advisers to several governments in Southeast Asia. The Europeans did not yet have a clear advantage in military and economic power over the stronger Asian states. As a result, the Siamese, while feeling it necessary to manipulate the rival Europeans, could also force them to leave. Although some states, especially in the islands, lost power and cities like Banten and Makassar declined, many Southeast Asian states remained dynamic in this era, so that, except on Java, European power was restricted largely to fringe areas like the Philippines and the Spice Islands.

Starting in the 1300s Theravada Buddhism dug deeper roots on the mainland, and Islam continued to spread throughout the Malay Peninsula, Indonesia, and the Southern Philippines. An age of commerce existed in parts of the region, especially the archipelago, at least until the later 1600s and some places much longer. There were also increasing urbanization and the strengthening of absolute monarchies in countries like Siam. And some smaller states were being absorbed into larger ones. On the mainland some 20 states in the fourteenth century had been reduced to fewer than 12 by the early eighteenth century, with Vietnam, Ayutthaya, and Toungoo clearly dominant. The economic changes, such as increasing maritime trade, were paralleled by a population increase to around 35 million by 1800. But during the 1600s the climate cooled significantly, causing less frequent rains and occasional famines in the once green lands. The side effects of climate change, however temporary, may have weakened Southeast Asian states in their competition with the West. Cooler European weather that also hurt European harvests may also have encouraged more Europeans to seek their fortunes abroad.

Southeast Asia became an even more crucial part of the developing world economy, with the Portuguese, Dutch, and Spanish exporting luxury items such as Indonesian spices but also bulk products such as tin, sugar, and rice from their newly colonized possessions. Some historians trace the birth of a true world economy to the founding of Spanish Manila in 1571, which became the first hub linking Asia and the Americas across the Pacific. The Manila galleons that annually carried agricultural products as well as Chinese silk and porcelain from the Philippines to Mexico for distribution in Spanish America and Europe symbolized the new reality. The galleons returned to Manila with European goods, mail, personnel, and vast amounts of silver to pay for Asian goods. The Spanish used much of the silver to purchase Chinese products. The silver shipments drained Spanish imperial coffers, however, and contributed to the decline of the Spanish Empire. The American silver gave Asian trade a great push, encouraging increased production of Indonesian coffee and spices, Philippine sugar, Chinese tea and silk, and Indian textiles. There was little Asian demand for most European goods until the Industrial Revolution began in England in the late 1700s and created marketable products such as inexpensive machine-made textiles, which is why Europeans had to resort to force to get what they wanted. The West did not come into a decaying and impoverished Southeast Asia but rather a wealthy, open, and dynamic region. But conditions changed significantly in the eighteenth and nineteenth centuries, as a growing European interest in obtaining minerals and growing crops for export began to overshadow other commercial activity.

CHAPTER 6

The Western Winds of Colonialism, 1750–1914

Frustrated by the Vietnamese emperor's refusal to liberalize trade relations with Western nations and protect Christian missionaries, the French, seeking to expand their empire in Asia, attacked Vietnam with military force in 1858 and over the next three decades conquered the country despite determined resistance. The blind Vietnamese poet Nguyen Dinh Chieu bemoaned the loss of his country's independence: "Rivers and mountains are overturned; whence this disaster, O Heaven? Sadly the white clouds cover the land. And now the West wind of autumn blows unceasingly across the world."[1] In this era most of the Southeast Asian states faced various crises, leaving them less able to thwart the more intensive European penetration made possible by the military, technological, and economic power generated by the Industrial Revolution. And capitalism in the West encouraged an endless quest to acquire new resources to be exploited and markets for industrial goods. One Malay teacher and scholar of Arab ancestry, Syed Shakkh al-Hady, observed ruefully in 1907 that "the Europeans . . . [came] replete with the weapons to win the battle of life and equipped with knowledge of the ways and means to make profit."[2] The result was a resurgence of colonialism, as all the major societies except the Siamese felt the Western winds of conquest.

In Indonesia, the Dutch greatly expanded their power between 1750 and 1914. The Dutch East India Company was abolished in 1799 because of debts and corruption, replaced by a formal colonial government charged with making the lands more profitable. The Dutch colonial regime concentrated its economic exploitation on the two most heavily populated and fertile islands, Java and Sumatra. In 1830 Dutch administrators introduced what they called the Cultivation System, which forced Javanese to grow sugar, a valuable commodity, on rice land. The government set a fixed price to pay peasants, even if world prices were high. Many peasants earned new income and some took advantage of improved irrigation facilities and massive forest clearing to grow more rice as well as sugar. But costs also rose faster than compensation, and rains washed dirt out of cleared lands, clogging rivers and harbors. Within a few years, peasants had to grow more sugar and work longer hours to earn the same profit as before. Sugar, meanwhile, enjoyed an ever-expanding world market and the peasants came to depend on sugar profits.

The Dutch colonizers and their collaborators prospered from their colonial policies, but many peasants ultimately became impoverished. A Dutch critic of the system, Douwes Dekker, described the results in his 1860 novel, *Max Havelaar*: "If anyone should ask whether the man who grows the products receives a reward proportionate to the yields, the answer must be in the negative. The Government compels him to grow on *his* land what pleases *it*; it punishes him when he sells the crop to anyone else but *it*."[3] Later, many peasants faced disaster when world commodity prices for sugar and coffee collapsed during the Great Depression of the 1930s.

The Dutch replaced the Cultivation System in the 1870s with a policy of free enterprise, which welcomed foreign investment and more Western-owned plantations. Many Chinese immigrated to the islands, becoming a commercial middle class and operating shops in every town and city. But the Dutch saw Indonesia as a supplier of tropical raw materials and a market for European manufactured goods and so invested little in industrial development.

Colonialism also fostered rapid population growth, particularly on Java, creating a terrible burden for contemporary Indonesia. In 1800 there may have been 10 million people on Java. The population grew to 30 million by 1900 and to 48 million by 1940, producing a landscape of densely packed villages and fewer trees. Dutch policies promoting social order such as reducing banditry contributed to population growth. By the late nineteenth century there was also better health care available, and people lived longer. Economic incentives encouraged women to have more children to provide more labor for the fields. Heavier labor demands on women may also have reduced the period they spent breast-feeding babies, thus making mothers fertile for longer periods of time. The result of a rapidly growing population was more people cultivating smaller plots and an increasing number of people with no access to land.

Population growth in Java fostered population movement. Many Javanese became plantation laborers, often migrating to Sumatra's east coast where a vast plantation economy developed to grow rubber and

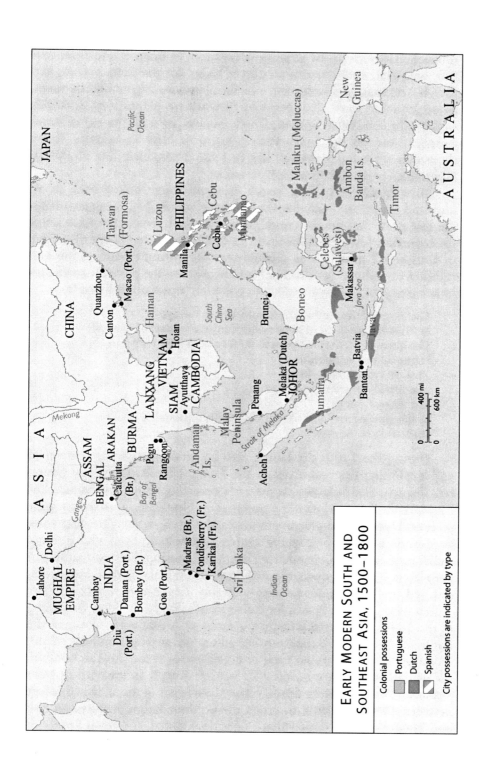

EARLY MODERN SOUTH AND
SOUTHEAST ASIA, 1500–1800

Colonial possessions
Portuguese
Dutch
Spanish

City possessions are indicated by type

tobacco. The movement of surplus Javanese to outer islands like Borneo, Sulawesi, and Sumatra continues today for the same reason, and forests are increasingly turned into farmlands to accommodate them. Some Javanese were also recruited to work on plantations in British Malaya, British North Borneo, Dutch Guiana (now Suriname) in South America, and on the South Pacific island of New Caledonia. Today thousands of Indonesians still live in these lands, including 90,000 in Suriname, far from their ancestral homes.

Most Javanese disliked Dutch rule and some looked back to an idealized past with nostalgia. One of these was R. Ng. Ronggawarsita, the last of a long line of court poets who had served Javanese kings for centuries. Just before his death in 1873, he wrote "Poem of a Time of Darkness," in which he remembered the glorious political life and stability of the lost "golden age" and bemoaned the powerlessness and hopelessness of the Javanese in the colonial "times of darkness":

> The lustre of the realm is now vanished to the eye
> In ruins the teaching of good ways for there is no example left
> The heart of the learned poet so coiled about with care
> Seeing all the wretchedness
> That everything is darkened
> The world immersed in misery . . .
> The time of doom
> In this time of madness to join the mad is unbearable . . .
> Starvation at the end.[4]

During the 1800s the Dutch also began consolidating control of and exploiting the resources of the Outer Islands, especially Sumatra, Borneo, and Sulawesi, sometimes resorting to violent tactics. For 30 years the fiercely Islamic Achehnese in Northern Sumatra strongly resisted Dutch attempts to dominate the area, a struggle that took thousands of lives before the Dutch triumphed. Even today many Achehnese seek independence from Indonesia. The self-sufficient people of Bali, although divided into several competing kingdoms, relished their independence and also put up a heavy resistance. The Dutch triumphed only at a high cost in lives on both sides. Beginning in the 1840s the Dutch launched a series of brutal wars to annex the Balinese. Attacking Balinese-ruled states on nearby Lombok island, Dutch soldiers sang about their enthusiasm for war: "And to Lombok off we go/And we are bored with peace/So we'll shoot with powder and lead/Those Balinese dead."[5] The Dutch sent in more armed forces between 1906 and 1908 to crush the holdout Balinese states on Bali and Lombok. After their valiant resistance failed, the royal family of

Klungkung in Eastern Bali, the last holdout kingdom, committed collective suicide, walking into the guns of the Dutch forces. A Dutch account from a Batavia newspaper described the horrific scene: "Little groups of five to six lance bearers made for the [Dutch] troops. They were immediately shot down. This maneuver repeated itself, then women and children also armed with lances and swords came out and the wounded began to stab themselves. It was now obvious that the prince and all the realm's lords and most prominent people had sacrificed themselves."[6] The Balinese defiance and preference for death over defeat gave the Dutch no satisfaction in victory.

By annexing scattered islands and states into the Dutch East Indies, the Dutch essentially created Indonesia as a political unit. But the colony, governed from Batavia (now Jakarta), remained necessarily decentralized, and there was little common national feeling. The colony included diverse peoples speaking many languages and maintaining distinctive cultures, making the later building of an Indonesian nation difficult. Unlike the Spanish, the Dutch put little emphasis on promoting cultural and religious change, and traditional cultures remained generally unchallenged. But the gradual spread of capitalism, with its individualistic orientation, eroded the more communal values of traditional villages. By 1900 the Dutch recognized the decline in human welfare and began building more schools and clinics under what they termed the Ethical Policy. But the improvements were limited, too little and too late. Few Indonesians had access to formal education, but those who did attend Dutch schools learned Western ways and the rhetoric of democracy and freedom. They could easily see that these fine ideas were not practiced in the colony.

Except in Portuguese and then Dutch-ruled Melaka, there was little Western influence in the Malay Peninsula until the late 1700s. Then the British became interested in the area as they were consolidating their position in India. Britain was becoming the strongest European power thanks to its leadership of the Industrial Revolution. Seeking a source for goods to be sold in China as well as a naval base in the Eastern Indian Ocean, the British East India Company purchased Penang Island, off Malaya's northwest coast, from a cash-strapped Malay sultan in 1786. Penang rapidly became a major free trade port for Western and Indian products as well as for local commodities such as tin, pepper, and spices. The local Malay population was soon outnumbered by Chinese, Indian, and Arab immigrants who came to trade and work. Each ethnic group practiced its own laws and customs, however, and with its diverse population, Penang represented in miniature an image of the Malaysia to come.

Britain soon became more deeply involved in the Malay world. In 1819 a British agent, Sir Thomas Stamford Raffles, capitalized on local political unrest to acquire sparsely populated Singapore Island at the tip of the Malay Peninsula. Raffles was alarmed by growing Dutch power and wrote that his actions broke the spell of Dutch invincibility, with the Dutch no longer being the exclusive sovereigns of the Malay world. A fine harbor and strategic location at the southern end of the Melaka Straits, the midpoint of shipping between China and India, quickly made Singapore the center for Britain's regional thrust and a great source of profit. Singapore welcomed Chinese immigrants, and the island became the major base for Chinese economic activity in Southeast Asia. For example, one of these immigrants, Tan Che Sang, arrived after spending many years in Melaka and Penang becoming a leading merchant. He and other Chinese merchants were instrumental in building the city. By the 1860s Singapore, with a mostly Chinese population, had become the successor to Srivijaya and Melaka as the crossroads of Southeast Asian commerce and the key China–India trade link. Britain obtained Melaka in 1824 from the Dutch in exchange for a West Sumatran port, Bengkulu, occupied by the British. From Singapore, Britain now governed the three ports of Penang, Melaka, and Singapore as a colony called the Straits Settlements. Increasingly, the historical Malay world was divided into British- and Dutch-ruled zones. With the 1869 opening of the Suez Canal, linking the Red Sea and the Mediterranean, European markets for Malayan products such as tin became much more accessible.

Chinese steadily immigrated to the region, and in the early 1800s more Chinese than ever were settling in Western Malaya, where they contracted with local Malay rulers to mine tin and gold. Demand for these metals in industrializing Europe increased dramatically, and rival Chinese communities fought wars with each other for control of minerals. Chinese miners established several towns, including Kuala Lumpur, that later grew into flourishing cities.

Political and social instability was common in some Malay states. With tin exports threatened, European businessmen in the Straits Settlements pressured sometimes reluctant British authorities to take a more active role in the Malay states. British officials were already concerned about the perceived threats from the rival Germans, French, and Dutch. By the 1870s local British officials began intervening in various Malayan sultanates, establishing political influence. They used the establishment of order and security as their rationale for intervention, but this masked the need of an industrializing trading nation for resources and markets. They convinced or forced sultans to accept a system of indirect rule

By the nineteenth century many Chinese settled permanently in Southeast Asia, raising families and often sending their children to local Chinese schools, such as this girls' school in Singapore, photographed in the early twentieth century. Some schools were sponsored by local Chinese organizations and taught in Chinese, while others were operated by Christian missions and used English, French, or Dutch in instruction. Library of Congress LC-USZ62-84233

with British advisers. Ultimately the political and economic systems of the Malay states were transformed as the British co-opted Malay rulers and the traditional aristocracy. By 1909 Britain had achieved formal or informal control over nine sultanates, including several northern states acquired from Siam. The various states kept their separate identities, but they were increasingly integrated with the Straits Settlements to form British Malaya. By maintaining the Malay sultans and aristocracy as symbolic leaders of their states, the British furthered the idea that Malays occupied a privileged position in the colony.

Under British rule millions of Chinese entered Singapore and Malaya, especially the western coastal states, to join the earlier immigrants and work as laborers, miners, planters, and merchants. The Chinese working in mines and plantations or as day laborers were known locally as *coolies*, a term, probably of South Asian origin, which indicated a manual worker of very low social status. One of these was Yap Ah Loy, who arrived from China as a penniless 17-year-old in 1854 to work in a tin mine. Eventually Yap became a rich merchant and mine owner. In 1865 he married Kok Kang Keow, daughter of a prominent Melaka Chinese family. From 1868 until his death in 1885, he served as the head, or *kapitan*, of the Chinese community in Kuala Lumpur, a town he helped found. Many Chinese stayed only a few years while others, like Yap, remained permanently, marrying locally or bringing their families from China. Through enterprise, cooperation, and organization, many Chinese became part of an urban-based middle class controlling retail trade. Many Indian immigrants or soujourners also came to the Straits Settlements as traders, craftsmen, and workers. And beginning in the 1880s the British imported Tamils from Southeast India to work on rubber and oil palm plantations, where they experienced the harsh realities and monotonous labor of estate life. By the 1930s there were 500,000 Indians in Malaya. Most Malays themselves remained in rural villages, living from small-scale trade, fishing, and farming. The Malay social system and its values, which emphasized aristocratic privileges, acceptance of status differences, and religious piety, differed greatly from the secular Chinese, who sought economic success and encouraged social mobility.

British rule transformed Malaya socially and economically. The Chinese and Indians eventually outnumbered the Malays. By 1931 the Chinese accounted for around 40 percent and the Indians for 14 percent of Malaya's population. A pluralistic society was developing: a medley of peoples who mixed but did not combine, a tossed salad rather than a melting pot. A Malay proverb described the new reality: "raven with raven, sparrow with sparrow." Each group largely maintained its own culture, religions, language, and customs. Most Malays lived in villages, most Chinese in towns or cities, and most Indians on plantations. Separate Christian mission schools, Chinese schools, and government Malay school systems meant that students mostly studied with others from their own ethnic or religious groups.

Meanwhile the British maintained their control of the colonies by governing the various communities through their own leaders: aristocratic Malay chiefs, wealthy Chinese merchants, and urban Indian traders and professionals. This policy of treating the main ethnic groups as separate communities transformed them into three separate ethnic blocs—Malay, Chinese, and Indian—with profound consequences for national and social unity. Malay intellectuals became increasingly concerned that Chinese immigrants might overwhelm the Malay culture.

These worries encouraged some Malays, mostly from commoner backgrounds, to work toward modernizing Islamic practice as a way to challenge the domination by the aristocracy and hence reform Malay politics to strengthen the Malays' hand in the competition with the Chinese.

The British, meanwhile, remained unconcerned with these social divisions and concentrated on their goal of extracting resources from Malaya. Economic development occurred largely along the west coast, where the planting of pepper, tobacco, oil palms, and especially rubber was encouraged, mostly on plantations, to meet Western resource and market needs. Tin and rubber became Malaya's major exports. Tin was shipped to Europe and North America to be used in manufacturing household utensils and to make tin cans and barrels for the storage of food and oil, which made life easier for Western families and for military forces stationed far from home. Ultimately some Chinese, Malays, and Indians benefited from the development of this export economy, but many others experienced stagnant or falling living standards. British tax policies encouraged Malay villages to grow cash crops, and many took up planting rubber trees. Such villages became integrated into the world economy but lost their traditional self-sufficiency.

The British also extended their power into the northern third of Borneo, inhabited mostly by Muslim Malays along the coast and animist hill peoples in the interior. In 1841 a wealthy English adventurer, James Brooke, intervened in a revolt by local Malays in Sarawak against the Brunei sultanate, which claimed ownership of the area. Brooke became *Rajah* (Governor) of Sarawak, based in Kuching, and he inaugurated 100 years of rule by an English family. The first rajah, James Brooke, had to defend his government against Chinese mining settlements used for autonomy and, more significantly, against the Ibans, an interior people much feared as warriors and headhunters who had long resisted coastal governments. The Ibans, animists whose economy was based on the shifting cultivation of rice, were annexed only after bloody military campaigns. Despite this violent annexation, the Brookes saw themselves, and largely governed, as benevolent autocrats claiming to protect local peoples from too-rapid change. Sarawak became an independent state under British protection, but the Brookes' relations with Britain and the neighboring Dutch were often strained. The Brookes expanded the state's frontiers by acquiring territory from declining Brunei and developed an economic base by encouraging Chinese immigration and cash crops. By 1939, Chinese represented a quarter of Sarawak's population. Some Chinese began growing pepper, and by the early twentieth century Sarawak became the major world producer of this valuable spice. World

War II ended the Brooke dynasty, since the rulers had to flee the Japanese invasion and lacked the resources to rebuild the state after the war.

Meanwhile, in Northern Borneo, a private British corporation, the Chartered Company, took over territory once ruled by Brunei and the sultanate of Sulu in the Southern Philippines. The company ruled British North Borneo, today known as Sabah, as a British protectorate from 1881 to 1941, operating the state in the interest of its British shareholders. Western-owned plantations grew rubber and tobacco. Brunei, once a major power in the region, became a British protectorate and flourished after the discovery of huge oil reserves in 1920.

France developed ambitions in Vietnam, which was engulfed in civil war and rebellion. In the 1770s rebels known as the Taysons, led by three brothers from the village of Tayson in Southern Vietnam, began a 30-year struggle against the Vietnamese emperors and their French allies. The inspirational Tayson leader Nguyen Hue sponsored economic expansion, rallied the people against a Chinese invasion, skillfully manipulated sentiment against foreign assistance to the emperors, and addressed growing poverty. The Taysons were social revolutionaries whose slogan was "seize the property of the rich and redistribute it to the poor,"[7] but they were also committed to a unified Vietnamese nation after many decades of division. In 1802 the armies of the powerful Nguyen family from central Vietnam, with French military assistance, defeated the Taysons and reestablished imperial rule over the country of 7 or 8 million people, which was comparable to the entire population of Britain. The most able Nguyen ruler was Minh Mang, who ruled from 1820 to 1841. A centralizer and modernizer interested in Western science, Minh Mang also persecuted Vietnamese Christians, whom he viewed as potential subversives, and promoted Confucianism, which by the early 1800s had became more deeply entrenched in Vietnamese life than ever before, earning him the hatred of the French.

But the Nguyen emperors were largely unable to revitalize Vietnam or resolve the social and economic problems that had inspired the Tayson Rebellion. *The Tale of Kieu*, a 3,300-line poem written by diplomat Nguyen Du in the early 1800s, reflected a growing criticism of the greed and hypocrisy of Confucian society. The poem, cherished by and familiar to every Vietnamese, sympathetically narrated the story of an intelligent, well-born, and beautiful young woman, Kieu, forced to become a concubine and then a prostitute while keeping a sense of honor and secretly remaining loyal to her true love. To many Vietnamese, Kieu symbolized the Vietnamese people mistreated by the upper-class Vietnamese and their French allies. Another critic of the imperial court and Confucianism was the feminist poet Ho Xuan Huong, who had been a concubine to several high officials. Using wit and sarcasm to attack the ills of society, she wrote freely about sex, championed women's rights, and also attacked polygamy: "One wife gets quilts, the other wife must freeze. To share a husband—damn it, what a fate! I labor as a wageless maid."[8]

By the late 1850s the militarily powerful and well-financed French, in pursuit of what they called a "civilizing mission" to spread French culture and religion, commercial gain, and control of the presumed Mekong and Red River routes to China, began their long, bloody campaign of conquest against a determined but badly outgunned Vietnamese resistance. In a quarter century of conflict, the French first conquered the south and then moved north. The blind Vietnamese poet Nguyen Dinh Chieu became a symbol of the Vietnamese resistance to the French when he wrote an oration honoring the fallen Vietnamese soldiers after a heroic defense in a battle in 1862: "You preferred to die fighting the enemy, and return to our ancestors in glory rather than survive in submission to the [Westerners] and share your miserable life with barbarians."[9] The French retaliated by seizing Chieu's land and property. The poet remained unbowed, refusing to use Western products such as soap powder and forbidding his children from learning the romanized Vietnamese alphabet developed by French Catholic missionaries. In verse spread by word of mouth and painstakingly copied manuscripts distributed throughout the land, Chieu rallied opposition. He heaped scorn on his countrymen who collaborated with the French occupiers and advised them to maintain the struggle for independence: "I had rather face unending darkness/Than see the country tortured/Everyone will rejoice in seeing the West wind [colonialism]/Vanish from [Vietnam's] mountains and rivers."[10]

Chieu had the talents and background to rally the Vietnamese against a French occupation. The son of a mandarin in southern Vietnam, Chieu overcame the handicap of blindness to become a physician, scholar, teacher, and renowned writer and bard, famous for his epic poems sung in the streets. These poems extolled the love of country, friendship, marital fidelity, family loyalty, scholarship, and the military arts. Chieu earned admiration for his loyalty to family, king, and country even if his blindness prevented him from taking up arms, as he lamented:

Rice fields are littered with our battle-killed
blood flows or lies in pools, stains hills and streams
Troops bluster on and grab our land, our towns

roaring and stirring dust to dim the skies
A scholar with no talent and no power
could I redress a world turned upside down?[11]

Chieu rejected the French offer of a financial subsidy and the return of his family land if he would rally to their cause. Today the Vietnamese continue to recite the stirring poems Chieu composed to aid the resistance.

By 1883 the French had annexed Vietnam. But it took them another 15 years to "pacify" the country against the heroic efforts of the *Can Vuong* ("Aid-the-King") rebel groups. Thousands of poorly armed Vietnamese waged guerrilla warfare, demonstrating anew the ancient tendency to resist foreign invaders against hopeless odds. As a French military officer affirmed in his report, the Vietnamese fought fiercely: "We have had enormous difficulties in imposing our authority in our new colony. Rebel bands disturb the country everywhere. They appear from nowhere, they arrive in large numbers, they destroy everything, and then disappear into nowhere."[12]

One of the rebellion's leaders, the mandarin Nguyen Quang Bich, rejected any compromise, replying in a letter to the French about their demand for surrender: "Please do not mention the word surrender any more. You cannot give any good counsel to a man who is determined to die [for his country]."[13] The Can Vuong rebels maintained the long tradition of resistance to foreign rule, a symbolic statement of Vietnamese determination to secure independence. In suppressing the struggle, the French massacred thousands, including the routine execution of surrendered or captured rebels. The Can Vuong showed some similarities with the later communists who struggled against the French and the U.S. forces in the twentieth century. The rebels employed a highly mobile form of guerrilla warfare, had strong support in the local population, arrested or executed collaborators with the new regime, and maintained an underground administration in the villages that competed with the local French puppet governments. Hence the rebels ruled the night; the French, the day. Furthermore, some of the rebel leaders developed reputations as Robin Hood figures, combining patriotism and social justice. The rebels remained a powerful symbol of resistance for generations. Meanwhile the imperial family lost much of its credibility because the emperor served the French as symbolic head of the colonial state.

By 1897 the French had created their Federation of Indochina, an artificial unit linking a Vietnam now broken for convenience into three separately ruled territories (Tonkin, Annam, and Cochin China) with newly acquired Cambodia and Laos. Both Cambodia and Laos had very different social, cultural, political, and historical legacies from those of Vietnam and relatively little in common with each other. The French maintained their rule by force and manipulation. By artificially dividing Vietnam, French colonial rule increased the cultural and linguistic differences between the regions but did not destroy the sense of common nationhood. Phan Van Tri, a poet writing in the late 1800s, reflected the patriotic views of many when he pined for national unity: "The nation, one tomorrow, will change its destiny to one of peace/ The South in common will enjoy reunion [with the north] in peaceful equilibrium."[14] French influence was especially strong in the south, where the administration was mostly French and the major city, Saigon, became known as the "Paris of the Orient." Several million Vietnamese, especially in the south, converted to Roman Catholicism. Those Vietnamese who adopted French culture, language, and religion were favored by the French for government jobs and other privileges but despised by other Vietnamese.

Vietnamese literally bow down before a French dignitary around 1890. Anxious to demonstrate their supremacy, the French demanded that Vietnamese officials pledge allegiance to the new colonial regime, even as thousands of rebels resisted the French for several decades. The French conquest of Vietnam brought an end to Vietnam's long independence. Adoc-photos/Art Resource, NY

Colonialism allowed the French to exploit the region's natural resources and also open new markets for French-manufactured goods. Powerful French commercial enterprises and top civil servants prospered, even if administering Indochina proved a financial drain on France. The colonial governments undermined the autonomy of Vietnamese villages by appointing their local leaders and increasing the tax burden to finance administrative costs. The French took land from the peasants and turned over perhaps half of the cultivated land to private landowners and investors. The colonial government also greatly expanded rice production for export, but such expansion favored large landowners rather than peasants. On rubber-tree plantations, workers faced dangerous and unhealthy conditions. By uprooting rural society, introducing competitive capitalism into once cooperative communities, linking the Vietnamese to the uncertainties of the world economy, weakening the imperial system, and otherwise exploiting the Vietnamese, the French also set into motion the forces that ultimately doomed their unpopular rule.

In the 1960s a peasant in central Vietnam recalled these years: "My father was very poor. He and my mother, and all of my brothers and sisters had to pull the plow. In the old days, people did the work of water buffalo."[15] French policies magnified the misfortunes of Vietnamese peasants, making a social revolution seem desirable. Such developments fueled widespread hatred of landlords. In some districts by the 1930s some 90 percent of the peasants were tenants farming land owned by others. The landlord problem in the Mekong delta and parts of Central Vietnam became particularly bad. The rural economy presented a stark picture of absentee land ownership, declining wages, and rising rents, an altogether combustible mix. Peasant poverty was steadily increasing.

The contents of Vietnamese peasant folk songs of the early twentieth century reflected the high levels of bitterness toward those, such as landlords, who profited from the French reconstruction of rural life:

What unhappiness strikes the poor
Who wear a single worn out, torn cloth
who tremble at the beatings of the communal drum
announcing the beginning of tax collection
the time of every unhappiness
Oh heaven, why are you not just?
Some have abundance while others are in want.[16]

The result of this bitterness was widespread peasant support for nationalists seeking radical change.

The changes instituted by the French in Cambodia and Laos were less dramatic than in Vietnam. Cambodia had long been dominated by Vietnam and Siam, which rankled Cambodian leaders. In 1856 a cautious King An Duong told a French emissary seeking closer relations: "What do you want me to do? I have two masters already, who always have an eye fixed on what I am doing. They are my neighbors, and France is far away."[17] In the 1850s the Vietnamese emperor allegedly claimed that Cambodia was like a child that must be maintained by Vietnam as its mother and Siam as its father. By 1863 Cambodia's rulers welcomed the French offer to guarantee their independence from Siamese and Vietnamese domination. In the 1880s the French transformed Cambodia into a colony. But Cambodia remained a secondary concern for the French and, since it was largely ignored, experienced less exploitation than Vietnam, except for the many rubber plantations the French developed. The Khmer monarchy remained in place and most peasants retained control of their land, but some Cambodians resented French control. The French also brought in Vietnamese as administrators and merchants, increasing Khmer-Vietnamese tensions.

The French united the rival Lao states along the Mekong River and the diverse hill tribes of the Laotian mountains into a common colonial entity, Laos, under the symbolic leadership of the Lao king of Luang Prabang. France did little to forge real national unity, improve social welfare, or encourage economic development except for building a few rubber-tree plantations. The result of French neglect was the retention of a traditional social structure but also less modernization.

But French control of Laos did have an impact on many of the hill peoples, including the Hmong. The original Hmong homeland was in mountainous southwestern China, where several million still live today. By the early 1800s, however, many Hmong were emigrating from China into Southeast Asia. Some moved into Northern Vietnam or Siam but most settled in the sparsely settled highlands of Laos, which by 1947 contained perhaps 350,000 Hmong. The Hmong were traders, horse breeders, and clothing and jewelry makers; they were known for their willingness to fight to preserve their independence. Seeking to make the mountain districts more profitable, the French introduced opium growing in the Laotian highlands as a source of revenue. Opium from Laos supplied the market in Vietnam, where French government monopolies thrived by selling it to Chinese immigrants and Vietnamese villages. As a result of French policies, many Hmong and some other Laotian hill peoples went from being rice farmers to opium growers, dependent on selling their crop to outsiders.

Vietnam, Cambodia, and Laos were not the only mainland areas to interest the expanding Europeans. Burma also fell under British colonization. It took Britain 60 years to conquer Burma, and the gradual loss of their independence proved devastating to the Burmese. But on the eve of British invasion, Burma seemed in a strong position. In the later 1700s the country had been revitalized under a vigorous new Konbaung dynasty, which expanded its borders by conquering neighboring states like Arakan and even defeated a traditional enemy, Siam, in a war. But there were growing problems posed by the gradual expansion of British power in Northeastern India, a traditional Burmese sphere of influence.

Even as the British encroached on Burmese territory, Burmese leaders were confident. One minister claimed that "the English are rich but they are not so brave as we are."[18] This attitude represented a false sense of their own power, however. The British had already developed a low opinion of Burma's leaders and came to despise the whole society. One British diplomat called the king and his court a bunch of clowns. Cultures clashed. In the 1830s a Burmese official told the British representative: "Your and our customs are so completely opposite on so many points."[19] Conflict was inevitable. The first Anglo-Burman War, resulting from a dispute over the Burma-India borderlands, raged from 1823 to 1826. The British captured the heavily populated Irrawaddy River delta, shocking the Burmese. After two years of hard fighting, the British pushed north toward the capital city, Ava, forcing the Burmese to sign a treaty awarding Britain parts of Northwestern and Southern Burma. The second war came in 1851, this time arising over the alleged Burmese persecution of British traders in Rangoon. Both sides suffered terrible casualties before agreeing to peace in 1852. As a result, the British acquired the Irrawaddy delta including Rangoon, breaking the spirit of the Burmese people.

Many Burmese began to feel an impending doom. Fear for the future was expressed in a fantastic literary activity, including drama, love poetry, and music. For example, Miyawaddy, a soldier, scholar, and longtime government minister from a prominent noble family, tried to salvage Burman traditions by writing plays set in villages and collecting folk songs, blending them together to create a new music. The court also commissioned scholars, brahmans, and officials to compile a great history of the Burmese people known as *The Glass Palace Chronicle*. There seemed a sense that the Burman cultural traditions might disappear. Based chiefly on ancient inscriptions, poems, texts, and chronicles, the *Chronicle* may or may not have accurately portrayed history but it represented the values of the era in which it was written. The desire to preserve Burman culture did not preclude interest in foreign ideas that might aid the country's survival. Miyawaddy, for example, appreciated Siamese music and culture, learned some Hindi (the major language of North India), and hired a Spaniard to translate English-language newspapers from India.

A new Burmese king, Mindon, who came to power in 1853, tried his best to salvage his country's prospects. In his journals British diplomat Henry Yule, who visited Mindon's court in 1855, described the king in his royal attire: "His dress was a long tunic of a lightly-colored silk, thickly set with jewels. Over the head was a gold plate."[20] A proponent of modernization, Mindon wanted good relations with the British. An idealistic, deeply religious, and learned man who avidly read books on philosophy, religion, politics, geography, and history, the king would be disappointed in his efforts. He introduced steamship navigation on the Irrawaddy River, promoted foreign trade, and attempted to break down barriers between the court and the Burmese people. Mindon's policies sparked a cultural renaissance, and the introduction of cheap printing presses spurred a literary revival. The multitalented Lady Hlaing, a member of an aristocratic family, wrote long, romantic court plays on the love lives of princes and princesses, and also introduced a new kind of song that combined dignity with melancholy. The British, however, constantly tried to humiliate Mindon and his government. And when they incorporated their Burmese territories into British India, it was a statement that Burma was so backward it did not even deserve its separate existence.

In the territories they controlled, the British tried to destroy Burmese culture. They weakened Buddhist institutions once supported by the kings and closed the Buddhist schools, which had fostered high rates of literacy. These were replaced with British schools run by the colonial government or Christian missions in hopes of westernizing the Burmese. In these schools Burmese traditions and leaders were belittled. Mindon failed to modernize his country and died in 1878, a broken man. He was followed by weaker leaders.

In 1886 the British completed their conquest of Burma in the Third Anglo-Burman War. The British marched north and captured the capital. Then, in the final insult, King Thibaw was given 45 minutes to pack, paraded through the capital in a bullock cart, and sent into exile in India. The Burmese kingdom was ended and the royal family exiled, but some Burmese resisted British rule for the next few years. The British policy of "pacification" was, in fact, bloody, as they destroyed whole villages and executed rebel leaders. In Southern Burma many Burmese lost their land or became deeply in debt to Indian immigrants. The British recruited non-Burman hill peoples into the government and army, increasing the divide between the majority Burmans and the ethnic minorities. The earlier sense of foreboding had been justified.

While Burma was being colonized, Siam became the only Southeast Asian country to maintain its independence. Burma and Siam, although longtime enemies, were similar in religion, government, and social structure, but the Siamese were more flexible and open to new ideas. For the Siamese, Buddhism and the monarchy served as the glue to hold the country together. Buddhism promoted consensus-building and conciliation, and Siam's class system allowed for greater upward mobility than Burma's, bringing fresh blood into the leadership. Furthermore, the Siamese had long been more involved in foreign trade, more open to immigrants, including many Chinese, and maintained close relations with China.

Geography and good luck also played a role. Because Burma bordered British India, it was engulfed in conflict with the West earlier than Siam. Siamese kings were aware that to the east the French were gaining control in Indochina while the British had ambitions to the south in Malaya. Siam was a strong state, however, under the vigorous Bangkok-based Chakri dynasty that came to power in 1781. An able political leadership had the time to mount a successful strategy to resist Western pressures. During the later 1800s and early 1900s, farsighted Chakri kings understood the changing nature of Southeast Asian politics and the rise of Western power. They promoted modernization policies and economic changes designed to ensure independence. Siam's kings followed a policy of yielding to the West when necessary and consolidating what remained of the kingdom. Several treaties with Siam in the early twentieth century allowed Britain and France to make Siam a buffer state between their colonies. Both nations were pressed to hold on to their other territories, wanted closer trade relations with Siam's ally, China, and feared a possible increase in British-French tensions. The price of political independence for the Siamese heartland was giving up claims to Laos and transferring Northern Malaya to Britain. Siamese leaders also acquiesced to commercial agreements that opened the country to Western businesses. Nonetheless, the Siamese retained some control over their destiny.

The first of the great Siamese kings, Mongkut, who ruled from 1851 to 1868, was probably the most perceptive and learned Southeast Asian leader of the mid-nineteenth century. The scholarly Mongkut had spent three decades as a Buddhist monk, specializing in education, and had studied English, Latin, and science. British photographer John Thomson, who traveled in Siam, noted the profound cultural differences between the British and Siamese. For example, Mongkut told the Englishman that it was a difficult task to keep all his 16 wives cheerful. The king coolly calculated that if many Western nations obtained rights in Siam, they would fight each other first, reducing the threat of invasion. Supported by other progressive officials, Mongkut, who hoped to divide the European powers, signed treaties with various Western nations that were often on terms unfavorable to Siam and invited Western advice to modernize his kingdom. Mongkut hired British women, including the wives of Christian missionaries, to teach English to his wives and sons. One of these teachers was Anna Leonowens, made famous a century later in *The King and I*. Based on her inaccurate book, this U.S. Broadway musical and then 1956 film misleadingly portrayed Mongkut, revered by Thais, and his progressive court as unsophisticated barbarians, an untrue, insulting picture that has resulted in a permanent ban on the film in Thailand.

The second great king was Mongkut's well-traveled son, Chulalongkorn, who ruled from 1868 to 1910, wisely emphasizing diplomacy and modernization. Chulalongkorn gathered a group of well-educated aristocratic advisors and started a broad reform program that included abolishing slavery, strengthening the bureaucracy, and establishing a Western-style government education system. Instead of rapid economic, social, and cultural changes, Chulalongkorn announced that he wanted "to see whatever is beneficial to the people accomplished gradually . . . and . . . unjust customs abolished. But it is impossible to change everything overnight."[21] The king stimulated economic growth by encouraging Chinese immigration and opening new land for rice production. Siam became one of the world's leading rice exporters by the early twentieth century. Chulalongkorn also began the building of a modern telecommunications and transportation system, especially railroads. But continuing Western economic pressures ensured that Western businessmen enjoyed many advantages. Nonetheless, Siam's economic development generally kept pace with that of its colonized neighbors but under Siamese rather than foreign direction. Siam remained independent and became increasingly modernized.

Siam's unique success in resisting colonialism and maintaining much of its traditional society and culture meant that Siamese did not face an identity crisis (unlike Filipinos), brutal challenges to cultural values (unlike Burmese), or severe economic displacement (unlike Vietnamese). Although it gave up some fringe territories, such as several Malay sultanates, to the British and French, Siam remained multiethnic, and ethnic diversity posed a challenge to national unity. Chulalongkorn's policies attempted to more closely integrate non-Thai peoples, such as the Lao people living south of the Mekong, the Malay-speaking Muslims in the far south, and the numerous Chinese immigrants, as well as highland peoples in the northern and western mountains, into the Bangkok-based state. Although success was mixed, a nation was being constructed by a centralizing government.

These decades also brought dramatic changes to the Philippines, where export of agricultural products intensified after 1750. Despite regional, ethnic, class, and familial loyalties that fragmented opposition to Spanish control, resentment against the conservative, corrupt, exploitative, repressive, economically stagnant, and racist rule of Spain had simmered for decades, especially among the *illustrados* ("enlightened ones"), educated and often affluent Filipinos, many of Spanish or Chinese mestizo ancestry. Some also criticized the domination of the Roman Catholic Church over education, intellectual life, and rural society.

Philippine nationalist sentiment was particularly significant among writers such as the anticlerical poet and novelist José Rizal, who came from a wealthy Chinese mestizo family and studied medicine in Spain and Germany before becoming a writer. He admired the religious tolerance in Germany, which was absent from the Spanish colonies. His best-known novel, *Touch Me Not* (also called *The Lost Eden*), published in Berlin in 1887, portrayed a stagnant colonial society obsessed with pettiness. One of the characters, Elias, in a conversation with a defender of colonial government and the Roman Catholic Church, articulated some of Rizal's critical views of Spanish colonialism and the power of the Roman Catholic religious orders.

> You accuse the [Filipino] people of ingratitude. Permit me, one of the suffering people, to defend them . . . you say that the [Roman Catholic] Religious Orders gave us the True Faith and redeemed us from error. Do you call external practices the True Faith or the stories of miracles and other fairy tales that we hear every day, the truth? Is this the law of Jesus Christ? A product of foreign manufacture has been imported here; we have paid for it. Because the forerunners were virtuous, are we to submit to the abuses of their degenerate descendants? Because we received great benefits, are we committing a crime in protecting ourselves against great injuries? But what would you say of . . . a people that obey because they are deceived; a Government that rules by deceit, a Government that does not know how to make itself loved and respected for its own sake. Forgive me, sir, but I believe that your Government is stupid and suicidal when it is glad that such things are believed.[22]

José Rizal, a doctor and dissident, became a symbol of the struggle against Spanish colonialism in the Philippines. His execution in 1896 made him a martyr, a status celebrated in this 1899 memorial broadside, with tributes written by varied admirers. Library of Congress LC-USZ62-43996

Rizal's writings earned him condemnation by top officials as a subversive, antipatriotic heretic, and he was publicly executed by the Spanish for alleged treason against the colonial government in 1896, thereby becoming a martyr. Rizal had earlier prophesied that "the day the Spanish inflict martyrdom [on me] . . . farewell Spanish government."[23] Indeed, Rizal's death united varied opposition groups and laid the foundation for armed resistance to Spanish rule.

Peasants, mostly impoverished tenants on landed estates, were also discontented, and popular movements and revolts expressing the suffering and hope of peasant society had long been common. Andres Bonifacio, a Manila clerk, formed a secretive revolutionary organization and vainly sought *illustrado* support. A revolution against Spain broke out in 1896. One revolutionary leader, Emilio Aguinaldo, a town mayor of Chinese mestizo ancestry, called on the people to rebel: "Filipinos! Open your eyes! Lovers of their native land, rise up in arms, to proclaim their liberty and independence."[24] The revolutionaries welcomed women into their movement, even while they maintained conventional attitudes and viewed a woman as, in the words of one leader, a "helper and partner in the hardships of life."[25] Yet women managed to play active roles in the movement, serving as soldiers, couriers, spies, and nurses. Gregoria de Jesus, the wife of a major revolutionary leader, fought alongside her husband, remembering later that "I was considered a soldier, and to be a true one I learned to ride, to shoot a rifle, and to manipulate other weapons. . . . I have known what it is to sleep on the ground without tasting food for the whole day, to drink dirty water from mudholes."[26] Despite the revolutionaries' heroic efforts, the Spanish had mostly contained the revolt by 1898, although they failed to capture all the leaders or to crush scattered resistance.

Military forces from the United States had engaged in occasional naval skirmishes in Southeast Asia throughout the 1800s, even landing troops in Vietnam in 1845 to force the release of a French missionary. After U.S. warships demolished a Sumatran port, home to a group of men suspected of aiding pirates in 1832, a U.S. physician with the fleet wrote that "without inquiring into or adjudging the facts a man-of-war . . . batters down the town [whose people are] . . . entirely innocent of the affair."[27] Some U.S. leaders advocated military action to gain trade agreements and occupy Southeast Asian ports, just as U.S. warships had forced the opening of Japan to the West in 1853. By the 1890s the United States, which already enjoyed the world's most advanced industrial economy, had stretched its national boundaries from the Atlantic to the Pacific, maintained an active trade with China, had used the threat of force to open Japan to Western trade, and was being encouraged by powerful business interests to build an empire abroad. But it was not until 1898 that the United States began to take a more active role in

Asia. In that year the United States challenged the decaying Spanish control of its Caribbean colonies in the Spanish-American War, which ended in 1902. Although the Caribbean islands of Cuba and Puerto Rico were the main focus of the war, the U.S. forces also intervened in the Philippines. This constituted the first of four ground wars U.S. forces would fight in Asia over the next eight decades.

In 1898 the U.S. fleet under Admiral George Dewey sailed into Manila Bay and destroyed the Spanish navy. The rejuvenated Philippine revolutionaries received initial U.S. support in their fight against Spain, but U.S. representatives made false promises of independence to revolutionary leaders to gain their support. Soon Filipinos were in control of much of the country. Aguinaldo declared independence and, with colleagues, established a republican government with a new semidemocratic constitution. The revolutionaries talked of uniting the Filipino people, but they were themselves deeply divided by regional and class origins, personal rivalries, and conflicting visions of the nation.

Initially few people in the United States cared about the Philippines. But as U.S. war efforts intensified and sparked nationalism in the United States, public opinion soon changed from indifference to a widespread demand that U.S. forces take over the islands. A powerful U.S. senator, Henry Cabot Lodge, argued, "It has been my firm belief that the Philippine islands would not only become an important market for us . . . but still more important would furnish a large opportunity for the investment of surplus capital."[28] The decision to remain as a colonizer after helping defeat the Spanish, thereby requiring the suppression of a nationalist revolution against colonialism, proved a brutal affair. U.S. President William McKinley's stated rationale for the conflict reflected the North American idea of Manifest Destiny, the notion that God supported U.S. expansion, while ignoring centuries of Filipino tradition and their deep desire for independence: "It is our duty to uplift and civilize and Christianize and by God's Will do our very best by them [the Filipinos]."[29] The India-born British poet and imperialist Rudyard Kipling urged the U.S. to assume world responsibilities: "Take up the White Man's burden/Send forth the best ye breed/Go, bind your sons in exile/To serve your captives' need."[30] McKinley, who admitted that he could not locate the Philippines on a world map, underestimated the Filipino opposition to the U.S. invasion. Altogether 125,000 U.S. troops fought in the islands during the Philippine-American War. More than 5,000 Americans and 16,000 Filipinos died in battle. Another 200,000 Filipinos died from famine and disease generated by the conflict or in guarded, fenced compounds set up by the U.S. forces to keep villagers from helping the revolutionaries or to protect them.

Defeating the revolutionaries proved a challenge. Angered by rising death tolls among U.S. soldiers, General Jacob Smith ordered his men to retaliate by turning Samar Island into a "howling wilderness. The more you kill and burn the better you will please me."[31] Forced to fight for every town, U.S. forces destroyed whole villages, looted Roman Catholic churches, and used torture, including water boarding, to gain information. Both sides committed atrocities. In many districts most of the population supported the revolutionaries, and the active participation of many peasants made this struggle the first modern war of national liberation. The elusive revolutionaries lived off the land and practiced a harassing guerrilla warfare that demoralized the U.S. soldiers, who had expected a quick victory. American forces controlled the towns; revolutionaries, the countryside. The revolutionaries kept up their spirits by singing, one of the most popular songs being "Bayan Ko" ("My Homeland"), written in 1896 during the anti-Spanish struggle:

My beloved country
. . . Blessed with unblemished beauty
But, alas, robbed of your longed-for freedom
Always weeping in poverty and pain
. . . A people who are now oppressed
in the morrow shall stand up
. . . and mark the dawn of freedom.[32]

People back home in the United States became deeply split over the war. There were many strong supporters, especially in the business community. One newspaper, *The New York Criterion,* asserted, "Whether we like it or not, we must go on slaughtering the natives, and taking what muddy glory lies in the wholesale killing until they have learned to respect our arms."[33] Many other people in the United States opposed the intervention and some joined organized protest movements. The writer Mark Twain, a strong opponent of the war, criticized American economic motives in his 1900 rewriting of "The Battle Hymn of the Republic":

Mine eyes have seen the orgy of the launching of the Sword
He is searching out the hoardings where the strangers' wealth is stored
He hath loosed his fateful lightnings, and with woe and death has scored
His lust is marching on.[34]

American critics also rejected such imperialism; one cynic wrote in a New York newspaper that "we've taken up the white man's burden, of ebony and brown. Now will you tell us Rudyard [Kipling], how we may put it down."[35]

By 1902, with the revolutionaries defeated and many of the illustrados co-opted, the United States began governing its new colony. Jacob Gould Schurman headed a presidential commission in 1902 to recommend policy and called the islands "a daughter republic of ours—a new birth of liberty and a beacon of hope to all oppressed [Asians]."[36] The U.S. policy, known as benevolent assimilation, emphasized reshaping Filipino society, with the United States as the preferred model for what some people in the United States sometimes called "our little brown brothers." The U.S. occupying forces established an elected legislature, filled mostly by Filipinos, but its decisions had to be approved by U.S. officials. In contrast to most Western colonizers, the U.S. administration fostered education, literacy, and modern health care. The schools produced a large number of Filipinos fluent in English, and Filipinos adopted many U.S. influences, even if U.S. dreams were unrealizable.

But U.S. rule also generally ignored peasant needs, perpetuating the power of the landed gentry and locking the colony into an economy now closely linked to U.S. market needs for cash crops like sugar and pineapples. A small group of landowners controlled the lives of millions of impoverished peasant tenants. These regionally based landowning families became the basis for the powerful business, industrial, and agricultural leaders who have dominated Philippine government, economy, and society ever since. But U.S. rule did not produce the general tyranny, so common in many other colonies, which would prompt massive rebellion and hatred of the colonizer. One frustrated nationalist even complained that the U.S. forces did not repress the Filipinos enough to spur massive opposition. And by the later 1930s Filipino and U.S. leaders were negotiating the terms for a transition to eventual independence, a situation that suggested that colonialism might not be a permanent condition for Southeast Asians.

CHAPTER 7

Colonial Impact and Changing Fortunes, 1800–1941

A chant popular among Vietnamese peasants in the 1930s lamented the results of colonialism: "Ill fortune, indeed, for power has been seized by the French invaders, who are bent on barbarous deeds. It's criminal to set out the food tray and find that one has nothing but roots and greens to eat."[1] From a global perspective, colonialism served primarily to link Southeast Asia more firmly to a world economy dominated by the West and to introduce Western ideas and technologies. But colonial policies also profoundly affected all aspects of life, and Southeast Asians responded to the challenges of colonial "ill fortune" in creative ways.

Conquest proved a shattering experience throughout the region. Although it ultimately brought an end to many local conflicts, colonialism also transformed once autonomous Southeast Asians into masses of subject peoples who enjoyed few political rights, with their values and systems of authority challenged. The broad outlines of colonial policy were developed in London, Paris, Amsterdam, Madrid, and Washington, and according to a French saying, "The colonies were created by the colonizer for the colonizer." In a few cases, the Western powers destroyed local democracies even as they tried to inculcate some Western values. For example, the Chinese who began immigrating to Western Borneo in the later 1700s to mine gold had established several small republics with general assemblies and executive councils, which even Dutch observers conceded were extremely democratic governments. But the Dutch crushed these republics, which resisted Dutch occupation, when they colonized the region in the 1850s. To maintain firm control, France, Spain, Portugal, and the Netherlands allowed little democracy in their colonies. Colonialism mostly meant government by stodgy and autocratic bureaucrats. The only colony with much self-government was the U.S.-ruled Philippines, which had an elected legislature. In British Malaya and Sarawak there was some local participation in city or state government. And the Burmese enjoyed a limited advisory role in government by the 1920s. Burmese participation increased in 1935 with a legislature containing some elected members.

Governments varied widely, but Europeans were always at the top of the administration and held ultimate political authority. Two broad types of colonial administration emerged: direct rule and indirect rule. Under direct rule, the administration was largely European even down to the local level. Traditional leaders, such as the Burmese kings, were removed or were symbolic only, as with the Vietnamese emperor. Direct rule was used in Burma, the Philippines, Vietnam, and parts of Indonesia. Some form of indirect rule was the general pattern in British Malaya, Cambodia, Laos, and parts of Indonesia. In this system, Europeans governed a district through the traditional leaders, such as Malay sultans, Cambodian kings, or Javanese aristocrats, and many traditional rulers and aristocrats eventually supported colonial rule to maintain their status. Colonial authorities used divide-and-rule tactics to play off one ethnic group or region against another, creating problems that still make national unity difficult. Colonizers drew up boundaries, creating artificial countries and the basis for later political instability. Colonial Burma, Indonesia, Malaya, and Laos lacked the largely homogeneous populations of many European nations, and some ethnic groups found themselves divided among several neighboring countries—for example, the Malays in Siam, Malaya, and Indonesia; the Lao in Laos and Siam; and the Khmers in Cambodia, Thailand, and Vietnam.

The transformation of economic life, which linked Southeast Asian societies more tightly to the world economy, was at least as significant as that of political reorganization. By 1914 the entire world was enmeshed in a vast economic exchange that particularly benefited the more powerful industrializing nations of Europe, North America, and Japan. Southeast Asians often produced goods such as Indonesian coffee and Malayan tin for markets thousands of miles away. The opportunities and demands of the colonial economy touched nearly everyone in some ways. By the early twentieth century, Western colonialism had brought a final end to slavery and forced labor, although both traditions had been declining for several centuries. King Chulalongkorn's modernization policies had the same effect in Siam. Southeast Asians had long participated in world trade as producers of many valuable products, from spices and sugar to tin and gold to carpets. Colonial governments

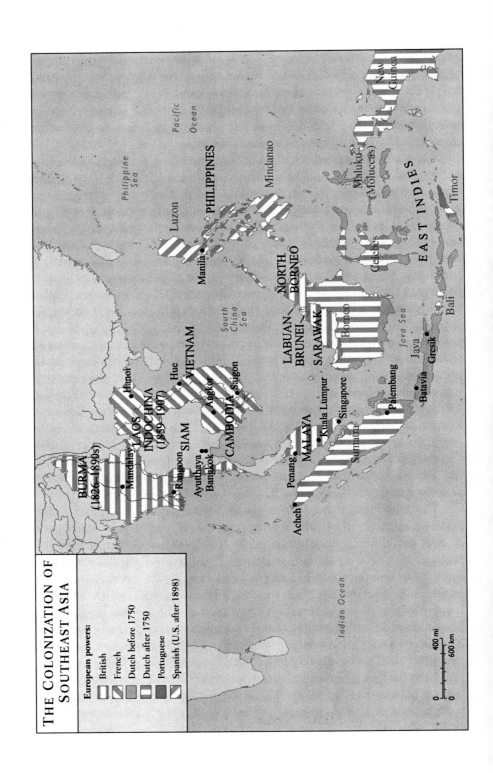

THE COLONIZATION OF SOUTHEAST ASIA

European powers:

British
French
Dutch before 1750
Dutch after 1750
Portuguese
Spanish (U.S. after 1898)

400 mi
600 km

Pacific Ocean

Philippine Sea

PHILIPPINES

Luzon

Mindanao

Manila

Maluku (Moluccas)

Celebes

EAST INDIES

Timor

South China Sea

NORTH BORNEO

LABUAN
BRUNEI
SARAWAK

Borneo

Java Sea

Bali

Java

Gresik

Batavia

Palembang

Sumatra

VIETNAM

Hue

Hanoi

Angkor

Saigon

CAMBODIA

LAOS

INDOCHINA
(1859–1907)

SIAM

Rangoon

Ayutthaya
Bangkok

BURMA
(1825–1890s)

Mandalay

MALAYA

Kuala Lumpur

Singapore

Penang

Acheh

Indian Ocean

wanted to extract this wealth, and trade was reoriented to Europe or North America. Businessmen from those countries controlled the large banks, import-export companies, and plantations.

The subsistence agriculture that sustained many Southeast Asians for centuries had been gradually declining as the chief economic activity since the 1400s and, in any case, could never produce enough revenues for colonial governments or investors. In the quest for revenues, colonial regimes promoted a shift from subsistence farming to cash crop agriculture by requiring taxes in cash rather than a share of the crop. Even rice, the basis of survival for millennia, became a cash crop in Burma, Vietnam, and Siam. A government report in British Burma in 1920 noted how the uncertainties of rice farming affected the peasants who grew the crop: "The soil did not really laugh with a crop when it was tickled with a hoe; it was equally likely to give an ugly leer . . . and the loans that were necessary . . . to provide food and clothes were to be obtained only . . . at a high rate of interest, which in a year of fever could not be paid."[2]

The age of the cash-crop-growing peasant, estate worker, and miner replaced the earlier age of commerce. Many Southeast Asians became involved in growing crops such as rubber, pepper, sugar, coffee, tea, opium, and palm oil; in cutting timber, mining gold and tin; or drilling oil for the world market. Their livelihoods now became subject to unstable global demand and the resulting fluctuations in the world price for their commodities, determined largely by the whims of Western consumers and corporations. The government turned over much land to Western-owned plantations, and Western companies owned most of the mines and oil wells. Plantation work involved long hours, strict discipline, monotonous routine, and poor food. On most rubber plantations, workers, including children, arose before dawn to tend the rubber trees and replace the buckets that collected the sap, trying to finish the labor before the blazing tropical sun made hard physical work unhealthy. Vietnamese writer Tran Tu Binh described the hellish life on a French-owned rubber estate: "Every day one was worn down a bit more, cheeks sunken, eyes hollow. Everyone appeared almost dead."[3] These activities also had an impact on the natural environment as forests were cleared for plantations or logged for timber to be shipped out of the region.

Many of the cash crops, such as cocoa, tobacco, and rubber, now being grown were not even native to the area. For example, rubber from Brazil was first introduced into Malaya and British Borneo in the 1870s and became the dominant cash crop in the 1890s. Rubber growing then spread to Sumatra, Southern Siam, Vietnam, and Cambodia. Demand for rubber increased worldwide after the invention of the bicycle, and then mass production of the automobile in the early 1900s opened up vast markets for rubber tires. By the early 1900s thousands of acres of forest were cleared for rubber growing, much of it on European-owned plantations. Malaya became the world's greatest exporter of natural rubber, supplying more than half of the world supply by 1920.

By the twentieth century Southeast Asia had become one of the world's most economically valuable regions, by 1950 exporting more than 50 percent of the world's rice and tin, 75 percent of its rubber, 20 percent of its palm oil, and 75 percent of its coconut oil. Dependence on a small number of exports, however, caused problems for many Southeast Asians. People in Malaya had little control over the rubber industry and fluctuating prices, for example, and this affected not only the rubber tappers and their families but also the shops, often owned by Chinese merchants, who sold them goods or extended them credit.

To enhance revenues, colonial officials emphasized construction of a transportation infrastructure, building railroads and road networks to link, for example, the Malayan tin fields and rubber plantations to the coastal ports. Colonies also became markets for Western

Rubber-tree plantations were particularly prevalent in Malaya, British Borneo, Southern Vietnam, and Sumatra. Plantations became a prominent part of the colonial economies, usually operated by European settlers or companies using local, Chinese, or Indian labor. Library of Congress LC-USZ62-60346

manufactured goods such as clothing and kitchenware, which often displaced traditional village handicrafts and undermined economic self-sufficiency. Some people, especially officials such as the Javanese aristocrats working for the colonial regime and many merchants, benefited from these changes and even grew wealthy. Some cash crop farmers achieved prosperity by responding to economic opportunities and improved irrigation infrastructure, especially when world prices for their crop were high. Living standards for some rural peoples improved, although they often had to work longer hours to earn the same profit as before. But a Dutch official in a 1900 report admitted that colonial rule had impoverished many Javanese: "During the past century the Netherlands has succeeded in reducing to complete poverty a very diligent and cultured people. The poverty of the Javanese is so abject that it deserves to become proverbial."[4]

Gradually Southeast Asians came to be integrated into the world economy as producers of raw materials and consumers of Western food imports and manufactured goods. Industrialization was limited, however. In the 1800s a few factories making cigars were established in Manila, mostly employing young women in the tedious work of rolling tobacco leaves. Many colonies became dependent on the export of one or two major commodities, such as rubber and tin from Malaya, rice from Burma, or rubber and rice from Vietnam. Government-licensed vice monopolies offering opium, alcohol, and gambling provided significant tax revenues. In French-ruled Vietnam, in fact, all villages were required to purchase designated amounts of opium and alcohol to enrich government coffers. By 1918 opium sales accounted for one-third of all colonial revenues in Vietnam, with the result that some Vietnamese became addicted to opium. Moreover, villages that bought too little alcohol or were discovered making their own illicit alcoholic beverages were fined, even though Vietnamese peasants had long made their own rice wine. Colonialism fostered considerable economic growth and some advances in communications, education, and health care but very little development, that is, growth that is balanced and equitable, benefiting the majority of people and providing new options. In most of Southeast Asia, development occurred only well after independence from colonial rule and then only in some nations.

Many Southeast Asians saw living standards and incomes drop in the early 1930s. The Great Depression that began in the United States in 1929 and rapidly spread worldwide generated problems as demand in the industrialized nations for commodities such as sugar, tin, and coffee fell. As the markets for their main exports declined, colonial revenues in Southeast Asia fell. Because rubber and tin provided the bulk of tax revenues in British Malaya, officials there had to make huge budget cuts, undermining educational services and road building, for example. In attempting to deal with the diminished world economy, the Western powers made international agreements to restrict production. One agreement that profoundly affected Southeast Asia confined rubber growing to large, mainly European-owned plantations, causing distress to many peasant growers, rubber workers, and the shopkeepers who exchanged goods for rubber. But the impact varied from place to place and some colonies began to recover in the later 1930s. Nonetheless, the economic problems increased discontent with colonial rule.

Some desperate populations responded by resorting to violence. In Malaya a peasant bandit, Nayan, who led a gang that robbed shopkeepers, landlords, and moneylenders, was celebrated in folk songs: "He was hunted like a wild buffalo/His image was fierce like a tiger/He searched for forgotten justice."[5] Some outlaws like Nayan were even seen by many peasants as victims of tyranny, as Robin Hoods who ostensibly robbed from the rich to give to the poor. Peasant rebellions against oppression or exceptional hardship were not unknown, especially in Vietnam, but unpopular government policies more likely prompted less extreme forms of resistance such as passive noncooperation, sabotage, spreading rumors, and evasion. Peasants might hide in the nearby jungle when the government tax collectors were spotted.

Like Nayan, most Southeast Asians were not passive observers of history. They had to negotiate, resist, or figure out how to capitalize on the policies challenging their livelihoods. Some urban Southeast Asians attempted to form labor unions or organize strikes. This was dangerous, indeed usually illegal, in colonial systems that protected Western-owned business. Yet strikes were fairly common. In the Dutch East Indies, railroad and dockworkers mounted several major strikes in the 1920s, all unsuccessful. The leaders were almost always arrested and added to the growing number of political prisoners in colonial prisons. Some unionists, such as Semaun, who became a leader of the railroad workers in Java at age 17 and later a key figure in the Indonesian communist movement. Isabelo de los Reyes founded the first true labor union in the Philippines in 1902. A former journalist and businessman who had been exiled by the Spanish, Reyes received little better treatment under U.S. rule. He was persecuted by U.S. business interests, vilified in the press, and jailed for leading strikes to promote better working conditions. Reyes's successor was also imprisoned and the union collapsed.

In the countryside, colonial policies greatly affected the peasant majority. As subsistence farmers before colonialism, they had chiefly sought security. Because an epidemic or drought could wipe them out, they wanted to minimize risk to ensure survival. Village societies spread the risk by promoting generosity and sharing while, in some cases, providing communal land for the poorest to use. They considered cooperation the best way to maintain the local environment for successful subsistence farming. But colonial policies often undermined these practices. Taxes increased and commercial agriculture took away some of the land to grow cash crops. The stability of peasant income was threatened.

Peasants responded to these challenges in diverse ways. Some rejected traditional values and used the capitalist economy to acquire a more entrepreneurial outlook, often prospering from shifting to cash crops. Others sought to avoid colonial policies through noncooperation or tax evasion. Peasant-based movements, usually local and short lived, emerged to reflect resentment of the changes fostered by capitalism. These movements sometimes had elements of modern nationalism, even if they mostly involved rural people who often looked to the past for inspiration. Some urban residents and peasants also joined religious cults and movements. Often using Buddhist, Muslim, or Christian religious symbols, such movements promised salvation in an afterlife and reaffirmed traditional values. They reflected the historical Southeast Asian

Manufacturing was limited during the colonial period, except for some factories that transformed local cash crops such as tobacco into commodities for the world market. This crowded factory in Manila, the Philippine capital, employed mostly women and girls to make cigars, a highly profitable export, from locally grown tobacco. Library of Congress LC-USZ62-80714

tendency to blend religions. Colonial governments usually cracked down on all of these movements as a threat.

One of the most important religious sects, the Cao Dai, was founded in 1925 by a low-level Vietnamese civil servant, Ngo Van Chieu, who was interested in spiritualism. During a séance, Chieu claimed to make contact with the supreme being, Cao Dai (the Supreme Palace on a High Throne), who was symbolized by a large eye. Chieu then organized a new religion, which grew rapidly. By 1940 the sect had several million followers, mostly peasants in Southern Vietnam. Followers of Cao Daiism believed that all religions should be unified, incorporating aspects of Christianity, Confucianism, Daoism, Buddhism, and spirit worship. Confucius, Buddha, and Laozi (the ancient Chinese founder of Daoism) were the three highest saints, followed by Jesus. The institutional structure resembled Catholicism, with a pope and separate hierarchies of men and women, each with their own cardinals and archbishops. But eventually disputes resulted in eight different versions of the Cao Dai church. The French, increasingly paranoid about dissent, cracked down on this perceived threat in 1940, forcing the Cao Dai underground. Today Cao Dai still flourishes, with churches all over Southern Vietnam and a spectacular cathedral in the city of Tay Ninh, near the Cambodian border.

Fostered by repressive or unpopular policies, rebellions punctuated colonial rule. The Saya San Rebellion in Burma was one of the most serious threats. Bands of Burmese had harassed the British for decades. The British called them "outlaws" and viewed "pacification" as purely a police problem, rather than addressing the desperation that fostered the violence. The Great Depression that began in 1929 finally sparked a major rebellion in 1930. It was led by a Buddhist monk, Saya San, whose followers were mostly peasants. He hoped to force out the British and then restore the traditional royal system of Buddhist government, with himself as king. Saya San also preached against the unpopular landlords, many of whom were Indian immigrants. The rebels were poorly armed, with only a few guns, but followers received tattoos that supposedly protected them from bullets. They attacked police stations, village chiefs, Indian merchants, and British residents. Saya San and his 15,000 followers fought so fiercely that they pushed the British out of many districts. The British responded with massive force and killed or wounded half of the rebels. Saya San himself was captured and executed, and the rebellion petered out.

Under colonialism, women experienced a different combination of hardship and opportunities than men. In Burma women may have seen their status improve because their men had lost their positions of power to the British colonizers and Indian immigrants. Elsewhere men took up cash-crop farming, which brought in much of the family's income, largely leaving responsibility for the food-producing farming to women and thereby increasing their workload. Increasingly, Chinese, Indians, and Arabs took over commercial life, robbing many women of their key role as small traders and leaving them to the lowest levels of village markets, decreasing their status as income earners for the family. Traditionally women had dominated textile production, weaving, spinning, dying, and often even growing the fibers. But after 1850 inexpensive factory-made textiles flooded in from Europe, and most people switched from local hand-woven cloth to machine goods. Many women lost their livelihood and independence, putting them in a position of greater dependence on men. A Javanese noblewoman, Raden Ajoe Mangkoedimedjo, wrote in a 1909 essay that "little by little [women] feel that their life is no longer of such value, considered by men only as ornaments as they are no longer contributing to the household coffers."[6] Poor women now faced the challenge of preserving their families while fulfilling all their other new responsibilities.

Were women impoverished or liberated by the decline of household weaving? Perhaps both. Weaving was hard work, even drudgery, but it could be done at home with friends and relatives while caring for children. Poor families lost income but could not afford to buy imported textiles. Women had to find other income sources. Some women now devoted their energies to farming, others to commerce or industry, which often took them away from the home and children. Today the factories of Southeast Asia are staffed largely by young, mostly unmarried women who live in crowded dormitories and work long hours. For rural women with little education and their poor families who desperately need their earnings, such factories offer the only income alternative to farm work or the commercial sex industry. A few women were able by the 1930s to get a Western education and enter professions such as teaching and nursing, but men dominated the better-paying occupations in commerce, government, and the professions, and they developed myths of male superiority to justify the new gender division of labor. Men increasingly became family providers, while women faced cultural biases and limits on their advancement in modern occupations. Some women joined movements to assert their rights, however. The European feminist movement had some influence in the late nineteenth and early twentieth centuries, but Southeast Asians adapted these ideas to their own sensibilities. Siamese feminists, for example, opposed polygamy and supported girls' education but also criticized women who violated cultural taboos.

The inspirational social activist, Raden Adjeng Kartini, who shared the problems women faced under the colonial system as well as in their own cultures, represented a new feminist consciousness. The daughter of a Javanese aristocrat, she rebelled against the confined lives of her social class, in which young women were expected to obey men, especially their fathers, without question, stay home, and train for marriage. Her father was progressive, however, and sent her to a Dutch primary school. A good student, Kartini wanted to complete high school and study in Holland, but that would have required her to leave home. Because Javanese custom discouraged aristocratic women from traveling without their families, her father would not permit it. Despite her father's progressive views, in conformity to aristocratic custom, at puberty Kartini was restricted to her family's home and ordered to prepare herself for an arranged marriage by learning domestic skills. But Kartini had larger ambitions. From her experience in Dutch-language schools and friendships with Dutch women, she drew a model of personal freedom contrary to that of her Javanese society, including a commitment to educate Javanese women in order to give them more options in life. Eventually she bowed to the wishes of her parents and entered an arranged marriage with a man she scarcely knew who already had two other wives. But he agreed to support her plan to open a school for girls, the first in Indonesia, which combined Javanese and Western values. Kartini died in childbirth in 1904, aged 25.

In the decade before her death, Kartini wrote a series of fascinating letters to Dutch friends in Java and Holland that reveal the contradictions in her thinking. She criticized the constraints of marriage, family, and society. Caught between two worlds, she was both repelled and attracted by her Javanese heritage. Although she had doubts about the advantages of marriage, she declared, "But we must marry, must, must. Not to marry is the greatest sin which the Muslim women can commit. And marriage among us—miserable is too feeble an expression for it. How can it be otherwise, when the laws have made everything for the man and nothing for the woman. When law and convention both are for the man; when everything is allowed to him." She thought women were repressed: "The ideal Javanese girl is silent and expressionless as a wooden doll, speaking only when necessary." She also condemned religious prejudice, whether by Christians or Muslims: "We feel that the kernel of all religion is right living, and that all religion is good and beautiful. But, o ye peoples, what have you made of it?" But she had hope for change: "I glow with enthusiasm toward the new time which has come. My thoughts and sympathies are with my sisters who are struggling forward in the distant West."[7]

Kartini's Dutch friends published her letters, and thanks partly to the royalties, the girls' schools Kartini founded multiplied after her death, educating thousands of Indonesian girls and ensuring her reputation. Although Kartini had criticized Javanese culture and admired Western ideals, in 1964 the Indonesian president named her a national heroine and honored her as the nation's *ibu* ("mother"). But conservatives accused her of abandoning Islam and Javanese culture, seeing her as an apologist for colonialism. Some contrasted her unfavorably to Rahma El-Yunusiah, a devout Muslim woman from Sumatra who taught Arabic and the Qu'ran and who refused any contact with the Dutch. Today Kartini is honored as a proponent of women's rights and a precursor of Indonesian nationalist sentiment.

Colonialism opened Southeast Asia to increased immigration from nearby regions. Indian trading communities developed in most major cities and many Indians settled in Malaya and Burma, but the Chinese arrived in much larger numbers. Between 1800 and 1941, millions of Chinese immigrated to the region to work as laborers,

Raden Adjeng Kartini (left), photographed in 1903 with her husband, Raden Adipati Djojoadiningrat, an influential aristocrat, became an inspiration to many Indonesian women. Before her early death in childbirth she challenged traditional gender expectations for girls by attending a Dutch-medium school and then opening the first girls' school in the Dutch East Indies. KITLV Leiden 15469

miners, planters, and merchants. They mostly came from two poor, overcrowded coastal provinces in Southeast China: Guangdong and Fujian. More than 20 million people of Chinese ancestry or ethnicity live in Southeast Asia today. Malaysia's population is 35 percent Chinese and Singapore's is 75 percent. Indonesia and Thailand each have between 3 and 5 million people of Chinese ancestry. Many cities such as Bangkok, Kuala Lumpur, and Singapore became substantially Chinese in population.

One of these Chinese immigrants, Ong Ewe Hai, left China by boat and arrived in Sarawak's main town, Kuching, in 1846, when he was 16 years old. He obtained some merchandise on credit for sale and also rowed a small boat up and down the river to collect jungle products from Dayaks and Malays. Eventually he became one of Sarawak's wealthiest and most influential merchants, and his oldest son followed in his footsteps as community leader. Unlike Ong, however, the majority of Chinese immigrated as coolies under a system that obligated them to pay off their passage by working for years in mines, plantations, or commercial enterprises. Many of these laborers later became shopkeepers, often prospering. Some, of course, remained poor. The men who pulled the rickshaws in Singapore, for example, faced a difficult life of physical hardship and low wages and often died young, sometimes from suicide.

The Chinese were, in general, adaptable and resourceful. An 1879 book by the British colonial official J. D. Vaughan listed dozens of occupations pursued by Chinese in the Straits Settlements, from bakers and barbers to bookbinders and carriage makers. The immigrant's dream was to make enough money to return to his native village a wealthy and respected man, and many did. But others remained in Southeast Asia permanently, marrying locally or bringing their families from China. Some Chinese blended local culture, in the form of clothing, literature, spicy foods, and language, with their own traditions such as Confucianism. But the majority preserved their own customs and languages. Over time the Chinese were transformed from sojourners into settlers. The majority of Chinese gravitated to the commercial sector, and through enterprise, organization, and cooperation, they formed a prosperous, urban middle class that controlled retail trade. A few became fabulously wealthy. Before the 1930s, colonial governments in Indonesia, Malaya, Sarawak, and Cambodia appointed rich Chinese businessmen such as Ong Ewe Hai as *kapitan chinas* to administer the Chinese communities.

Fueled by immigration, the 20 to 25 million people who lived in Southeast Asia by 1600 grew to 30 or 35 million by 1800, and to 140 or 150 million by the 1930s. Vastly increased population contributed to the growth of cities—such as the colonial capitals of Manila, Jakarta, Rangoon, and Kuala Lumpur—which governments needed as administrative and communication centers. Like Angkor Thom, Ayutthaya, or Melaka centuries before, most modern cities attracted diverse populations, including many immigrants or migrants from nearby districts. Food stalls, restaurants, religious buildings, and schools aimed at particular ethnic groups provided social, cultural, and religious diversity.

Despite some tendency for people to prefer others of their own culture, many ignored the ethnic barriers. Some descendants of Chinese, Indian, and Arab immigrants assimilated into the surrounding culture. Friendships and even marriages defying ethnic categories were not unusual in some places. For example, much of Thailand's political and economic leadership today has some Chinese ancestry resulting from assimilation or intermarriage. Similarly many Vietnamese, Khmer, Lao, Burmans, and Filipinos have Chinese ancestors.

Colonial schools, where they existed, also fostered cultural and social change. Although colonizers often justified their rule as a way of bringing progress to Southeast Asia, few governments devoted many resources to improving education. The U.S.-ruled Philippines had the best record, with 25 percent of the total colonial budget spent on education and 75 percent of children attending primary school. At the other extreme was French Indochina, which spent little money on schools. As a result, literacy rates varied, and by 1940 ranged from 50 percent in the Philippines to 10 percent in French Indochina and Dutch Indonesia. Independent Siam made education widely available for both boys and girls.

Christian missions, which emphasized Westernization, were largely responsible for the local population's health and education. Mission hospitals practiced Western medicine and denounced folk medicine. Both the mission and government schools taught Western values and European or American history. Students learned about the English king Henry VIII and Emperor Charlemagne of the Franks but little about Southeast Asian history. Children in the U.S.-ruled Philippines, a tropical and mostly Roman Catholic land, learned English from books showing U.S. youngsters throwing snowballs, playing baseball, and attending Protestant church services. Burmese students had to take Christian names and wear Western clothes. But mission schools also taught new agricultural methods, hygiene, sanitation, mathematics, writing, and Western languages, all of which gave a small group of educated Southeast Asians skills they could use in the colonial economy and the lower levels of colonial administration. The Spanish had founded Santo Thomas Catholic University in the Philippines in 1611, and a second university, the Ateneo de Manila, in 1859, while the British established Rangoon University in 1920. But before the 1950s, those few who were able to obtain a university education generally had to do so in Europe—and discovered, on returning to Southeast Asia, that many jobs were reserved for people of European ancestry. The colonial regimes generally supported Christian missionary activity and usually favored Christians in hiring. Many Vietnamese and some Chinese became Christian, as did various hill peoples, but few Theravada Buddhists or Muslims abandoned their faiths. Facing discrimination in the colonial system, educated Asians sought social and political equality for themselves.

The Western emphasis on individualism taught in the schools conflicted with traditional community values. To counteract this influence, some Southeast Asians developed alternatives to Western education, often by expanding traditional religious schools, such as the Islamic schools of Malaya and Indonesia. Some of these alternative schools, however, mixed Eastern and Western ideas. For example, in 1922 Ki Hajar Dewantoro, the leader of a mystical Javanese religious organization, established the *Taman Siswa* ("Garden of Pupils") schools as a counterweight to both Islamic and Christian schools. His schools placed an emphasis on Indonesian history, music, and dance as well as self-expression and social equality. Students and staff wore Javanese rather than Western clothes. Many graduates became leaders of Indonesian nationalism.

The dramatic confrontations of old and new art forms generated significant new ones, most notably in theater, which had long been an integral part of Southeast Asian cultures. In addition to providing aesthetic pleasure and emotional release, theater functioned as a channel for communication to reach the largely illiterate populations. At the end of the 1800s, for example, a popular urban theater mixing music, acting, and dancing known as *bangsawan* ("noble people") spread widely, particularly in Java, Sumatra, Malaya, and Sarawak. The music and stories combined Indonesian, Indian, Middle Eastern, Chinese, and Western influences. *Bangsawan* reflected ethnic diversity and musical mixing in a genuinely popular theater tradition. Theatrical troupes, many owned by Chinese, were equally at home performing before kings and noblemen, town fairs, and village folk. In 1993 the Sarawak writer Hajjah Maimunah Haji Daud remembered the appeal of theater troupes when she was a child: "The audience was well and truly transported to the land of fantasy peopled by legendary heroes and heroines who were forever young and beautiful. The good characters triumphed over the evildoers."[8] This Malay-language theater flourished from the 1920s through the 1950s. Colonialism fostered cultural changes throughout the region and spurred the mixing of Eastern and Western influences. A new Malay dance, the *joget*, combined folk and Western dance steps and songs. Even though the partners never touched, the dance was criticized by Islamic purists opposed to such suggestive body movements. The traditional arts such as gamelan music or shadow plays were also challenged by Western imports such as gangster movies and jazz.

New musical styles mixing Eastern and Western influences began to appear during the colonial era. Perhaps the earliest Indonesian popular music was *kroncong*, a romantic blend of Javanese and European (especially Portuguese) music that emerged out of the urban mix in the nineteenth century. The *kroncong* style was languid, with a gentle melancholy in its lyrics and melody, and relied on distinctive instrumentals. *Kroncong* blended Western instruments such as the guitar and violin with the complex rhythmic patterns of the Javanese gamelan. Originating in the slums and suburban villages of Jakarta, *kroncong* sprang from the lower classes and was especially popular with Indonesian sailors and soldiers, as well as disreputable Javanese youth gangs known as "*kroncong* crocodiles." Gang members dressed flamboyantly, drank heavily, and gambled. This rebellious spirit was also common in twentieth-century popular music around the world such as jazz, reggae, rock, and hip hop. *Kroncong* was an adaptable style that could be used for romance, nostalgia, dancing, and even topical commentary.

Despite the foreign influence and a lowbrow image, the music gradually became strongly identified in the public mind with the Indonesian soul. By the 1940s anti-Dutch nationalists adopted *kroncong*, some even attempting to elevate it to a national music. *Kroncong* was transformed from popular music to a nationalist symbol. Although younger Indonesians have developed new forms of music since the 1950s, *kroncong* still has an audience among the generation who grew up in the early and mid-twentieth century. And a few Western composers such as Claude Debussy and Colin McPhee who observed performances by Javanese and Balinese gamelan orchestras incorporated gamelan influences into their music.

In Indonesia, the Philippines, and Vietnam a modern literature also developed that reflected both alienation from colonial rule and an awareness of rapid social and cultural change. To avoid the secret police and censorship, Vietnamese writers often used historical themes to discuss contemporary problems. Because they could not openly discuss politics, however, Indonesian writers focused on psychological problems, indicating that the colonial system was causing mental anguish and disorientation. Novels and poems reflected the tensions between East and West, old and new. The Sumatra-born novelist Armijn Pane, for example, portrayed the educated Indonesian beset by doubts in his daily life, caused by his two contradictory personalities, one modern and liberated, and the other, traditional. His characters searched unsuccessfully for meaning and purpose. In Pane's novel *Shackles*, published in 1940, one of the leading characters expressed his confusion about life: "Can you imagine having three radios, all of them turned on, but each of them turned to a different station? . . . That is exactly like it was inside my head. So many different voices, I couldn't understand even one of them."[9] Many works reflected an atmosphere of despair, as writers placed their own views in the mouths of fictional characters. Ultimately, these transformations and dislocations of the colonial era, often reflected in the literature, fostered the nationalism that would emerge throughout Southeast Asia in the twentieth century.

CHAPTER 8

Fighting for the Cause of National Freedom, 1900–1950

In 1930 the newly formed Indonesian Nationalist Party met to develop a platform for action, to respond to the challenges posed by colonialism. Their statement urged Indonesians to be zealous in the cause of national freedom, which was the only way, they argued, that the Indonesian people could reshape the nation in their own interest. Nationalist movements originated in Europe in the eighteenth century and then spread to the Americas and India before moving into Southeast Asia in the late nineteenth century. Nationalism involved a sense of common feeling transcending class and ethnicity among people who desired to express that wider community by establishing an independent country. Nationalism's first Southeast Asian stirrings came in the Philippines, leading to the ultimately thwarted revolution against Spain in 1896. By the 1930s nationalism was a growing force in Indonesia, Vietnam, and Burma, all places where colonial rule was particularly oppressive and unpopular. Nationalism also influenced Siamese politics but was a weaker force in Cambodia, Laos, Malaya, and the U.S.-ruled Philippines.

Some of the earliest nationalist activity emerged in the Dutch East Indies, where diverse new cultural organizations, representing a more modern way of thinking, formed in the early 1900s. Groups like *Budi Otomo* ("Noble Endeavor"), founded by Javanese aristocrats in 1908, began to envision a unified nation. Other early nationalists sought national freedom while building a culture and language to unite the diverse population. Malay was the mother tongue for many peoples in Western Indonesia, especially in Batavia and Eastern Sumatra, but elsewhere it served primarily as a trading language, widely used in the marketplace. Nationalist intellectuals began using Malay as the basis for a new unifying national language, which they called *Bahasa Indonesia*. Some now wrote in Bahasa Indonesia rather than Javanese, Balinese, or another regional language. New literary and cultural magazines as well as newspapers and books promoted the new language and a modern culture. Gradually Bahasa Indonesia became the language of the national media and education.

New ideas about national identity and the perceived threat from Western culture also reshaped religious traditions. Some Muslims, impressed with but also resenting Western economic and military power, sought modernization by purging Islam of practices based on old Hindu-Buddhist influences, such as mysticism and the sharp division between commoners and aristocrats, which they believed held Indonesians back by promoting cultural and social conservatism. A movement called *Muhammadiyah* ("Way of Muhammad"), founded on Java in 1912, and its allied women's organization, *Aisyah*, represented this trend of Islamic thought, known as modernist. Adherents criticized local customs they considered backward and promoted the goal of an Islamic state. They stressed the five pillars of Islam, devalued the writings of religious scholars after Muhammad, and favored the segregation of men and women in public, a custom in the Middle East and South Asia long ignored by most Indonesians. Muhammadiyah also attracted support in the Outer Islands. In 1912 the colony's first true political movement, a modernist Islamic organization called Sarekat Islam (SI; "Islamic Union"), was founded by Javanese batik merchants. Led by Haji Umar Said Tjokroaminoto, a charismatic aristocrat, SI had 2 million members by 1919.

After the Bolshevik victory in the second Russian Revolution of 1917, some SI members became attracted to Marxism, which derived from the ideas of the nineteenth-century German thinker Karl Marx. Marx viewed historical change as a result of struggles between opposing social classes, criticized capitalism for exploiting workers, and believed that socialism would eventually replace capitalism, thereby removing the ruling class. Eventually, he contended, the state would whither away and everyone would be free from oppression. The most extreme Marxists, the communists, sought the violent overthrow of both capitalism and governments that oppressed the working classes. In seeking a more radical approach to confront colonialism, some SI members began working with Dutch communists. The Dutch colonial government responded with repression, however, exiling many SI leaders. Finding the organization too conservative, Marxists left the SI and established the Indonesian Communist Party (PKI) in 1920, devel-

Sarekat Islam (the Islamic Union) was the major early nationalist organization in Indonesia. Its leaders, including these from Kediri in East Java, dressed in traditional Javanese clothing, were mainly merchants and devout Muslims who shared a disdain for Dutch rule and commercial competition from the local Chinese. KITLV Leiden 8094

oping a more revolutionary strategy to achieve independence. The PKI attracted support chiefly from nominal Muslims in Java, who resented both Dutch colonialism and more dogmatic Muslims, and the group grew rapidly, gaining many peasant and urban worker members. Overestimating its strength, the PKI launched a poorly planned uprising in 1926. The government responded with massive force, crushing the uprising and executing the PKI leaders.

The destruction of the PKI and the decline of SI left a vacuum for other nationalists. Organized women's groups arose originally with the goal of improving Indonesian women's lives, but in 1928 the Congress of Indonesian Women began openly advocating for independence. More influential politically, the Indonesian Nationalist Party (PNI) was established in 1927 and mostly led by Javanese aristocrats. PNI stood for a new national identity encompassing all the Indies. Sukarno (1901–1970), the key founder, was born into a wealthy aristocratic family, with a Javanese father and Balinese mother. As a youth, Sukarno studied with the SI leader Tjokroaminoto, learning both politics and *wayang kulit* stories, often based on Hindu epics from India and popular on Java for centuries.

Like the characters in these stories, Sukarno showed a tendency to bring together seemingly contradictory ideas, such as Islam—which emphasized the sovereignty of God—and atheistic Marxism, which rejected organized religions as a diversion from the realization of oppression and action to overcome it. He told an American journalist that he was a Muslim, Christian, and Hindu simultaneously. In 1941 Sukarno wrote: "What is Sukarno? A nationalist? An Islamist? A Marxist? . . . Sukarno is a mixture of all these isms. . . . I have made myself a meeting place of all trends and ideologies. I have blended them . . . until finally they became the present Sukarno."[1] After studying engineering, he dedicated his life to politics and to achieving a free Indonesia. A splendid orator, the fiery, charismatic Sukarno attracted a large following through his use of Javanese religious and cultural symbols, and he became the mass popularizer of Indonesian nationalism.

In 1928 Sukarno created the slogan "one nation—Indonesia, one people—Indonesian, one language—Indonesian." He even designed a flag and wrote a national anthem. The PNI was the first group to really think of the Indonesian nation as a goal that could soon be reached. The Dutch authorities arrested Sukarno for treason in 1929 and exiled him to a remote island prison for the next decade—which made Sukarno a martyr and increased his popularity. At his trial, Sukarno delivered a passionate, inspiring defense speech that stressed the greatness of Indonesia's past as a building block for the future:

> All interests of imperialism, social, economic, political, or cultural, are opposed to the interests of the Indonesian people. The imperialists desire the continuation of imperialism, the Indonesians desire its abolition. . . . The P.N.I. awakens and reinforces the people's consciousness of its "grandiose past," its "dark present" and the promises of a shining, beckoning future. . . . What Indonesian does not feel his national heart beat with joy when he hears about the greatness of . . . Srivijaya . . . Mataram . . . Madjapahit. . . . A nation with such a grandiose past must surely have sufficient natural aptitude to have a beautiful future. Among the people again conscious of their great past, national feeling is revived, and the fire of hope blazes in their hearts.[2]

Although Sukarno appealed to Indonesian traditions, Indonesia's nationalist leaders were mostly westernized, secular, and educated men from wealthy backgrounds, with little in common with average people. Sutan Sjahrir, a Holland-educated nationalist from Sumatra, reflected his estrangement from the people he hoped to lead while writing a letter to his wife in 1935 from a remote prison: "Why am I vexed by the things that fill their lives, and to which they are so attached? Why are the things that contain beauty for them and arouse their gentler emotions only senseless and displeasing for me? We intellectuals here are much closer to Europe or America than we are to the primitive Islamic culture of Java and Sumatra."[3] With their best-known leader, Sukarno, in jail, the PNI grew slowly throughout the 1930s.

The strongest nationalist thrust in Southeast Asia emerged in Vietnam by the early 1900s. Some nationalists there worked for reform or self-government within the French system, such as trying to influence colonial policies and persuade officials to reform Vietnamese society along Western lines. Others, such as the passionately revolutionary Phan Boi Chau (1867–1940), sought a complete end to French rule. Born into a mandarin family, Phan may have been the first to consciously refer to Vietnam as a "nation" in the modern conception as a political unit. He formed several revolutionary organizations but was a poor strategist. By the time of his death as a French prisoner in 1940, Phan had earned a reputation as the most inspirational nationalist of his generation, the symbol of patriotism and resistance, even if his efforts failed. As he wrote in his prison diaries, "It has been but a yearning to purchase my freedom even at the cost of spilling my blood, to exchange my fate of slavery for the right of self-determination."[4]

Unable to dislodge French rule, the older, Confucian-educated nationalist leaders such as Phan gradually lost their leadership to younger, French-educated intellectuals. Activism shifted to groups like the Vietnamese Nationalist Party (VNQDD), whose members were drawn mostly from the urban middle class and traditional village leaders. Because there was little possibility of fostering change through peaceful protests, the VNQDD had few options other than terrorism via bombing French buildings and assassinating colonial officials. A premature uprising sparked by the organization in 1930 prompted violent French repression, which destroyed most of the nationalist groups except for the communists, who were better organized, underground, and benefited from having some leaders and many members living outside Vietnam. This proved a turning point in Vietnamese history. An imprisoned non-communist nationalist lost all hope after the ferocity of the repression, pleading with the French to have mercy: "Many simple peasants, interested only in their daily work in the rice fields, living miserable lives like buffaloes and horses, have been compromised in this reprisal. There are tens of thousands of men, women, and children who have been massacred. I beseech you in tears to redress this injustice which otherwise will annihilate my people, which will stain French honor, and which will belittle all human values."[5]

Now, with the elimination of most of their rivals, the communists, under the leadership of Ho Chi Minh, enjoyed a favorable position from which to lead Vietnamese nationalism. Born Nguyen Sinh Cung in central Vietnam in 1890 to a mandarin family that had supported the anti-French resistance, Ho received a high school education, then in 1911 signed on as a merchant seaman on a French ship. He would not return to his homeland for another 30 years. Ho hated colonialism and dreamed of an independent Vietnam, later telling an American journalist, "The people of Vietnam often wondered who would help them to remove the yoke of French control. Some said Japan, others Great Britain, and some said the United States. I saw that I must go abroad and see for myself."[6] While a seaman, he visited several ports in the United States, developing a distaste for U.S. racism but also an admiration of its freedom. After working as a cook in London, the young Vietnamese settled in Paris, working as a cook and photo retoucher. He spent his free time reading books on politics, eventually joining the French Socialist Party. In these years he changed his name several times, to Nguyen O Phap ("He Who Hates the French") and then Nguyen Ai Quoc ("Nguyen the Patriot").

Nguyen Ai Quoc became famous among Vietnamese exiles in Europe for his efforts in 1919 to address the delegates meeting at the Paris Peace Conference to reach a final settlement of World War I. Determined to force the issue of independence for colonized peoples, he attempted to enter the meetings and to present a moderate eight-point plan for changes in France's treatment of its Indochinese colonies, including the introduction of personal freedoms, local representation in government, and release of political prisoners, but he was not admitted to the proceedings. Disillusioned with the Western rhetoric of freedom, he joined the French Communist Party, which promised to abolish the French colonial system. While nationalists and communists did not necessarily share the same goals, the young Vietnamese concluded that communism and revolution were the most effective strategy for promoting nationalism. He moved to Moscow and then spent two decades organizing a communist movement among Vietnamese exiles in Thailand and China. The revolutionary took on a new name, Ho Chi Minh ("He Who Enlightens"). Eventually Ho became a worldwide symbol of national assertion, opposition to Western imperialism, and sympathy for the plight of the poor peasants and women in Asia.

In 1930 Ho and his colleagues established the Indochinese Communist Party (ICP). The ICP developed its strongest following in Northern and Central Vietnam. The party was weaker in Southern Vietnam, where many groups contended for influence and the French secret police presence was stronger. Many Vietnamese now viewed revolution rather than reform as the only answer to colonial exploitation and repression. During the 1930 rebellions, ICP-allied groups, mostly comprised of peasants whose lives had been made even more desperate by the Great Depression, seized several provinces in Central Vietnam, holding off the French military for months. Although the French killed or imprisoned thousands of ICP members and supporters, they could not destroy the movement.

Vietnamese Marxists linked themselves to the patriotic traditions of the past, including the Trung Sisters and Le Loi, who fought the Chinese, and the Can Vuong rebels, who opposed the French. One of Ho Chi Minh's best-known poems, "The History of Our Country from 2879 B.C. [sic] to 1942," emphasized resistance to foreign aggression and praised the Tayson rebels for their defeat of China in 1788. Another Vietnamese Marxist, Hoai Thanh, writing in 1943, glorified the links with the past: "And, so it seems we are not lost after all. Behind us we have the immense history of our people. Between us and that immense history there is still a road we can travel, still spiritual cords attaching us."[7] Given the country's long history of resistance to foreign occupation, it was perhaps inevitable that Vietnamese communism took on a strongly nationalist flavor. Yet some Vietnamese intellectuals also put Vietnamese tradition on trial, often criticizing Confucianism and patriarchy for holding the country back. During the 1930s, while Ho's relations with the Soviet Union ebbed and flowed, the ICP developed a strategy of including all nationalist forces in a Marxist-led united front that worked toward revolution and independence. In 1941 Ho established the Viet Minh (Vietnamese Independence League), a coalition of anti-French groups that waged war against both the French and the Japanese, who occupied Vietnam during World War II.

Elsewhere another powerful anticolonial nationalism movement developed in Burma, although it was less radical than in Vietnam. Despite granting the Burmese some limited self-government by the 1930s, British rule was repressive, and Burmans were outraged to be governed as part of British India. They resented the large Indian community that had come in under British rule, because many Indians were wealthy merchants, landlords, or moneylenders who were viewed as taking advantage of the local population. Anti-Indian riots erupted during the 1930s. The British also favored some of the ethnic minorities such as the Karens in Eastern Burma, especially those who became Christian, and mostly recruited the police forces from these groups. This policy of divide and rule increased ethnic tensions.

Nationalism in Burma arose among the urban intellectuals, especially university students and graduates in Rangoon. These nationalists used Buddhism as a rallying cry to press for reform. Some favored women's rights, and in 1927 they elected a woman, Ma Thein May, as vice president of the first student union at Rangoon University. Nationalists debated with each other how much to cooperate with British rule and became impatient for more reform. Ba Maw, who served in the colonial regime, told a political meeting in 1937 that "my political struggle revolves around the clock. I, and indeed all Burmans, are determined to order our own progress according to our own clock but the British government wants to order our progress according to a British clock. I have never been able to accept this theory which makes the British clock set my time."[8] Many hill peoples, such as the Karens, however, fearing ethnic Burman domination of nationalism, favored the British policies.

A militant student movement emerged whose members called themselves *thakins* ("lords"), a symbol of youthful defiance of British rule. The thakins reflected various strands of opinion. Some thakin leaders were Marxists and secularists concerned with social and cultural issues. Another key leader, Thakin Nu, was a devout Buddhist who had translated several Western books into Burmese, including the writings of Karl Marx.

Although students lived in a colony that restricted political activity, university life offered many pleasures, posing a challenge to political activists. When not studying for examinations students had ample time to make friends, attend theatrical performances and musical concerts, and enjoy tennis tournaments or regattas on the nearby lake. There was also some campus interest in feminist issues, including the growing popularity of Western-style clothing for women. Students also debated politics. The thakins supported or led student strikes and protests that put the British on the defensive. In 1936 a major student strike erupted at Rangoon University. Campus tensions had increased after the university expelled Thakin Nu, the Student Union president, and disciplined the student newspaper editor, Thakin Aung San, for protesting university policies on issues such as scholarships and exams. The Student Union called a strike and both male and female students blockaded examination halls. Students in 32 secondary schools joined the strike. The unrest forced university authorities to grant some student demands, such as introducing scholarships for poor students and allowing student representation on the university board. Later both Thakins Aung San and Nu became leaders of independent Burma. Aung San had grown up on stories of Burma's past and aroused audiences with references to their "imperishable memories" and "historic destiny."

As nationalism swept through Southeast Asia, it was not confined to the European colonies. It emerged in Siam, for example, as an outgrowth of tensions between the aristocratic elite and the rising middle class. The push for nationalism began with the kingship of Chulalongkorn's son, Rama VI, who became king on Chulalongkorn's death in 1910. He was the first Siamese king to have extensive education abroad, including earning a law degree from Oxford University. A talented poet, writer, and actor, he wrote more than 200 works, from translations of Shakespeare to books of history. Rama VI was also a reformer and founded the Wild Tiger Corps, a scouting organization that became a paramilitary group with its own clubhouses, uniforms, and rugby team. Eventually Rama VI became a cultural nationalist, pushing the revival of Buddhism, attacking the Chinese minority, and negotiating an end to some unfavorable treaties forced on his predecessors by Western nations. His successor, Rama VII, who was crowned in 1925, was more conservative, stressing the position of the royal family and questioning whether Siam was ready for representative democracy: "The King is the father of his people and . . . treats them as children rather than subjects. The obedience the king receives is the obedience of love not of fear."[9]

By the 1920s a middle class of civil servants, military officers, lawyers, journalists, and teachers had emerged in Bangkok. Most had not come from the nobility and many had studied abroad, especially in England. They wanted more influence, power, and status, and they resented the privileges and wealth of the monarchy and aristocrats. Their discontent was fueled by the Great Depression, which forced salary and budget cuts. In 1932 midlevel military officers and professionals surrounded the palace with tanks and took power in a bloodless coup. The new leaders called themselves "nationalists," intent on strengthening the nation in a time of trouble. The king, whose Chakri family had ruled since the late 1700s, agreed under pressure to become a constitutional monarch. Like the British monarchy, the Thai monarchy became largely symbolic but continued as a force for national and cultural identity. Although they talked about introducing democracy, the new leaders did little more than put in place a few of its trappings. The focus of national loyalty henceforth had three pillars: "Nation, Religion and King."

Military leaders ran the government through the 1930s, pursuing nationalist policies, including restrictions on Chinese economic power. They also sponsored a Pan-Thai movement, which aimed to unite all the speakers of the varied Tai languages, including diverse groups in Eastern Burma, Southwest China, and Laos, with those of Siam, and to spread Thai language and culture as well as Buddhism to the ethnic minorities in Siam. The Siamese had commonly referred to themselves as Thai for several centuries. In the late 1930s the prime minister, Phibun Songkhram, officially renamed the country Thailand (Land of Free People), a more political label in contrast to the cultural identity of Siam. He adopted a Western calendar and urged his people to live modern lives, including dressing in a modern Western fashion with hats and shoes. During the late 1930s Thailand forged an alliance with the rising Asian power of imperial Japan. Phibun's government introduced features of a fascist regime, including a militarized educational system and youth organizations. By 1941 Thailand was a considerably different nation than it had been in 1930.

Nationalism was much weaker in Cambodia, Laos, and Malaya, which had experienced less disruption than Burma, Indonesia, and Vietnam from colonialism. However some discontent simmered below the surface. Occasional rebellions broke out in Laos, such as a Hmong movement in 1918 to establish a separate state, but the uprisings never gained enough widespread support to seriously challenge French control. Although the Lao people could look back into history for an example of a major Lao state, Lan Xang, the people themselves had later been divided into several rival states, allowing the French to colonize the territory. Lao nationalists wanted to reunite the Lao, as one leftist group argued in 1941: "Clannishness took the place of what we term love of nation or patriotism as the Lao of one district seemed to be unaware that the Lao of another district were their brothers. The horizon of our ancestors was quite narrow-minded."[10] A few Cambodian and Laotian leftists had connections to the better-organized Vietnamese communists, who supported their efforts. Meanwhile, the deep ethnic divisions in Malaya discouraged the evolution of a national movement that could challenge British authority. Most people there focused on their own ethnic communities, with many Chinese donating money to political movements and disaster relief in China. The Malayan Communist Party, organized in 1930, gained most of its support from poor Chinese residents. Malay nationalism had a chiefly cultural focus. Numerous magazines, newspapers, and books debated whether Islamic practices and Malay customs needed to be modernized to meet the challenges posed by a growing Chinese population.

The occupation of Southeast Asia by Japanese forces from 1941 to 1945 proved a turning point for the region, giving a boost to the forces of nationalism and weakening Western colonialism. Before 1941 colonial authority seemed strong, and only Vietnamese nationalism was well organized and mass based. Then, in a few weeks, everything changed. European and U.S. officials, businessmen, planters, and missionaries were either in retreat or in prison camps, and the Japanese were in charge.

The Great Depression of the 1930s had devastated the Japanese economy, resulting in a repressive military government that invaded China in 1937 in search of resources and markets. Now allied with Nazi Germany and fascist Italy, the Japanese wanted access to the oil, rubber, and other resources of Southeast Asia. Japan bullied Thailand and the new pro-Nazi French government, which controlled Vietnam, to allow the stationing of Japanese troops. Then, to neutralize possible U.S. opposition, the Japanese attacked the U.S. naval base at Pearl Harbor, Hawaii, on December 7, 1941, quickly followed by a rapid invasion of Southeast Asia. With superior naval and air strength, and with the British and Dutch preoccupied by the war in Europe, the Japanese easily overwhelmed the colonial forces there. Within four months the Japanese controlled most major cities and heavily populated regions. The hasty evacuation of many European and American officials and residents seemed to many local peoples as an act of desertion, damaging Western prestige.

Even today there remains some bitterness toward the Japanese, now directed against Japanese economic power. Western and Southeast Asian films have often painted the Japanese as brutal, ruthless conquerors, and many were. But the variety of Japanese motives and behaviors makes it hard to generalize. Japanese control shattered the mystique of Western colonialism and invincibility. The Japanese talked of "Asia for the Asians," but this rhetoric masked their desire for resources, especially the rubber, oil, and timber of Indonesia, Sarawak, Brunei, and Malaya. Few Japanese knew or cared much about Southeast Asian culture, and many Japanese were as arrogant as the Europeans they replaced. But some local commanders were sympathetic to the local population.

Japanese domination was brief, less than four years, and yet it generated much change. In many places, tensions and conflicts between ethnic groups increased due to economic hardship and selective repression. For example, in Malaya and Sarawak the Japanese policy of favoring the Malays and punishing the Chinese created considerable antagonism between the two groups that persisted long after the war. In Burma many hill tribes cooperated with the British in attacking Japanese positions, while the Burman thakins allied with the Japanese occupiers as a strategy to gain eventual independence.

Occupation also caused much economic and physical hardship, destroying the link to the world economy. Western companies closed, causing unemployment. Meanwhile, Japanese forces seized natural resources and food. By 1944 living standards for most people were in steep decline, with severe shortages of essential goods. The Japanese drafted thousands of people, especially Javanese, to work as slave laborers, building railroads, bridges, and roads in Burma, Thailand, and Malaya. Few who survived were ever able to return. One Javanese who did later wrote, "People died or lived, just like pebbles that caught in a sieve. And I was like a grain of sand that escaped."[11] The Japanese also conscripted young women, especially Filipinas, to serve as prostitutes (called "comfort women" by the Japanese) for their soldiers. As their war effort faltered, however, the desperate Japanese resorted to ever more repressive policies, and Southeast Asian civilians increasingly experienced casual brutality. Sybil Kathigasu, a Malayan Indian thrown into a dank prison for angering the police, reflected on the regular beatings: "They seemed desirous of battering the truth out of my body. Each unsatisfactory answer I gave—and they were all unsatisfactory—was followed by a dose of intense physical pain."[12]

Although often harsh, Japanese rule did offer some benefits to Southeast Asians. Abruptly cutting ties to the West had a profound psychological impact. The Japanese needed experienced local help and promoted Southeast Asians into government positions once reserved for Westerners. Many of these Indonesians or Malays or Burmese were, in fact, better educated than the people they replaced. Abang Haji Mustapha, a Malay leader in Sarawak who cooperated with the Japanese, defended his actions in a speech, criticizing the limited opportunities under British rule: "The British received exorbitantly high salaries, their lowest being higher than the highest salaries of the native inhabitants. All commercial enterprises yielding high returns were monopolized by the British and the profits derived were remitted to England."[13] The Japanese sought to purge Western cultural influences and suppressed Christianity, closed mission schools, and encouraged Islamic or Buddhist leaders; these policies fostered a renaissance of indigenous culture. Literature flourished in Indonesia. The Japanese occupation "destroyed a whole set of illusions and falsehoods and left man as naked as when he was created in the garden of Eden,"[14] the Indonesian writer Sitor Situmorang later argued in an essay.

The Japanese also promoted nationalism, at least indirectly, through their recruitment of Southeast Asian leaders. Under colonialism most nationalists had been in jail or exile and hence powerless. The Japanese tried to use them, creating an uneasy alliance between imperial authorities and nationalists such as Sukarno. The Japanese generally gave nationalist leaders little real power, however, and cynically saw them as window dressing to organize public support for the Japanese cause. But some Japanese officers were sympathetic and pursued pro-nationalist policies in Indonesia and Burma. Nationalists enjoyed a new role in public life, using the Japanese to recruit mass support. They now had access to radio and newspapers, which they used to spread the nationalist message. For example, Sukarno had little choice but to urge Indonesians to cooperate with the Japanese but also told them in 1943: "This is not a test imposed merely by the [Japanese occupation] government. It is a test of History. Let us set ourselves to face this test of History with spirit."[15]

Japanese policies also mobilized young people. In both traditional and then colonial societies, youth were mostly powerless and expected to obey their elders. The Japanese saw young people as uncorrupted by Western values, and they established youth organizations, ranging from scout troops to paramilitary forces. The armed paramilitary groups became the basis for nationalist armies in Indonesia and Burma that resisted the return of Western colonialism after the war.

Most Southeast Asians, who had little reason to support the colonial powers, hoped the Japanese might be an improvement. But the sense of liberation that the Japanese initially brought soon changed to widespread hostility as economic conditions and repression became worse. Resistance seemed hopeless but some Southeast Asians actively opposed Japanese rule. Predominantly Chinese guerrillas, many of them communists, went into the mountains and waged resistance in Malaya. Both communist and pro-U.S. guerrilla forces in the Philippines also fought skirmishes with the Japanese occupiers.

The strongest resistance to the Japanese came in Vietnam. Vietnamese communism might never have achieved power so quickly had it not been for the Japanese occupation, which discredited the French administration and imposed great hardship on most of the population. Japan's waning war effort and the imprisonment of the French in 1944 created a power vacuum in Vietnam. The Viet Minh, led by Ho Chi Minh, were now armed and trained by a few U.S. advisers who had been sent in to help anti-Japanese forces. With this U.S. assistance, the Viet Minh moved out of their bases along the Chinese border and expanded their influence in Northern Vietnam. By attracting thousands of poor peasants, the Viet Minh rapidly gained strength. Ho declared: "Our people suffer under a double yoke; they serve not only as buffaloes and horses

to the French invaders but also as slaves to the Japanese plunderers
... Let us [all Vietnamese] unite together."[16] Viet Minh popularity was
aided by a terrible famine, which killed 2 million Vietnamese in 1945
while scarce food was exported to Japan. By 1945 the great majority
of the people in Northern and Central Vietnam probably supported the
Viet Minh, and in many districts in Southern Vietnam the Viet Minh
organized local village administrations with peasant help.

Japanese fortunes waned by early 1945 as the United States began
bombing Japanese installations in Southeast Asia. In some of these attacks, major towns and cities were leveled, especially in Burma, North
Borneo, Sarawak, and the Philippines. In an attempt to generate local
support to resist the Western challenge, Japanese officials helped set up
a committee to prepare for Indonesian independence, and Sukarno addressed the members, telling them that together the united Indonesian
people would renew their struggle to forever end Dutch colonialism:
"The [Dutch] enemy . . . must be met with every means at our com-
mand that can be used as a weapon, from the cannons . . . to the boiling
water that is heated in the kitchen. . . . Every city, every village, every
house—yes, every heart must become a fortress."[17] The Japanese also
allowed Burman nationalists to establish a government.

As Japanese fortunes declined, however, some nationalists began
secretly working with the Western Allies. The Burmese nationalist army
changed sides and helped push Japanese forces out. Unable to convert
Southeast Asian resources rapidly enough into war materials, its forces
badly overstretched, and rocked by a string of military reversals and
the atomic bombings of Hiroshima and Nagasaki by the United States,
Japan surrendered in August 1945. Thai opposition leaders who had
spent the war years in the West returned to Thailand and replaced
the former military government with a pro-Western one. Tired of
economic deprivation and brutal repression, most people welcomed
Japanese defeat, and some even accepted the return of Western forces,
especially in Malaya, British Borneo, and the Philippines, which the
United States granted independence under pro-U.S. leaders in 1946.
In most places, however, the returning Westerners faced a situation of
growing volatility.

The end of war allowed for immediate political change in Vietnam,
Burma, and Indonesia. In Vietnam the Japanese surrendered to British forces who moved into Saigon and then prepared the ground for
a French return. Meanwhile the Viet Minh marched into Hanoi and
declared the end of French colonialism. With this event, known as the
August Revolution of 1945, a Vietnamese government headed by Ho

Chi Minh was in control of the capital and in a position to administer the country, the first non-French regime in more than 80 years. Ho addressed a cheering crowd of thousands, including several U.S. military officers who had advised Ho and his forces during the Japanese occupation. In his stirring speech, Ho echoed themes from the American declaration of independence.

All men are created equal. They are endowed by their Creator with certain inalienable rights. Among these are life, liberty, and the pursuit of happiness." These immortal words are from the Declaration of Independence of the United States in 1776. Taken in a broader sense, these phrases mean: "All peoples on earth are born equal; all peoples have the right to live, to be free, to be happy." The Declaration of the Rights of the Man and Citizen of the French Revolution of 1791 also proclaimed: "Men are born and remain free and with equal rights." Nevertheless for more than eighty years the French imperialists, abusing their "liberty, equality, and fraternity," have violated the land of our ancestors and oppressed our countrymen. Their acts are contrary to the ideals of humanity and justice. They have exploited us without respite, reduced our people to the blackest misery and pitilessly looted our country. They have despoiled our ricelands, our mines, our forests, our raw materials. . . . Vietnam has the right to be free and independent. All the people are determined to mobilize all their spiritual and material strength, to sacrifice their lives and property, to safeguard their right to liberty and independence.[18]

Ho would have welcomed support from his wartime ally, the United States, and he wrote a series of plaintive letters to President Harry S Truman that went unanswered. But it was clear in Northern Vietnam that the Mandate of Heaven once enjoyed by Vietnamese emperors had passed to Ho and the Viet Minh.

For many Vietnamese the August Revolution was the formative experience of their lives, fostering a deep sense of solidarity and readiness to sacrifice. But the French were not willing to accept Ho's government, and they even had some allies among Catholics and pro-Western nationalists. Although the Viet Minh occupied Northern Vietnam, Chinese troops moved into the area to disarm the Japanese. This provocative move generated a Vietnamese fear of a permanent presence by their traditional enemy. Commenting that "it is better to sniff French [manure] for awhile than to eat China's forever,"[19] Ho patiently negotiated with the French for a peaceful independence, paving the way for the withdrawal of Chinese troops. But French leaders, in control of the south, were determined to regain domination of the whole of their valuable colony. In 1946 Ho warned French negotiator Jean Sainteny, a longtime acquaintance, that a war would be costly and unwinnable: "You will kill ten of my men while we will kill one of yours, but you will be the ones who will end up exhausted."[20] When negotiations failed, the Viet Minh had to secure the independence of North Vietnam through a brutal war with France between 1946 and 1954.

Burma emerged devastated from the Japanese occupation, with most cities blasted into rubble by Allied bombing. The British, facing a well-armed nationalist army and weary of conflict, elected to negotiate independence with the charismatic nationalist leader Aung San, who enjoyed wide popularity as the leader of the thakin group known as the "thirty comrades." In an interview with reporters in 1946, Aung San, a strong secularist, proclaimed a "nationalism compatible with the welfare of one and all, irrespective of race, religion or class or sex. That is my nationalism."[21] In 1948 the British left, but newly elected Prime Minister Aung San and several other top officials were assassinated by a ruthless political rival. Aung San was replaced by his longtime thakin colleague, U Nu, an idealistic Buddhist. Soon many ethnic minorities, fearful of Burman domination, as well as several communist groups,

Aung San, the charismatic leader of the Burmese nationalist movement, addresses a mass meeting in Rangoon. He first emerged as a student leader at Rangoon University and then led anti-British Burmese paramilitary forces during World War II. Collection International Institute of Social History, Amsterdam

declared their secession and organized armies. For the next four decades a complex civil war troubled the country, and the central government rarely controlled much more than half the nation's territory.

Meanwhile, the Dutch had no plans to allow their most valuable colony, Indonesia, to become independent. They quickly occupied key areas of the country but then faced the nationalist forces. The Indonesian Revolution of the late 1940s was a bitter and bloody conflict. In the 1952 novel *A Road with No End* by the Sumatran author Mochtar Lubis, the revolutionary Hazil claims, "This music sings the struggle of [humanity]. This is the revolution we have begun. But the revolution is only a means to attain freedom, and freedom is only a means to enrich the happiness and nobility of human life."[22] Although the main nationalist leader, Sukarno, pursued a policy of negotiation, the Dutch used massive violence to suppress the revolutionaries and the Indonesians fought back. In a story about the brutal battle to control the east Java city of Surabaya, the Sumatran writer Idrus noted that, for the revolutionary soldiers, "everything blurred: the future and their heartbreaking struggle. They only knew that they had to murder to drive out the enemy and stop him trampling their liberated land. They killed [the Dutch soldiers] with great determination, spirit and hunger."[23] At the center of the anticolonial struggle were youth. For them this was a transforming experience that built patriotism and morale. The United States, fearing regional instability, pressured the Dutch, dependent on U.S. aid to recover from World War II, to give up the fight in 1950, and they did. The nationalist thrust had now produced several new nations in Southeast Asia. But the struggle for independence throughout the region, and the building of states capable of improving the lives of their people, had only just begun.

CHAPTER 9

Revolutionary Wars and Nation Building, 1950–1975

In 1950 a small group of leading Indonesian writers published a moving declaration promoting "universal humanism" and "human dignity." Their beliefs were shaped by the nationalist struggle against the Dutch as well as their familiarity with European Enlightenment values such as democracy, free thought, and tolerance. They claimed, "We are the legitimate heirs to the culture of the whole world, a culture which is ours to extend and develop in our own way. We are born of the common people. For us, revolution implies the discarding of old and outmoded values and their replacement by new ones. Our fundamental quest is humanity."[1] These writers hoped that Indonesia could combine the most humane ideas of East and West to become a beacon to the world, open to all cultures and showing respect for the common people. These bold and noble aspirations, with their recognition of a connection to the wider world, reflected a new sense of possibility as walls of colonialism crumbled or were knocked down. But the idealism was soon dashed by the realities of the years just after the end of World War II. Most nationalists argued that the longing for dignity could only be achieved after securing independence, either through negotiation or revolution, and by building new nations.

The writers had been inspired in part by the irreverent Sumatran poet Chairul Anwar (1922–1949), who believed that the Indonesian Revolution against the Dutch had destroyed the old colonial society and allowed for the possibility of building a new, open society. A true bohemian who was undisciplined in his personal life, Anwar had risen from poverty—his family was too poor to send him to secondary school—to master the Dutch, English, French, and Spanish languages. Influenced by both Western books and by Indonesian sensibilities, Anwar excited

Indonesian writers with his pathbreaking poems that stretched the possibilities of the Indonesian language. But Anwar had died of syphilis when just 27 years old, and others were left to carry on the campaign to foster change while preserving continuity.

During the 1940s and 1950s most of the Southeast Asian countries gained their independence, but the euphoria proved short lived. The new nations now faced the severe challenges of overcoming economic underdevelopment, promoting national unity in ethnically divided societies, and dealing with opposition to the new ruling groups. These leaders also had to forge new relationships with the former colonial powers and the new superpowers of a Cold War world—the United States, the Soviet Union, and China. The new international situation helped shape Southeast Asian politics and relations with the wider world. The years between 1950 and 1975 were marked by impressive progress in many areas but also by wars, revolutions, insurgencies, and dictatorships, among other problems. Although all countries faced severe challenges, the peoples of Indochina experienced the most wrenching conflicts related to the Cold War.

The Vietnamese independence declared by Ho Chi Minh in 1945 faced formidable opponents. The French, back in control of Southern Vietnam and desperate to retain all of their valuable empire in Indochina, refused to give up their claims over the whole country. In an interview with a French magazine in 1946, Ho Chi Minh challenged French leaders to avoid conflict over Viet Minh control of Northern Vietnam: "If they force us into a war, we will fight. The struggle will be atrocious, but the Vietnamese people will suffer anything rather than renounce their freedom."[2] The struggles in Indochina beginning in the 1940s were indeed atrocious and involved many countries, including the United States. Ho's strategy relied on an idea, as he told the *New York Times* in 1946: "We have a weapon every bit as powerful as the most modern cannon: nationalism! Do not underestimate its power."[3] For Indochina war was the main fact of life for some 30 years.

During the First Indochina War, from 1946 to 1954, the French attempted, with massive U.S. economic and military aid, to maintain their colonial grip. Worried about growing communist movements in Asia, the United States shifted from supporting the Viet Minh during World War II to opposing all left-wing nationalists in Southeast Asia while helping the French rebuild after the war. Leaders in the United States believed that Britain and France needed the resources from their colonies to regain prosperity and weaken their own communist movements. Sending in a large military force, the French pushed the Viet Minh out of the northern cities with brutal tactics that alienated the population. Ho asked Vietnam's men and women to "use guns, swords, spades, hoes or whatever weapons they had to resist."[4] The French, finally, could not overcome an outgunned but determined Viet Minh with a nationalist message. In areas they controlled, the Viet Minh won peasant support and new recruits by transferring land to poor villagers. French observers referred to a "quicksand war" bogging down their forces. French general Jacques-Philippe Leclerc complained that fighting the Viet Minh was "like ridding a dog of its fleas. We can pick them, drown them, and poison them, but they will be back in a few days."[5] After a major military defeat in 1954 when Viet Minh forces overwhelmed a French base at Dienbienphu, in the highlands near the border with Laos, and took thousands of French prisoners, the French abandoned their efforts, negotiated a peace agreement at a conference in Geneva, Switzerland, in 1954, and went home.

The agreements negotiated at Geneva left the Viet Minh in control of the northern half of Vietnam and provided that elections would be held in 1956 to determine the fate of South Vietnam. But although Northern and Southern Vietnamese spoke different dialects and often had different customs, few Vietnamese wanted separate nations. Ignoring the Geneva agreements, which it had not signed, the United States quickly filled the political vacuum left by the French departure, pressing the discredited emperor Bao Dai, a renowned playboy and longtime French puppet, to appoint an anticommunist leader, Ngo Dinh Diem, as president of South Vietnam. Diem had nationalist credentials but had lived outside of Vietnam, including in the United States, for years. With U.S. support, Diem refused to hold reunification elections. Even U.S. President Dwight Eisenhower conceded that the elections had to be prevented because Ho would win 80 percent of the vote in a free election. But not all Vietnamese shared pro-Ho sentiments and some, especially in the south, feared communist ideology. The stage was set for what Americans called the Vietnam War and what many Vietnamese termed the American War. World historians often refer to it as the American-Vietnamese War or the Second Indochina War.

The roots of the war were planted in the 1940s when the United States emerged as the dominant world power. The Cold War between the United States and the Soviet Union, however, strongly influenced U.S. foreign policy, which focused in the 1950s on defeating communism around the world. The Chinese communist victory in China in 1949, and then the Korean War from 1950 to 1954—in which U.S.-led and Chinese–North Korean forces fought to a stalemate—increased

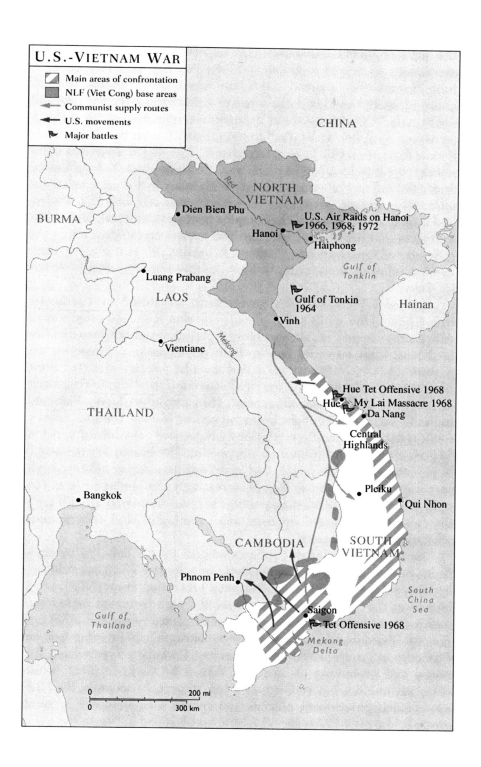

U.S.-VIETNAM WAR
Main areas of confrontation
NLF (Viet Cong) base areas
Communist supply routes
U.S. movements
Major battles

CHINA

BURMA

NORTH VIETNAM

Dien Bien Phu

U.S. Air Raids on Hanoi
1966, 1968, 1972

Hanoi

Haiphong

Red

Gulf of Tonkin

LAOS

Luang Prabang

Gulf of Tonkin
1964

Hainan

Vinh

Mekong

Vientiane

THAILAND

Hue Tet Offensive 1968

Hue   My Lai Massacre 1968
Da Nang

Central
Highlands

Bangkok

Pleiku

Qui Nhon

CAMBODIA

SOUTH
VIETNAM

Phnom Penh

South
China
Sea

Gulf of
Thailand

Saigon

Tet Offensive 1968

Mekong
Delta

0   200 mi
0   300 km

U.S. fears of Asian communism. U.S. leaders feared radical nationalist movements as threats to global stability. The U.S. Secretary of State, John Foster Dulles, claimed that if "Indochina should be lost [to communism], there would be a chain reaction throughout the Far East and South Asia."[6] Concerns about a possible communist sweep through Southeast Asia, known as the "domino theory," soon provided the rationale for action. U.S. leaders were especially worried about any communist threat to its allies Thailand and the Philippines. But the United States did fail in Vietnam, a country with many historical reasons for mistrusting foreign powers on "civilizing" missions, and U.S. leaders had little understanding of the complex historical, cultural, and political forces that had shaped Vietnam and were overconfident about the prospects of Americanizing Vietnam. Reflecting this attitude, President Lyndon Johnson announced, "I want to leave the footprints of America there."[7]

In North Vietnam, Ho's government, supported by the Soviet Union and China, built a disciplined state that launched programs to address the inequalities of the colonial period. Land reform redistributed land from powerful landlords to poor peasants. However, the government's authoritarian style and socialist policies alienated some among the middle class and the small Roman Catholic minority, many of whom, with U.S. encouragement, then moved to South Vietnam. In South Vietnam, President Diem, an ardent Roman Catholic from a wealthy mandarin family, established a repressive government based in Saigon, cracking down hard on opponents. The United States poured in economic and military aid, and increasing numbers of military advisors were sent to stabilize Diem's increasingly unpopular regime. The rigid Diem talked of winning popular support but allied himself with the rural landlords and opposed any meaningful land reform, thus alienating many peasants.

Soon the dynamics of conflict changed. By the late 1950s, dissidents, including many southerners who were former Viet Minh soldiers, had formed the communist-led National Liberation Front (NLF), often known as the Viet Cong. Diem responded with increased repression, murdering or imprisoning thousands of suspected rebels and other opponents. Buddhists resented the government's policies favoring Roman Catholics in government positions, aiding Catholic refugees from the north, and promoting an ideology shaped by Catholic ideas, while many nationalists viewed Diem as a U.S. puppet. Meanwhile, the NLF assassinated government officials and spread their influence in rural areas. By the early 1960s the NLF, now openly aided by North Vietnam, controlled large sections of South Vietnam and thousands more U.S. advisors assisted Diem's army. In 1963 U.S. leaders gave up on Diem and sanctioned his overthrow and assassination by his own military officers.

As violence intensified, the United States escalated the conflict by the mid-1960s into a full-scale military commitment. With South Vietnamese forces growing weaker, President Johnson increased the U.S. contingent, using as an excuse an alleged attack by North Vietnamese patrol boats on two U.S. warships in the Gulf of Tonkin, just off the North Vietnamese coast, which may never have occurred. In 1965 Johnson ordered a massive intervention of ground troops and an accelerated air war against military targets in North and South Vietnam. By 1968, 550,000 U.S. troops were in South Vietnam. Diem was succeeded by a series of military regimes that enjoyed some local support but never achieved much credibility with the majority of the South Vietnamese population. Military supplies and thousands of North Vietnamese troops regularly moved south through the mountains of Eastern Laos and Cambodia, along what came to be known as the Ho Chi Minh Trail.

For many Vietnamese, the war was essentially a continuation of the First Indochina War to expel the French and reconstruct a damaged society. Some historians argue that the fate of Vietnam was already decided earlier when the Viet Minh declared independence in 1945 and then humbled the hated French colonizers in the First Indochina War. Even Ho Chi Minh's death in 1969 did not change the situation much. Land reform was perhaps the key issue of the war, and the communists advocated changes, promising to put land in the hands of the peasants who worked it. Some U.S. policies, especially the massive bombing, also backfired. One of the thousands of women who fought for the NLF, Anh Vien, later told an American researcher, "The first days I felt ill at ease—marching in step, lobbing grenades, taking aim with my rifle, hitting the ground. But as soon as I saw the American planes come back [to bomb], my timidity left me."[8]

Americans decided who governed in South Vietnam but did not consult these officials on decisions to commit more U.S. troops. While Americans proclaimed a desire to win the "hearts and minds" of the South Vietnamese, American policies and actions often ignored the consequences for the local people. Pham Duy, a folk singer in South Vietnam who disliked both the Saigon government and the NLF, wrote in a song: "The rain of the leaves is the tears of joy/Of the girl whose boy returns from the war/The rain on the leaves is bitter tears/When

American troops fighting in Vietnam in the 1960s and early 1970s faced an often hostile local population. The strategy known as "search and destroy" required American soldiers to search villages and detain residents suspected of supporting the communist-led National Liberation Front. National Archives NWDNS-127-N-A185020

a mother hears her son is no more."⁹ Because the South Vietnamese army, mostly conscripts, suffered from low morale and high desertion and casualty rates, Americans did much of the fighting. U.S. strategists viewed Vietnam chiefly in military terms, measuring success by the body count, free fire zones, search and destroy missions, and massive firepower. A top U.S. military strategist believed the United States could only overcome the communist forces with "more bombs, more shells, more napalm . . . until the other side cracks and gives up."¹⁰ Vietnam became the most heavily bombed nation in world history, with the United States dropping nearly triple the total bomb tonnage used in World War II. The use of chemical defoliants to clear forests caused massive environmental damage. Thanks to the toxic chemicals sprayed on the land and water, Vietnam today has the world's highest rate of birth defects and one of the highest rates of cancer.

The U.S. strategy of massive force, combined with the communists' determination, brought about a military stalemate by 1967. Neither side could achieve victory. The Tet Offensive of 1968, in which communist forces occupied or attacked the major cities during the Vietnamese New

Year holiday, was a turning point. In the United States and around the world people watched on television as communist guerrillas attacked the U.S. Embassy in Saigon and U.S. Marines fought their way, block by block, against fierce resistance into key cities. Although the communists were pushed back from the cities, had some of their infrastructure exposed, and suffered high casualties, Tet proved a psychological and political setback for the United States.

By the late 1960s a majority of Americans had turned against a war that seemed to have no end, a quagmire in which U.S. soldiers were being killed or injured for goals that seemed unclear. The new president, Richard Nixon, was forced by public opinion to begin a policy of "Vietnamization," which relied increasingly on South Vietnamese troops to do the fighting, and to begin a gradual withdrawal of U.S. troops, finally negotiating a peace agreement with North Vietnam. In 1973 most U.S. ground forces left Vietnam, although the United States continued air and logistical support for the South Vietnamese. By 1975 the NLF and North Vietnam had defeated the South Vietnamese army. As communist units marched into Saigon, more than 70,000 anticommunist South Vietnamese fled the country in a panic. Vietnam was now reunified under communist leadership.

One top U.S. official, General and former Ambassador Maxwell Taylor, later concluded that the United States lost because they never understood the Vietnamese on either side. He overestimated the effectiveness of U.S. policies and also overestimated the willingness of the U.S. public to support a prolonged war without a clear purpose or expectation of victory. William D. Ehrhart, who served with the U.S. Marine Corps in Vietnam, reflected the disillusionment of the war felt by some U.S. veterans and the sense that, as General Taylor suggested, citizens of the United States never understood the Vietnamese: "We are the ones you [Americans] sent to fight a war you didn't know a thing about. It didn't take us long to realize the only land that we controlled was covered by the bottoms of our boots."[11] The war's human toll was appalling, for both the United States and Vietnam, costing the United States 58,000 dead and 519,000 physically disabled. Around 4 million Vietnamese were killed or wounded, 10 percent of the total population. By 1975, however, the fighting had ended and Vietnam could turn at last to reconstruction.

Laos was a pawn in the larger conflict between the United States and the North Vietnamese. Anticolonial sentiment in Laos grew during and after the Japanese occupation of World War II. In 1953 the French, wearying of their Indochinese experience, granted Laos independence under a conservative, pro-French, Lao-dominated government that left-wing nationalists considered to be a facade for continued Western domination. The U.S. intervention, which began in the late 1950s and continued until 1975, was a response to, but also helped intensify, an internal conflict between U.S.-backed right-wingers rooted in the Lao landowning aristocracy, neutralists, and the Pathet Lao, who were revolutionary nationalists allied to the Vietnamese communists.

In 1960 right-wing forces advised and equipped by the U.S. Central Intelligence Agency (CIA) seized the government, initiating a major crisis. As fighting intensified, the Pathet Lao gained control over much of the northern mountains while the government controlled the south and Mekong valley. U.S. intervention converted the Laotian government into a client state that had little credibility and was bloated with corruption. Its U.S.-financed army was ineffective. The Pathet Lao had support among some of the hill peoples, but a large faction of the Hmong people led by Laotian General Vang Pao sought increased autonomy. Promising them permanent U.S. support and protection, in 1960 the CIA recruited a secret army that eventually numbered some 45,000 soldiers, largely drawn from among the Hmong and Mien peoples. Unknown to the U.S. public, the secret army attacked North Vietnamese forces along the Ho Chi Minh trail and fought the Pathet Lao. Some 30,000 Hmong, 10 percent of their population, died during the conflict. American bombing depopulated large areas of the highlands, including Hmong districts, forcing many into refugee camps. The entire war imposed a terrible toll on Laotian society, killing some 100,000 Laotians. In 1975 the Laotian government collapsed and the Pathet Lao took full control of Laos amidst a background of war weariness and a desire for stability. Thousands of anticommunist Hmongs, Mien, and Lao fled into Thailand, many eventually reaching the United States.

Like Laos, Cambodia became part of what some observers called the "sideshow" to the war raging next door in Vietnam. Cambodian nationalism had gained strength during and after World War II. By 1953 France granted the country independence under the young, charismatic, and widely popular Prince Norodom Sihanouk, who had resigned as king to enter politics. In 1955 Sihanouk and his supporters won the first free election, and as president, Sihanouk ruled as a benevolent autocrat but with occasional repression to protect an inefficient economy and his own power monopoly. The multitalented but mercurial president also wrote popular songs, directed films, and wrote angry letters to U.S. newspapers protesting U.S. policies. Sihanouk diplomatically maintained Cambodian independence and peace in the face of the growing warfare on his borders. Despite historical Cambodian fears of Vietnamese expansion, he calculated that the Vietnamese communists would eventually triumph and expressed sympathy for the Vietnamese revolution. During the 1960s Vietnamese communist forces roamed the border area while U.S. warplanes secretly bombed Cambodian territory. Sihanouk was powerless to stop either action.

Sihanouk also faced growing problems in the form of economic stagnation, political corruption, and resentment of his autocratic power. The *Khmer Rouge* ("Red Khmers"), a tiny communist insurgent group led by alienated intellectuals mostly educated in French universities, concentrated on building a small support base of impoverished peasants in the northern mountains. But Sihanouk remained popular among the majority of peasants, many of whom owned their own land. Sihanouk's royal heritage gave him the aura of a "god king" in the ancient Cambodian monarchial tradition but one with a common touch. But military officers and the urban business community were restless and envied the U.S. money and arms flowing into South Vietnam, Laos, and Thailand. They also feared the North Vietnamese and resented Sihanouk's dictatorial rule.

Khmer Rouge soldiers, mostly from poor peasant backgrounds, were usually armed with Chinese-made assault rifles. Overcoming U.S. bombing and the Cambodian army, the Khmer Rouge came to power in 1975, soon depopulating the cities and launching a campaign to kill all Cambodians they believed to be their enemies. AP Photo/Neal Ulevich

In 1970 Sihanouk, on vacation in France, was overthrown by pro-U.S. generals and civilians with possible U.S. backing, beginning a tragic era in Cambodian history. South Vietnamese and U.S. forces soon invaded Eastern Cambodia in search of bases of the Vietnamese communist forces. The invasion energized the small Khmer Rouge movement. Cambodia's new leader, the inept Lon Nol, was not consulted in advance about the invasion. His government lacked much legitimacy outside the capital city, Phnom Penh, and became increasingly dependent on U.S. aid for virtually all supplies. The army, paid and equipped by the United States, suffered from corruption and low morale. Meanwhile, to counteract the rapid deterioration of the government forces and the growing strength of the Khmer Rouge, U.S. planes launched an intensive air assault through the heart of Cambodia's Mekong basin agricultural area, where most of the people lived. The bombing killed thousands of innocent civilians and terrified much of the remaining population. Rice production declined by almost half, raising the possibility of mass starvation. Amid the chaos and destruction, the Khmer Rouge, now cynically allied with Sihanouk, rapidly enlarged its forces, recruiting from among the displaced and shell-shocked peasantry. From 1970 until 1975 between 750,000 and 1 million Cambodians perished from the conflict between the Khmer Rouge and the U.S.-backed government. In 1975 Khmer Rouge forces reached Phnom Penh. As U.S. forces and a few Cambodian allies flew out, the Khmer Rouge seized the government and launched a new and terrible era of repression, hardship, and killing.

During these years the other nations of Southeast Asia avoided the destructive warfare rocking Indochina but faced serious challenges of their own. Indonesia experienced some of the most serious turbulence. Given the diversity of islands, peoples, and cultures, Indonesian leaders became obsessed with creating national unity. However, their national slogan, "unity in diversity," expressed a goal more than a solid reality. During the 1950s and early 1960s Indonesia was led by the charismatic nationalist hero but unpredictable president Sukarno, whose strength was bringing different factions together and creating solidarity in a huge nation in which villagers on remote islands and cosmopolitan city dwellers on Java knew little about each other. Sukarno's personal style and political leadership were rooted in the traditional cultural ideals of Javanese kings. Increasingly authoritarian, Sukarno argued that "our democracy is not a battlefield of opponents. Our democracy is nothing else than a search for synthesis, a search for an accumulation of ideas and energies."[12] He also sought a role on the world stage, sponsoring a major international conference at the Javan city of Bandung in 1955 to help shape a Non-Aligned Movement that included countries like Burma, Cambodia, China, India, Yugoslavia, and Egypt and sought a middle way between the two superpowers.

The parliamentary system of the early 1950s involving many political parties, most of them representing regions, ethnic groups, or religious factions, proved unstable and divisive. Regionalism grew as Outer Islanders resented Javanese domination. Sukarno's nationalistic but poorly implemented economic policies contributed to a severe economic crisis by the early 1960s, as well as deepening divisions between communist, Islamic, and military forces. In an essay the pro-communist novelist Pramoedya Ananta Toer described the failures: "Jakarta reveals a grandiose display with no relationship to reality. Great plans, enormous immorality, no screws, no nuts, no bolts, no threads, no valves, no flywheels, no belts and no washers for the machinery we do have."[13]

By 1965 Indonesia had become a turbulent mix of explosive social and political pressures and experienced its greatest crisis as an independent nation. After a failed attempt to seize power by a small military faction with communist sympathies, a group of long-discontented conservative generals, angered at Sukarno's friendship with communist nations such as China and apparent favoritism toward the Indonesian Communist Party (PKI), arrested Sukarno and quickly launched a brutal campaign to eliminate all leftists, especially those affiliated with the large PKI, which had rebuilt its influence among many poor peasants and nominal Muslims in Java. The resulting bloodbath killed at least 500,000 and perhaps even as many as 1 million Indonesians, including many Chinese. Most PKI leaders were killed or arrested, with thousands of leftists such as the writer Pramoedya Ananta Toer held in remote prison camps for years. Sukarno died in disgrace in 1970. A government headed by General Suharto took power in 1966 and ruled until 1998, moving Indonesia in new pro-Western and authoritarian directions. They made it a crime to slander or show disrespect of the government or officials.

The Philippines achieved independence from the United States on July 4, 1946, and the U.S. president, Harry Truman, proclaimed in a radio broadcast that the two countries would be closely bound together in a political and economic alliance for many years. But the new nation soon faced problems sustaining its democratic approach. The huge economic gap between rich and poor, regional and ethnic loyalties, and a primary orientation toward the family shaped society and politics. A small group of landowners, industrialists, and businessmen, often termed the "hundred families" and who had prospered under U.S. rule, manipulated elected governments to preserve their political and economic power. The new constitution also protected U.S. economic interests. Personal and family rivalries, rather than ideological differences, separated the political parties. Free elections involved enough violence, bribery, and fraud that disillusioned Filipinos often derided them as mainly decided by "guns, goons, and gold."

Furthermore, many nationalists believed continuing U.S. influence hindered the creation of a truly independent Filipino identity and culture. Several major U.S. military bases near Manila symbolized this reality. The powerful U.S. influence in popular culture was undeniable. American films, TV programs, music, comics, and books had huge audiences. A prominent local critic, Doreen Fernandez, wrote in 1989 that Filipinos "sing of White Christmases and of Manhattan. Their stereos reverberate with the American Top 40."[14] Although outside influences on Filipino culture were often superficial and exaggerated by observers, Filipinos have never fully created a clear national identity out of the diverse mosaic of languages, regions, and colonial traditions. Furthermore, many among the Muslim minority of around 5 percent have felt alienated from the Christian majority, fostering insurgencies seeking autonomy in the southern islands.

Economic inequality and social divisions have fueled chronic conflict in the Philippines. The leftist Filipino poet Amado Hernandez portrayed the gap between the rich and poor in his poem "The Kingdom of Mammon": "On every side there's pleasure and distraction, fiesta and dancing, night-long, day-long/who dares whisper that thousands have no roofs above their heads/that hunger stalks the town."[15] Impoverished rural areas fostered various insurgencies to bring revolution. The communist-led rebellion from 1948 to 1954, led by the *Hukbalahap* (People's Anti-Japanese Army) guerrilla fighters (better known as the *Huks*), capitalized on peasant discontent in Luzon. Only heavy U.S. assistance to the government and promised reforms suppressed the rebellion. However, most of the reforms were never enacted. In the 1970s the communist New Peoples Army (NPA) formed and soon controlled many rural districts. Like the *Huks*, the NPA attracted support from rural tenant farmers and urban slum dwellers with a promise of radical social and economic change. In 1972 President Ferdinand Marcos, who was ineligible to run for reelection, used the restoration of law and order as an excuse to suspend democracy and arrest his political opponents, probably with the support of the Nixon administration in the United States. For the next 14 years he ruled as a dictator and resolved few problems.

Like Indonesia and the Philippines, Thailand struggled to create national unity and stability. Thai nationalists sought a Thai-oriented national culture, but ethnic diversity posed political problems. The impoverished northeast, where one-third of the population lived, was mainly ethnic Lao, often viewed by Thai from the central plains as unpolished and inferior. Many northeasterners looked on the Bangkok-based national government with wariness. A communist insurgency backed by China emerged there in 1965, with the guerrillas capitalizing on the national government's neglect of the region's development. In the south, where many Malay-speaking Muslims resented Buddhist domination, various communist and Islamic insurgent groups also operated during the 1960s and 1970s.

Thai society has never been rigid, but it promoted respect for those in authority and valued social harmony, and this conservatism contributed to authoritarian governments and bureaucratic inertia. Thailand's political history after 1945 was characterized by long periods of military rule followed by short-lived democratically elected or semidemocratic governments. Coups d'état by one or another military faction were common, as Thais strove for a balance between order and stability on the one hand and democracy and personal self-determination on the other. In 1970 King Bhumibol reflected the tension between conservatism and change when he warned against the idea that "the destruction of old established things for the sake of bringing about the new would lead to entirely good results, since surely there must be some good in the old-fashioned things."[16]

Not until the 1970s would a true mass politics develop as opposition movements challenged the long-entrenched, corrupt, and often repressive military regime. Many Thais resented U.S. influence and the various military bases, mostly in the northeast, that the Americans used to support their military efforts in Laos and Vietnam. The presence of many free-spending American soldiers created a false prosperity in Bangkok and the cities near military bases while also posing a challenge to Buddhist morality. Staunch Buddhists were outraged by the sleazy bars, gaudy nightclubs, and brothels that often exploited poor Thai women and served the U.S. and foreign visitors but also attracted eager Thai men. Disenchanted with the military regime and their U.S. allies, university students played a particularly large role in confronting the dictatorship. In 1973 the military regime was overthrown after mass demonstrations, bringing political liberalization. One student expressed the feeling of elation: "I sense freedom. . . . Like many other Thais, I have wanted it for a long time, but now that we seem to have it, I feel bewildered. I don't quite believe it yet."[17] Student activists spread out to villages and factories to generate "bottom up" change by engaging peasants and workers in the struggle for change.

For the first time in Thai history, real democracy and debate flourished, fostering new ideas. Progressive writers and musicians promoted what they termed "art for life, art for the people," often extolling the hardworking peasants. For example, the radical thinker and poet Jit Poumisak wrote of the rice farmer: "Every time you grab a fistful of rice/Remember it is my sweat you swallow/To keep on living/. . . But to grow rice is the bitter work/That only we farmers must taste."[18] The fragile civilian government allowed these cultural activities but proved unable to resolve major problems such as poverty. Right-wing military men and bureaucrats became alarmed at challenges to their power and privileges. Thai society became increasingly polarized. Finally, in 1976, bloody clashes between leftist students and right-wing supporters of the military led to another military coup and martial law. In the process, soldiers and thugs killed or wounded hundreds of students and arrested thousands. The return of military power reestablished order, but the massacres discredited the new government after the use of brutal force against dissidents.

By the 1960s, Burma had also come under military domination. Aung San's successor, U Nu, promoted democracy, which, he wrote in an essay, "involves self-restraint, tolerance, and forbearance, three virtues with which, unfortunately, human nature is not richly endowed."[19] U Nu's fears that democracy might fail in Burma proved prescient and he faced mounting problems, including corruption, economic stagnation, and a civil war pitting various ethnic and communist armies against the central government. Some of the minority groups in Eastern and Northern Burma, including Kachins, Karens, and Shans, had formed armies to fight for autonomy or independence. In a poem a Burmese poet described U Nu's inability to resolve the nation's many challenges in the 1950s: "In the blast of the whirlwind/A leaf caught up, spinning/Whirling and eddying/And floating in the wind."[20]

In 1962 the army seized control from U Nu's ineffective civilian government, which had been unable to quell various secession movements. General Ne Win and his military colleagues have run the country ever since. Skeptical that democracy would work in a badly fragmented nation, military rulers suspended civil liberties, imposed censorship, discouraged contact with Western nations, and devoted most government revenue to the military to fight insurgencies and keep the loyalty of soldiers. To fund their armies, the insurgents, and increasingly the national army, often relied on revenues from growing and exporting opium. Ne Win imposed his own version of socialism in which the military took over industries, banks, and commerce, and discouraged foreign investment. Military leaders issued an ideological statement that argued that, "Burma does not believe that man will be set free from social evils as long as pernicious economic systems exist in which man exploits man and lives on the fat of such appropriation."[21] But the inefficient system proved unable to supply much more than basic goods, forcing people to find other items on the black market. Stagnation and repression fostered growing dissent by the 1980s, and various ethnic insurgencies seeking autonomy continued to fight the regime, but the military kept tight control of the political and economic system.

Governments proved more stable and somewhat democratic in Malaya after independence. After World War II the British established formal colonial control in Sarawak and Sabah while seeking to dampen political unrest in Malaya and Singapore. A British proposal to form a multiethnic Malayan nation with Chinese residents treated as political equals to Malays generated an upsurge of Malay political feeling. The United Malays National Organization (UMNO) formed to promote Malay nationalism and negotiated with the British about the Malayan future, and Britain agreed to a federation providing special guarantees of Malay rights. These developments alarmed many Chinese. In 1948 the mostly Chinese Malayan Communist Party began a guerrilla war from mountain bases to defeat the colonial government. By 1956 the insurgents had been defeated. UMNO and moderate Chinese and Indian parties formed a coalition to win elections.

In 1957 the Malayan Federation became independent under a government headed by UMNO and its aristocratic leader, Tengku Abdul Rahman. Predominantly Chinese, Singapore remained outside the federation as a British colony. The Malayan arrangement favored the Malays politically, since they had the majority, but Chinese were granted liberal citizenship rights and maintained strong economic power. Many Malayans were hopeful that this arrangement would work. As a character in Malay writer Ibrahim Omar's story "Isolated Village" comments, "Now is no longer the time of our ancestors. Now is not the time of the white people. Now we rule ourselves. And we must help each other help ourselves."[22]

British leaders suggested the idea of a Malaysia federation as a way of ending their now burdensome colonial rule over Singapore, Sarawak, and Sabah, even though the various states were historically and ethnically distinct from Malaya. The Malaysian federation, linking Malaya,

Singapore, Sabah, and Sarawak, was formed in 1963 essentially as a marriage of convenience. In the years that followed, Malaysia struggled to create national unity out of deep regional and ethnic divisions. The new, hurriedly formed Malaysian nation faced many political problems, including some disenchantment in Sabah and Sarawak over Malayan domination. Singapore left the federation in 1965, becoming an independent state.

The Singapore exodus allowed UMNO to exercise more influence over federal Malaysian policies. Given the need to reduce political tensions, sustain rapid economic growth, and preserve stability, ethnic group leaders cooperated through political parties, which allied in an UMNO-dominated ruling coalition, known since 1971 as the National Front. But below the surface, tensions simmered. The 1967 novel *Minister*, by popular Malay writer Shahnon Ahmad, included speculation about a future in which Malays had been driven into the forests while Chinese controlled the rest of the country. Some critics believed the fictional story helped spark street fighting between Chinese and Malays following a heated election in 1969, which generated a nationwide state of emergency and the suspension of parliamentary government, the most significant crisis of the young nation. Parliamentary government was restored in 1970. But the crisis intensified concerns that freedom of speech and press might spark ethnic tensions, prompting the government to ban public discussion of "sensitive issues" such as ethnic relations. After 1970 governments pursued policies designed to reshape Malaysia's society and economy within a modified democratic system. And the growth of mass communications such as television began to knit the nation more closely together and link it even more to the wider world.

Malaysian writer and journalist Sri Delima offered an observation on the coming of television to a once remote Malay village in the 1970s and the social changes and cultural debates it brought:

> When Pak Ali bought the TV set he knew he was buying it for the whole village. Most of the village folk of course cannot even dream of owning or even renting a set. On Hindustani [Indian] film nights the front room of Pak Ali's house is packed. The audience overflows down the steps and into the garden, for the village's 300 families are all Hindustani-film fans. The elders talk of religion and rubber, of politics and the new village chief. Though their eyes are fixed on the TV set, they keep up a dignified discussion, for they do not quite approve of the love scenes in the film. The women, sitting on the steps with babies in their laps, are frankly enthralled. Standing far back in the shadows

are the village's young men and girls. There are very few, for most have gone off to town to chase the dream of a better life. "Modern Drama" night is different. Elders and young people alike get involved in the issues thrashed out on the TV screen—morality, parent-child relations, marriage and divorce, poverty—all hotly relevant to their lives. When a character in the TV play proses away against the new permissiveness, the elders nod their heads and pretend not to hear the rude remarks of the young, hissed from the darkness of the garden.[23]

By the mid-1970s, only Malaysia and Singapore had at least partial democracies. Vietnam, Cambodia, and Laos all had authoritarian communist governments. Indonesia and Burma had been under military rule since the 1960s and, after a brief period of democracy, Thailand was again governed by generals. A dictator also governed in the Philippines. And few of the countries showed much economic dynamism, but seeds of change had been planted. Migrants crowding into cities came into contact with people from different backgrounds, generating some cultural mixing. Expanding educational systems helped foster larger middle classes seeking more influence. Industrialization created new kinds of jobs. Nations were slowly being built, in the form of institutions and in people's minds. In the years to follow, the pace of change would accelerate in every area of life.

CHAPTER 10

Diverse Identities, "Tigers," and Changing Politics since 1970

I n the 1980s Linus Suryadi, a well-traveled Javanese Roman Catholic arts activist and poet, used the ancient Buddhist ruins at Borobodur as a backdrop to discuss the changes taking place in his country:

> At Borobodur it is almost incredible
> The statues of Buddha are without heads
> I see only Javanese peddlers
> Groups of tourists sightseeing
> Shops and restaurants are also there
> Hotels and markets at the foot of the temple
> When it is lush the *Boddhi* tree falls with a crash
> There is no replacement
> There is another version without the centers
> For shopping and handicrafts
> There is another meaning without the reality
> Of the sacred building commercialized
> The legacy replaced by arenas for entertainment
> A diverse identity.[1]

The men and women who built and worshipped at Borobodur more than 1,000 years ago lived in a society that was also shaped by global influences but nonetheless very different from the society their descendants know today.

Southeast Asia changed dramatically during the 1960s and 1970s and even more in the decades to follow. Some nations achieved considerable economic development, as their leaders, inspired by the example of Japan's industrialization in the late nineteenth century and then rapid recovery following World War II, encouraged their people to "Look East." They mixed capitalism with activist government to spur economic growth. Indonesia, Malaysia, Singapore, and Thailand all gained reputations as "tigers" in the 1980s because of their economic dynamism. Lively market economies developed, but the governments also played a major role in stimulating trade and growth and maintained somewhat authoritarian political systems to ensure social stability. By the 1990s experts talked about a vibrant Pacific Rim that also included Japan, China, Taiwan, and South Korea. Some forecast a so-called Pacific century in which these nations would lead the world economically and increase their political strength.

Generally, ethnic Chinese have constituted the region's most significant economic force, with their money and initiative fostering much of the economic growth in Singapore, Malaysia, Thailand, Indonesia, and the Philippines since the 1960s. However, many Southeast Asians have also resented the Chinese for their economic power, their pride in their ancestral culture, and their continuing ties to China. Anti-Chinese violence has erupted occasionally, and some governments have tried to restrict Chinese business activities by favoring indigenous entrepreneurs. In the 1970s thousands of Chinese left by choice or were expelled from Vietnam. Tensions between Chinese and the local Muslim peoples sometimes emerged in Malaysia and Indonesia, encouraging many middle-class Chinese to emigrate to Western nations.

Such rapid economic progress also had negative consequences. Industrial activity and the expansion of agriculture, mining, and logging contributed to environmental destruction. Today forests are being rapidly cut down or flooded by power-generating dams to serve the needs of farmers, loggers, businessmen, and politicians. The deforestation affects an incredible diversity of plant and animal life, endangering such animals as the gibbons of Java and the orangutans of Borneo. Rivers and bays are more often brown than blue, from the silt carried downstream from the mountains.

In 1997 most of these rapidly developing countries faced severe economic crises, part of a broader collapse for the Asian economies and a downturn for the world economy. The reasons for the troubles varied from country to country, but they included poorly regulated banking systems, overconfident investors, and too much favoritism by governments toward well-placed business interests. The dislocations hit all social classes. The crisis eventually bottomed out, and several of the countries began to put their economies back on a modest growth basis by the early twenty-first century, helping to raise living standards for their growing populations. However, the global economic crisis of 2008

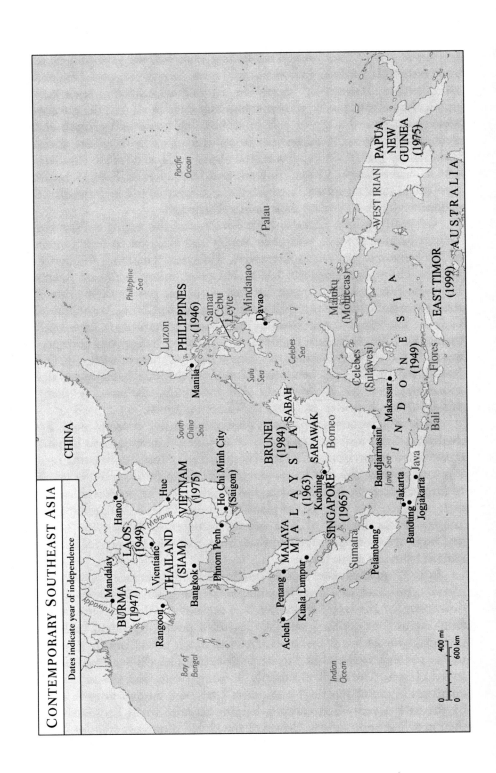

CONTEMPORARY SOUTHEAST ASIA

Dates indicate year of independence

CHINA

BURMA (1947)
Mandalay
Rangoon
Irrawaddy
Bay of Bengal

LAOS (1949)
Vientiane
THAILAND (SIAM)
Bangkok

Hanoi
Hue
VIETNAM (1975)
Ho Chi Minh City (Saigon)
Phnom Penh
Mekong

South China Sea

Pacific Ocean

Philippine Sea

Luzon
PHILIPPINES (1946)
Samar
Cebu
Leyte
Manila
Mindanao
Davao

Palau

Sulu Sea

Celebes Sea

BRUNEI (1984)
SABAH
SARAWAK
Kuching
Borneo

MALAYA (1963)
M A L A Y S I A
SINGAPORE (1965)
Kuala Lumpur
Penang
Acheh

Sumatra
Pelambang

Bandjarmasin
Java Sea
Jakarta
Bandung
Jogjakarta
Java

I N D O N E S I A (1949)

Makassar
Celebes (Sulawesi)
Maluku (Moluccas)

Bali
Flores

EAST TIMOR (1999)

WEST IRIAN

PAPUA NEW GUINEA (1975)

AUSTRALIA

Indian Ocean

400 mi
600 km
0

threatened prosperity by prompting budget and job cuts as export markets and foreign investment dwindled.

By 2008 there were some 578 million people living in Southeast Asia, a huge increase from the 20 to 25 million four centuries earlier. Several countries have quite large populations, including some 230 million people in Indonesia (the fifth largest country in the world), 85 million each in the Philippines and Vietnam, some 65 million in Thailand, 54 million in Burma, and 27 million in Malaysia. Population growth outstrips resources in countries like the Philippines, Indonesia, and Vietnam, sometimes resulting in domestic unrest, from riots to full-blown insurgencies. At the same time several nations, including Singapore and Thailand, have seen falling birth rates—a result in part of increasing affluence. Human rights abuses resulted from governments squashing dissent or combating criminal activity. But despite occasional political upheavals, the destructive wars of the earlier years have not been repeated. And, in some cases, dictatorships were eventually replaced by more open regimes.

Indonesia is now the colossus of Southeast Asia, stretching from east to west the same distance that the United States spans from California to New York. The rapidly growing population includes more than 700 ethnic and linguistic groups scattered across some 13,000 islands. The Javanese from the overcrowded island of Java account for around half of the total population. But the regional, ethnic, and cultural diversity has created tensions and violence, which helped bring down Sukarno's regime in 1964. The turmoil of the mid-1960s led to a new government known as the "New Order," headed by Javanese general-turned-President Suharto, the son of a poor peasant. Between 1966 and 1998, Suharto's government mixed military and civilian leadership but allowed only limited dissent and opposition, and these policies achieved stability. Golkar, a political coalition allied to Suharto and the military, dominated stage-managed elections and the political agenda. The Suharto government pursued a strongly pro-Western foreign policy, allying Indonesia with the United States and promoting Western investment. Top leaders, including members of Suharto's family, controlled lucrative business enterprises. One of the world's most corrupt leaders, Suharto and his family acquired more than $15 billion in assets from their companies, which received government favoritism, and from access to public coffers. Concerned with limiting the potential for disorder, Suharto restricted the airing of opposing viewpoints.

Indonesia also became dependent on the fluctuating world price for oil from Kalimantan (Borneo) and Sumatra. By the 1980s oil represented 80 percent of export earnings. However, the decline of world oil prices by the 1990s provided fewer funds for the national budget, forcing Indonesia to accumulate an enormous foreign debt. The rapid development of mining, forestry, and cash crop agriculture inevitably has taken a terrible toll on the environment. Rain forests have been clear cut so rapidly for timber and plantations that forest fires have become common in the once green lands of Sumatra and Kalimantan, causing terrible air pollution in Indonesia for months at a time and creating a thick, unhealthy haze every year that spreads to neighboring nations.

In many respects, however, the New Order improved Indonesian life, bolstering the country's economic position and fostering the emergence of an educated urban middle class. Reduced inflation, increased per capita income (to around $1,000 per capita annually), improved life expectancy (to age 62), higher rates of adult literacy (82 percent), and an annual growth rate of nearly 5 percent by the 1990s were all major improvements over the early 1960s. But one-third of the population remained very poor. Income disparities between classes and regions widened while corruption became a major problem. In a short story from the 1980s, the writer Taufiq Ismail had a children's chorus voice his criticism of a society in which government officials and predatory businessmen solicited bribes and grabbed public funds for themselves: "Indonesia, Land of Robbers. My true homeland stiff with thieves. In the future, I shall plunder while my wife, she shall seize."[2] The wealthy frolicked in nightclubs, casinos, or golf courses built across the street from slums or on land appropriated from powerless villages. Even so, a vibrant popular culture developed, including poets, novelists, and theater groups whose innovative work gained international acclaim. The flamboyant bohemian poet W. G. Rendra critiqued his nation's development policy in 1990:

> I see developed countries giving economic aid
> and as a result many people from the Third World
> are losing their lands so the rich can play golf
> Or so a dam can give electrical power
> to industries with foreign capital.
> And the unfortunate people . . . get compensation
> for every square meter of their land
> with money that has the same value
> as a packet of American cigarettes.[3]

Innovative musicians influenced by Western rock also addressed social and economic problems, including Rhoma Irama, the master of the *dangdut* musical style and Indonesia's first true entertainment superstar. Dangdut originated as a fusion of Western rock and the highly popular

Indian film music, with some influences from the older Malay folk traditions. Dangdut was rooted in the urban lower class in which Rhoma was raised and which "thumbed its' nose" at the elite culture. Since the late 1970s his songs have addressed poverty, human rights abuses, the struggle of the underdog, and the betrayal of the nationalist promise. One of his songs condemned "people who lust, in their cunning, for power/Have we now returned to the law of the jungle/With the strong oppressing the weak?/When will we ever see justice done."[4] Rhoma also made several popular films including Indonesia's first rock musical in 1980. Rhoma's music, movies, and flamboyant performance style earned him a huge following among urban slum dwellers and rural folk, especially youth, who saw their values reflected in his music and agreed with the message of one of his more famous songs: "the rich get richer and the poor get poorer." Rhoma's music also contained a strong Islamic quality, full of moral teaching, which may have helped inspire a revival in Islamic ideas. By the 1990s other more rebellious folk rock, hard rock, and hip hop musicians had eclipsed him in popularity.

Many Indonesians disliked the New Order. Given the elimination of left-wing forces, Islam provided the chief opposition to the establishment. With 87 percent of Indonesians either devout or nominal Muslims, Suharto discouraged Islamic militancy as a threat to national unity in a multifaith country. Some Muslims have opposed the government's secular policies and desired a more Islamic approach to social, cultural, and legal matters. Muslim conservatives denounce casinos, racy magazines and films, and scantily clad female pop singers. However, relatively few Muslims have actively sought an official Islamic state. A progressive and democratic strand of Indonesian Islamic thought has favored liberal social and political reform, and the traditional Javanese emphasis on harmony, consensus, and tolerance was incorporated into the national political process and Islam. The numerous Islamic liberals and moderates offer a stark contrast to the more dogmatic forms of Islam common in countries such as Pakistan and Saudi Arabia.

Nonetheless, many Muslims blamed the government for poor living standards and what they viewed as immoral activities, a resentment enhanced by the widely reported lavish lifestyles and massive corruption among some government and business leaders. One group of Muslim-oriented students given public trials for oppositional activities in 1979 articulated the litany of complaints against the system: "The lop-sided character of our society's social existence [is] typified by one group that gets richer by the day without having to perform any meaningful work, alongside millions of unemployed people who are forced to sell their dignity as humans simply to avoid starvation. Social justice is far from a reality. . . . Our political life is frozen."[5] And many Indonesians also disliked Javanese domination of the government and military.

By the 1990s Indonesian society was filled with increasing ethnic and class tensions, insecurities, student protests, and labor unrest. Riots aimed at the influential Chinese business community sporadically erupted in several cities. President Suharto showed a willingness to use force to repress regional opposition, as in East Timor, a Portuguese colony just gaining its independence but occupied in 1975 by Indonesian forces despite much local opposition. Indonesian troops and sympathizers killed thousands of East Timorese until the United Nations forced a referendum in 1999 in which the majority of Timorese voted for independence. Renamed Timor Leste, the tiny new country of around a million people had few resources, however, and most people have remained poor. Since independence, the East Timorese remain dependent on international aid and have struggled to end lingering violence and establish political and social stability. Suharto also sent in troops to suppress other secessionist movements, including in North Sumatra, where the devoutly Islamic Achehnese have sought independence for decades. Suharto responded to challenges at home by cracking down on dissidents. One of them was Sukarno's daughter, Megawati Soekarnoputri, who took over as leader of an opposition party in 1994.

In 1997 the Indonesian economy collapsed, throwing millions out of work and raising prices for essential goods. Student riots led to Suharto's resignation, and the country fell into a turmoil of protests and ethnic clashes. Meanwhile, the political system became more open, as various nationalist, Muslim, and promilitary groups jockeyed for power. Many civilians, particularly among the urban middle class, desired a more participatory system, and in 1999 free elections were held. The new president, Abdurrahman Wahid, the respected but nearly blind and unpredictable leader of a moderate Muslim organization, was unable to establish legitimacy, however. He resigned under pressure and was replaced by Vice President Megawati Soekarnoputri, who became Indonesia's first woman president. Like her father, Megawati followed secular, nationalist policies to promote stability and showed little faith in grassroots democracy, resolving few problems. Disillusioned with her faltering, indecisive leadership, in the 2004 elections, Indonesians rejected Megawati and elected a Javanese general, Susilo Bambang Yudhoyono, as president.

The fall of Suharto brought unprecedented freedom of the press and speech, but removing New Order restrictions allowed long-simmering ethnic hostilities to reemerge. Conflicts between Muslims and Christians on several islands and regional rebellions have continued. Islamic militants gained strength and a few extremists linked to the international Islamic terrorist network Al Qaeda were responsible for bombings in tourist districts on Bali in 2003 and 2005, adding to the growing tensions and raising questions about the long-term stability of Indonesian democracy. Complicating the political problems, in late 2004 more than 150,000 people in Northern Sumatra perished in a tidal wave that destroyed cities and washed away villages. This was followed by earthquakes, volcanic eruptions, droughts, and other natural disasters. Efforts to recover from these major setbacks dampened but did not destroy economic growth. And although the influence of Islam has increased, and many more women than before choose, or are pressured, to wear head scarves or full veils, most Indonesians remained moderate in their faith and supportive of democracy. The secession movement in Acheh has waned. Much remains uncertain, including whether this vast and diverse country with so many built-in tensions can remain united. Reflecting the unease about the challenges, a character in a satirical play about the passing of an aging monarch (Suharto) during a period of confusion asserted that "the more one is confused the safer we all are."[6]

Indonesia was not the only nation to experience political turbulence at the end of the twentieth century. Festering Islamic and communist insurgencies in the Philippines provided an excuse for President Ferdinand Marcos to declare martial law in 1972 and rule as dictator until 1986. During the Marcos years, economic conditions worsened, rural poverty became more widespread, the population grew rapidly, and political opposition was limited by the murder or detention of dissidents, censorship, and rigged elections. The dictator, his family, and his cronies looted the country for their own benefit, amassing billions. All the while, the United States strongly supported his government in order to protect business investments and military bases.

Although the Philippines had enjoyed one of the most robust economies before World War II, it now lagged well behind most of the other non-communist nations in Southeast Asia in development, due in part to poor political leadership. The majority of rural families were landless, and child malnutrition was common. The government built high walls along city freeways so that affluent residents would not have to view slums along the route. Across the street from the glittering pavilions of Manila's Cultural Center, whose landscaped gardens were a monument to Marcos's splendor, homeless families slept in the bushes. The First Lady, Imelda Marcos, a former beauty queen from a wealthy family, had sponsored the cultural center as part of an effort to make

Manila the Athens of Asia and as an example for the Filipino people, who, she believed, needed symbols of national prestige more than food and jobs: "Yes, the Filipinos are living in slums and hovels. But what counts is the human spirit, and the Filipinos are smiling. They smile because they are a little healthy, a little educated, and a little loved. And for me the real index of this country is the smiles of the people, not the economics index."[7]

In Manila a tiny minority lived in palatial homes surrounded by high walls topped with bits of broken glass and barbed wire, with the gates manned by armed guards. They worked in air-conditioned high-rise office buildings. But the vast majority of the capital's people lived in improvised housing in slums, building shacks out of bits of bamboo, cardboard, corrugated metal, and a few cement blocks. The countryside remained impoverished. The writer F. Sionel Jose expressed this reality in a 1979 novel: "Looking fretfully at the land around him, he realized that in all the years nothing in the countryside had changed, not the thatched houses, not the ragged vegetation, not the stolid people. Changeless land, burning sun—the words turned in his mind."[8] To find work and escape poverty, many Filipinos migrated, temporarily or permanently, to other Asian countries, the United States, or the Middle East, in search of work. The emigrants have become part of what Filipinos ruefully call a "3D" culture, referring to the dirty (domestic work), dangerous (factory work), and difficult (entertainment) jobs available to them overseas. Some 10 million Filipinos lived abroad by 2006, and many of them were women who worked as nurses, maids, or entertainers and often faced exploitation, sexual abuse, and harassment. Some have done well abroad, and Filipino doctors and nurses, for example, make important contributions to North American health care. Filipinos abroad send some $1 billion a year back home to their families.

The failures of the Marcos years generated public protests in 1986. In the cities, much of the opposition gathered around U.S.-educated Corazon Aquino, whose husband, Benigno Aquino, a leading opposition figure, had been assassinated. Corazon Aquino, from a wealthy Chinese mestizo family, headed an opposition slate when a flagrantly stolen presidential election ignited massive protests under the banner of "People Power." Street demonstrations involving students, workers, businessmen, housewives, secretaries, pop singers, and clergy demanded justice and freedom and created a spectacular nonviolent revolution. Crowds sang, blocked tanks, and surrounded military garrisons. Marcos and his family fled into exile in the United States. Filipinos burst into the presidential palace to see what their taxes had bought for the

Marcos family. In a country where the per capita income was around $800 a year, hungry people saw a dining table piled with caviar and champagne, rooms filled with priceless treasures, and closets bursting with exquisite clothes and thousands of pairs of shoes.

In the aftermath, Corazon Aquino became president and reestablished democracy. But the hopes that the nation could resolve its serious problems proved illusory. Aquino's factionalized ruling coalition included many figures tied to the same wealthy interests that had always dominated politics. Some two-thirds of Congress members came from the same hundred or so landowning families who were favored during and after U.S. colonial rule. The Philippines returned to a turbulent democratic pattern but became more open to dissenting voices. Aquino, herself a member of one of these influential families, voluntarily left office at the end of her term in 1992. Her successors had rocky presidencies. One of them, Joseph Estrada, a former film star with a reputation for heavy drinking, gambling, and womanizing, was impeached for corruption and vote-rigging. In 2001 another woman, Gloria Macapagal-Arroyo, who had a Ph.D. in economics and was the

The blatantly fraudulent Philippine election of February 1986 provoked a military coup, which swelled into the largely nonviolent nationwide "People Power" democratic revolution. Here, unarmed civilians show their support for mutinous soldiers by forming a human shield around them and making an "L" sign for "Laban," or "Fight." AP Photo/Alberto Marquez

daughter of a former president, became president but also faced allegations of corruption. She was reelected in 2005 amid controversy but faced constant challenges questioning her legitimacy, and she narrowly escaped impeachment attempts.

Two decades after the overthrow of Marcos, the public seems somewhat disillusioned with the mixed results. Filipino leaders struggled to find the right formula for positive change, but none of the subsequent governments successfully addressed poverty, found a way to reduce the fastest population growth in Asia, or seemed willing to curb the activities of influential companies exploiting marine, mineral, and timber resources. A Roman Catholic priest noted how economic exploitation and environmental destruction by local and foreign entrepreneurs have remained characteristic for decades: "A plunder economy, that's the post World War II Philippine history: plunder of seas, plunder of mines, plunder of forests."[9] The income gap continues to grow, and the poor have limited access to health, welfare, and related services. Vigilante violence has grown in rural areas, and several Muslim rebel groups remained active in the south. Government inaction left reform activities largely to the citizen or church-run grassroots groups that address poverty, legal inequalities, human rights, social welfare, labor exploitation, and environmental destruction.

Political leaders also took a significant nationalist step in 1991 by refusing to renew the agreements allowing U.S. military bases on the islands, a historical turning point that cost the nation many millions of dollars a year in U.S. payments and lost jobs. Although many Filipinos admire the United States, others resent U.S. political, economic, and cultural power in their country, reflected in a hit song by the popular group, the Apo Hiking Society, entitled "American Junk": "Leave me alone to my Third World devices/I don't need your technology/You just want my natural resources/And then you leave me poor and in misery/. . . American junk, Get it out of my bloodstream/. . . Got to get back to who I am."[10]

Also with a long history of dictatorship, as in Indonesia, Thailand struggled to maintain democracy. Many Thais welcomed the end of the turmoil that troubled the country during the democratic blossoming from 1973 to 1976, but the repressive atmosphere of military dictatorship became chilling. During the 1980s the longtime communist insurgency in the northeast ended after the government switched to a political strategy to co-opt the revolutionaries. Many of the former communist guerrillas and leftist students later became successful in business and the professions, the academic world, or democratic politics. Some became involved in the nongovernmental organizations promoting issues like environmental protection and women's rights that became increasingly active and influential in the 1980s and 1990s.

By the 1980s Thailand had developed a semidemocratic system combining traditions of order and monarchy with Western notions of representative government and accountability. Several power centers emerged, including the military, the political parties, and the big business community, with the king playing a mediating role to promote political moderation and stability. Money has lubricated elections, with most successful candidates coming from wealthy families, often of Chinese ancestry. Some pop songs have skewered unresponsive local politicians mainly interested in securing wealth and power: "The candidates' adverts tell us all about their good deeds/They bring along movies to entertain us in the villages/They say they can solve all kinds of problems/. . . here will be lots of roads and canals/You won't have to raise buffaloes/. . . But . . . we are still using buffaloes/And they have become very rich."[11] But the rapidly expanding urban middle class increased its political importance and generally supported an expansion of democracy that would give them more influence.

From the 1970s until the late 1990s, Thailand enjoyed high rates of economic growth, which considerably expanded the urban middle class, many of whom supported a more open, democratic society. The large Chinese minority still controls much of the wealth, and the top of the economy is mostly dominated by men of Chinese ancestry. Foreign investment played an important economic role in Thailand, and despite a growing manufacturing sector, the export of commodities such as rice, rubber, tin, and timber remained significant. Bangkok contains some 6 million people and produces more than half of the nation's wealth. Many Thais enjoyed high per capita income and high standards of public health by Asian standards. Indeed, thousands of people from North America and Europe travel to Thailand each year for high-quality but inexpensive medical treatment. By 2000 life expectancy was nearly 69 years and, thanks to improved education for women, adult literacy was more than 90 percent.

But the wealth has been inequitably distributed among ethnic groups and regions. Perhaps a quarter of Thais are very poor, most of them in rural areas. And the economic miracle was, in many respects, built on the backs of women, many from rural districts, working in urban factories, the service sector, and the commercial sex industry. Millions of Thai women have identified with the songs of popular singer Pompuang Duangjian, herself the product of a poor village, who often dealt with the harsh realities faced by many female migrants: "So lousy poor, I just have to risk my luck. Dozing on the bus, this guy starts chatting me up. Say's he'll get me a good job."[12] Pompuang herself had only two years of primary school education and worked as a sugar-cane cutter before starting a music career. With much of her money stolen by lovers, managers, and promoters, she was unable to afford treatment for a blood disorder and died at age 31.

During the later 1990s, pro-Western democrats, supported by much of the Bangkok middle class, governed the country and promoted political and economic liberalization. A new constitution adopted in 1997 guaranteed more civil liberties, protected free speech, and reformed the electoral system. In some regions grassroots activists have sought local solutions to local problems. A lively free press emerged. However, the Asian economic crisis of 1997 hit Thailand particularly hard and weakened the liberal-dominated government, which struggled to restore economic growth.

In 2001 a new nationalistic party led by one of Thailand's richest men, the media magnate and billionaire Thaksin Shinawatra, swept in to power on a platform of helping the rural poor and reforming the entire Thai system. Both big business and the rural voters often ignored by Bangkok supported him. Although Thaksin remained hugely popular in the countryside, he lost support in the cities by weakening democratic institutions, strengthening the state, shifting more power to big business, enriching himself and his family, and buying rural support by increasing government hand-outs, all of which his critics believe were authoritarian attempts to weaken democracy, with the potential to bankrupt the country. Furthermore, his harsh policies of using police force to defuse growing unrest by Malay-speaking Muslims in the south only inflamed the discontent, resulting in terrorist attacks, including bombings, arson, and drive-by shootings that have killed more than 2,000 people since 2004. In 2006 middle-class demonstrations in Bangkok against Thaksin became more frequent and tensions increased, until the military seized power and exiled Thaksin. The new government, supported initially by many in the Bangkok middle class and led by technocrats, maintained a fairly open society and promised an eventual return to democracy, a goal supported by most Thais. But dissent simmered, especially among Thaksin supporters. In 2007 the army gave up power and allowed free elections, which were won by Thaksin's allies. Worried that Thaksin would return to Thailand and power, an unwieldy opposition coalition of royalists, some liberal democrats, some who favor military rule, and sections of the Bangkok middle class mounted demonstrations that kept

Thai politics in turmoil in 2008. The protestors sought a new constitution providing for some appointed members to parliament that would favor urban voters while marginalizing the rural population. The courts forced out two successive pro-Thaksin prime ministers for corruption and voter fraud. Meanwhile pro- and anti-Thaksin supporters struggled in the streets, courts, and parliament, and even in the main airports, leaving the tourism-based economy in disarray, the nation deeply divided, and the political future clouded.

At the same time, Thailand also suffered from environmental problems. Rapidly growing Bangkok became one of the most polluted cities in Asia, drenched in toxic smoke from factories and automobiles despite efforts by local environmental groups to clean up the air. The nation's once abundant rain forests disappeared rapidly, sparking an environmental movement among the Thais. Angkhan Kalayanaphong, the most popular poet in Thailand for years, pleaded for Thais to save the forest from commercial logging in "Bangkok—Thailand":

Dense woods in dense forests; slowly
The rays of half a day mix with the night . . .
Rays of gold play upon, penetrate the tree-tops
rays displayed in stripes, the brightness of the sun.
You trees . . . make the sacrifice again and again.
Do you ever respond angrily? You have accepted your fate
which is contemptuous of all that is beautiful.
But troublesome are the murderers, the doers of future sins.
Greedy after money, they are blind to divine work.
Their hearts are black to large extent, instead of being honest and
upright.
They have no breeding, are lawless.
Thailand in particular is in a very bad way.
Because of their (commercial) value parks are purified (destroyed)
Man's blood is depraved, cursed and base.
His ancestors are swine and dogs. It is madness to say they are Thai.[13]

Although the Thais have a reputation for flexibility and adaptability, the rush of changes has been destabilizing. Migrants fleeing rural poverty continue to flock to Bangkok in a search for employment, causing severe crowding. Child labor laws are abused. Successive governments have been unable to substantially resolve many of the longstanding social and economic problems, especially after the economic collapse of 1997, which threw many Thais out of jobs and left half-finished buildings dotting city skylines. Nearly a million women work as prostitutes, many of them servicing "sex tours" of Western men; AIDS has become a skyrocketing problem. Thais have often defined their personal goals as *sanuk*, a multipurpose word that can mean "easy going," "fun," "carefree activity," "pleasant environment." But it has become increasingly difficult to find sanuk amidst the problems and tensions spawned by modernization. And yet Thais have reason for optimism, possessing a talent for compromise and a Buddhist religion that teaches moderation, tolerance, and a belief in the worth of the individual. These form the basis of their democratic spirit and the desire for a more equitable distribution of wealth.

Whatever Thailand's problems, however, they have paled in comparison to Burma's, where problems resulted partly from a turbulent recent history and its general isolation from the world. Ethnic Burmans constitute about 75 percent of the country's people, mostly living in the Irrawaddy valley, but there are dozens of ethnic groups in the mountains and fringe areas, many of whom have actively sought secession or autonomy. To combat regional rebellions, the military seized power in 1962 and established an unproductive socialist economy while limiting contact with other nations and restricting tourism. Under Burma's harsh, corrupt military regime, few outside the ruling group have prospered despite Burma's valuable natural resources such as timber, oil, gems, and rice. By 1987 Burma was ranked by the United Nations as one of the world's ten poorest nations, with an annual per capita income of $200 and average life expectancy of 59. However, by the 1980s, as a result of the military keeping a tight control of the government and economy, economic stagnation and political repression had fostered dissent and the various ethnic-based secession movements continued.

In 1988 mass protests led by students and Buddhist monks demanded civil liberties. These demands were met with gunfire as soldiers killed hundreds and jailed thousands. The longtime dictator, Ne Win, retired and the generals now in charge tightened their control and increased repression. Claiming to restore precolonial names, the military regime also renamed the country Myanmar, and the capital, Rangoon, became Yangon. In 1990, under international pressure, the generals allowed elections but with many restrictions. The opposition, however, quickly organized and won a landslide victory even though most of its leaders were in jail. Aung San Suu Kyi, daughter of the founding president, Aung San, had returned from a long exile in England to lead the democratic forces, and her party had the most votes. She soon gained fame as an eloquent orator. But the military refused to hand over power, put Aung San Suu Kyi under house arrest, and rounded up hundreds of other opposition supporters. Refusing to compromise in exchange for her freedom, she became a courageous symbol of principled leadership, winning a Nobel Peace Prize in 1991 for her role in defying the military leaders. She said that she did not consider herself a martyr because other Burmese had suffered much more than she had.

During the 1990s the Burmese army relentlessly put pressure on secessionist groups, co-opting or destroying most of them. Meanwhile, opium grown in the eastern highlands became a major illegal export for both the government and the remaining ethnic armies. At the same time, the government began welcoming foreign investment, and Western, Japanese, Chinese, and Southeast Asian corporations invested in Burma, especially in the timber and oil industries. The generals cleverly manipulated politics while slightly relaxing their grip. With most pro-democracy leaders in jail, opponents had to be careful. Cartoonists circulated their political drawings and rock groups released their recordings through underground channels. Writers congregated at outdoor teashops to discuss ideas or, in hushed tones, politics. With Aung San Suu Kyi's National League for Democracy sidelined, a group of former protesters known as the 88 Generation, out of prison but with few job prospects, have risked rearrest by forming an informal network to publicize the issue of political prisoners and organize peaceful demonstrations. Meanwhile, some older Burmese dream of restoring the monarchy ended by the British in 1885. The Asian economic crisis of 1997 prompted many investors to pull out, spurring speculation that the declining economy might force the military to release opposition leaders and open the system to attract foreign support. Yet growing revenues from the exploitation of offshore oil reserves and the resurgence of foreign investment in the 1990s allowed the regime, now led by General Than Shwe, to solidify its power and marginalize the opposition even more while diminishing the willingness of other countries to punish Burma for gross human rights violations. The paranoid and reclusive military leaders isolated themselves even more from the outside world and their own people in 2005 when they announced that they were immediately transferring the government from Rangoon to Naypyidaw, a remote town in Central Burma, where they devoted huge funds to construct rapidly a lavish capital that was virtually off-limits to all but senior officials.

The depth of public resentment toward a repressive regime that ruled by fear became clear in 2007, when mass demonstrations erupted in response to the government's unilateral decision to dramatically raise fuel costs. Student protestors were soon joined by thousands of Buddhist monks and sympathizers. The military responded with fierce brutality, beating, arresting, and torturing demonstrators. Dozens died. The demonstrations were crushed, and the government leaders, ignoring condemnation by the outside world, remained isolated and largely scornful of the people and their aspirations for a more open system. The repression was tested after a terrible cyclone devastated the Irrawaddy Delta in 2008, leaving more than 100,000 people dead, missing, or homeless. In the aftermath the ruling generals allowed only limited aid from abroad, leaving most of the survivors to fend for themselves with the help of local citizen organizations and the Buddhist clergy.

The contrasts between stagnant, authoritarian, closed Burma and prosperous, open Thailand since the 1970s are striking. In the early 1950s both nations had economies of similar size and growth rates, but the gap between them has become wide. Burma's life expectancy, 55 years in 2000, amounted to 14 fewer years than Thailand's. Both nations have had a long history of military dictatorship, but only the Thais, unwilling to tolerate a repressive atmosphere, made a transition to a more open government. Thais did not develop a hatred of Western models or fear contact with the outside world, as the Burmese did during their colonial period. While Thailand opened its economy to the world after World War II, the Burmese chose isolation. Burma's percentage of the world rice trade fell from 28 percent in the 1930s to 2 percent by the 1990s. Burma also had a much larger ethnic minority population than Thailand, and although many Burmese have accommodated themselves to military rule—valuing stability and worried about a return to civil war—the government must address the aspirations of all groups if it is to have any real legitimacy with its own people and the international community in the long run.

Malaysia's experiences were completely different from those of Burma and even of neighboring Indonesia, achieving much more political stability and economic progress. Malaysia politically links the Southeast Asian mainland with the archipelago, and it is characterized by the geographical division between the mainland and the Northern Borneo states of Sabah and Sarawak. There are also major ethnic divisions. Malays number slightly more than half of the federal population, allowing them to dominate politics and the bureaucracy. But most Malays live in rural areas. Chinese, more than one-third of the population, generally monopolize the urban economy. Indians, 10 percent of the population, are divided between urbanites and rural plantation workers. Various non-Muslim peoples, including Kadazans, Ibans, and other Dayak peoples, are numerous in Sabah and Sarawak.

Malaysia maintained a limited democracy after the state of emergency in 1969 and 1970 that followed communal fighting. The system included regular elections in which the National Front coalition of parties controls the process and most of the media. By limiting civil liberties and free debate the system restricts the ability of opposition political groups to compete in elections on a level playing field. Even so, some opposition members have gained election to Parliament. On the other hand, a few dissidents were jailed as political prisoners. Some middle-class grassroots pressure groups also emerged to lobby for consumer, environmental, human rights, or religious issues, with mixed success. Because the government or its allies control the print and broadcast media, dissidents use the Internet to spread their views. Ethnic identity remains central to politics, which is based on managing and preserving, rather than completely eliminating, ethnic divisions.

Datuk Seri Dr. Mahathir Muhammed, a medical doctor and Malay nationalist, became prime minister in 1980. A descendant of a Muslim Indian immigrant, he was the first non-aristocrat to become the nation's leader. In power for more than two decades, Mahathir skillfully handled global recession and adopted a sometimes anti-Western foreign policy. But his autocratic leadership style allowed little tolerance for opponents, and he arrested or sidelined several potential successors who questioned his policies, including the popular deputy president, Anwar Ibrahim. The major opposition to Mahathir's party, UMNO, came from a Malay party advocating an Islamic state and a mostly Chinese party pursuing a liberalizing agenda. UMNO claimed to be both pro-Islamic and pro-modernization, attracting support from many non-Malays who feared Islamic militancy. Mahathir retired in 2003 and his replacement, Abdullah Ahmad Badawi, tended to take a less nationalistic stance but proved unable to maintain mass support. In 2008 an opposition coalition of moderate Malay, liberal Chinese, and Islamist parties led by Anwar Ibrahim won nearly half of the seats in Parliament, shocking the National Front and demonstrating the potential to reshape the political system.

Malaysia has enjoyed considerable economic progress since 1970. Benefiting from abundant natural resources and entrepreneurial talent, high annual growth rates into the late 1990s enabled Malaysia to surpass nations like Portugal and Hungary in national wealth and to achieve a relatively high per capita income and considerable export-oriented light industry employing cheap labor. Rubber and tin still constitute the export mainstays, but these industries have faced competition from synthetic rubber and a decline in world demand for tin. As a result, Malaysian leaders promoted economic diversification, and timber, palm oil, and especially oil became valuable export commodities. At the same time, the manufacturing sector has grown rapidly, and Malaysians now build their own automobiles. But economic growth came at the price of toxic waste problems, severe deforestation, and air pollution. In 1997 the Malaysian economy, like those of its neighbors, collapsed but, partly by ignoring Western advice and imposing more government controls on the economy, Mahathir's policies restored high growth by the early twenty-first century.

The 1969 communal violence resulted in the New Economic Policy (NEP) aimed at redistributing more wealth to Malays, but average Malay incomes still lag considerably behind those of most Chinese while Tamil plantation workers and many Borneo Dayaks are often even poorer than Malays. The NEP fostered a substantial Malay middle class, but critics wondered whether most Malays benefited much.

In a 1966 novel, *No Harvest but a Thorn*, Malaysian writer Shahnon Ahmad described the fatalistic, inarticulate world of the Malay peasant, tied to the land and tradition while also struggling against the forces of nature to sustain a meager existence. But peasant life changed considerably in the years to follow. Rural development policies, including land schemes and mobile health clinics, improved life for many. By 2000 official poverty rates had dropped from some 50 percent in 1970 to around 20 percent, and life expectancy reached 71. Yet large pockets of urban and especially rural poverty remained. Better irrigation and mechanized equipment benefited many peasants, especially those with more capital, larger fields, and political connections, while others without connections faced less security, making for a growing gap in villages between rich and poor. Lack of rural employment prompted many Malays to migrate to towns, where they worked in low-paying jobs. Many young women labored in electronics and textile factories located in urban free-trade zones where foreign companies enjoy tax benefits to establish enterprises. The Malay rock group Kembara celebrated these hardworking people in a popular 1980s song: "Work, work, work. I am the blue collar worker/Machines have become my companions."[14] Migrants unable to find good jobs became part of urban life.

Today, some 40 percent of Malaysians live in cities and towns. More than 10 percent reside in bustling Kuala Lumpur, whose jammed freeways, glittering malls, downtown monorail, one of the world's tallest buildings, and high-rise condominiums contrast with growing shantytown squatter settlements and countless shabbily dressed street hawkers hoping to sell enough of their cheap wares to buy a meal. Since the 1980s televisions, stereos, and videocassette recorders have been nearly universal in the urban areas and increasingly common in the rural areas. Many Malaysians own personal computers and cell phones. The stresses of big city life are exacerbated by the nearly

1 million vehicles hitting the city streets every work day. The pervasive traffic congestion led to the expression: "Ours not to reason why, ours but to drive and sigh."

Malay society has become more diverse since the 1970s. Islamic resurgence has increasingly influenced public life, and Islamic movements with dogmatic, sometimes militant, views attracted the support of many young Malays, especially rural migrants to the city, alienated by a westernized, materialistic society and looking for an anchor in an uncertain world. These movements caused a deep rift between secular and devout Malays and today increasingly divide Muslims from Christians, Hindus, and Buddhists. These movements—which sometimes reject modern technology and products, discourage contact with non-Muslims, and require women to dress modestly—often alarm secular Malays and non-Muslims who view the movements as moving Malaysia backward. In response, Malay women's rights group use Islamic arguments to oppose restrictions favored by conservatives, and they find some support among the numerous women holding high government positions. Sisters of Islam, for example, founded in the 1980s by the politically well-connected academic Zainab Anwar, espouses an Islamic faith that supports freedom, justice, and equality and fights against strict interpretations of Muslim family law.

Youth alienation and unhappiness over job prospects were by-products of rapid development, but not all Malays chose religion as a bulwark. Some aimless, urban young people instead adopted selective features of Western popular culture, from punk hairstyles to "heavy metal" and rap music. Increasing numbers of teenagers and young adults, especially Malays, enjoyed "hanging out" at fast food restaurants, shopping malls, and public squares in order to relax, listen to music, and relieve tension after work or school. Meanwhile, many non-Malays resented government attempts to build national unity and identity, such as the increasing emphasis on Malay language in education and public life. Yet increasing numbers of non-Malays became fluent in Malay, the language of instruction in most schools and colleges.

Many patterns deeply rooted in history, such as cultural resilience, a genius for adaptation, and the incorporation of foreign peoples and ideas, remained important as Malaysians addressed the accelerating pace of change over the past few decades. They hoped to maintain stability and development benefiting all ethnic groups, address rural poverty, create a stronger sense of common Malaysian consciousness, and foster tolerance so that all Malaysians felt they had a continued place in one of Asia's most promising nations.

Malaysia and Singapore shared many historical and cultural links, but in 1965 Singapore, whose Chinese leaders had a different vision of the nation than did the Malay federal leaders, left the federation. Singapore became one of the world's smallest nations, situated on a tiny island 25 miles long and 15 miles wide. But the 5 million people were also among the world's most prosperous and productive, despite few resources. In Asia only Japan enjoyed a higher standard of living. Singaporeans could expect to live 80 years and enjoyed an adult literacy rate of 88 percent. The country's per cápita annual income of $10,000 was third only to that of Japan and Brunei in Asia and more than triple that of Malaysia, the next highest in Southeast Asia. With hardly any rural land remaining for farming, Singapore depended heavily on world trade. The predominance of Chinese, some 75 percent of the population, made Singapore unique in Southeast Asia and helped explain its separation from Malaysia, less than a mile away across the strait.

Singapore mixed freewheeling economic policies with an autocratic leadership that tightly controlled society. The country has been run like a giant corporation, efficient and ruthless. People pay a stiff fine if caught spitting, littering, or even tossing used chewing gum on the street. The rigid laws were satirized by a pop group, the Wah Lau Gang, in a song: "I cannot spit, cannot litter, chew chewing gum at all."[15] Lee Kuan Yew, a local-born, British-educated Chinese lawyer who led Singapore for nearly four decades, justified such restrictions by claiming that "Asian" values required stability over individualism and that Western-style democracy was dangerous in a diverse society vulnerable to more powerful neighbors.

The highly educated, enterprising population, combined with policies favoring economic growth and foreign investment, has turned Singapore into an industrializing economic powerhouse and world financial center. The city became a hub of light industry and high technology as well as headquarters for many corporations. It was also in the vanguard of the information revolution, becoming one of the world's most wired societies. Everyone studied English in school, and Singapore has world-class universities with international faculties. Business people and professionals from around the world flocked to this globalized city, just as they flocked to Srivijaya and Melaka centuries ago. Picturesque but congested Chinese commercial districts, village-like Malay neighborhoods, and farms have been replaced by high-rise apartment blocks, shopping complexes, food courts, professional buildings, luxury hotels, and multistory parking garages. One of the world's most modern cities, Singapore is also one of the world's healthiest societies, enjoying, for example, the world's lowest rate of infant mortality. But Singaporeans had to juggle their ethnic heritages with Singapore's cosmopolitan environment, a challenge discussed by one of the city-state's major artistic voices, Dick Lee, in a 1989 song: "Traditional, International/Western feelings from my oriental heart/How am I to know, how should I react?/ Defend with Asian pride? Or attack?/The mad Chinaman relies/On the east and west sides of his life."[16]

Increasingly middle class, few Singaporeans were interested, or willing to take the risks, in opposing the electoral system in which little serious internal opposition to the ruling party is permitted, despite a parliamentary structure. Only a few small opposition political parties and their courageous leaders have defied a rigged voting system by running for Parliament. Those who publicly challenge the government and its policies, however, face harassment, public humiliation, ruinous lawsuits, and even prison. Local and foreign critics believe Singapore must find better ways to balance rapid economic growth, increasing prosperity, and stability with more personal expression and tolerance toward dissent.

Even wealthier than Singapore, the tiny sultanate of Brunei, on the northwestern coast of Borneo, is a relic of history. Brunei, which became independent from Britain in 1984, would be an unremarkable backwater if it did not have large reserves of oil and gas. This oil supported one of the world's last absolute monarchies, an Islamic state in which the sultan, one of the world's richest men, ruled without opposition over a mostly Malay population with a Chinese minority of 20 percent. Oil wealth also produced the highest per capita income in Southeast Asia, some $23,000 a year, as well as high life expectancy (74 in 2000) and literacy rates. About 60 percent of the population of 350,000 lived in towns.

Brunei diversified its economy in agriculture and light industry while wisely investing the oil profits. However, the government has also restricted civil liberties, tolerated no opposition, and discouraged nonconformist ideas. Members of the royal family, factionalized between pro-Western modernizers and Islamic conservatives, hold most top positions. But corruption and wasteful spending tarnished their reputation. A growing educated middle class may one day tire of the lack of democracy. Meanwhile, the sultan maintains the support of the population by funding a generous welfare program including subsidized health care, housing, and food prices and free education through the university level. Bruneians live as if in a medieval sultanate but with modern conveniences.

After years of war and destruction, Vietnam faced a daunting challenge of reconstruction amid lingering tensions resulting from the bitter divisions. Political and economic mistakes by the government, natural disasters, a long U.S. economic embargo, and the devastation of the war all contributed to severe postwar problems. Between 1978 and 1985, 500,000 "boat people," many of them ethnic Chinese, risked their lives to escape Vietnam in rickety boats. Some faced death or harm at sea from pirates, storms, or hunger. After spending months or years in crowded refugee camps in Southeast Asia, most of the refugees were resettled in North America, Australia, or France. More than 1 million live in the United States today, many in "Little Saigon" neighborhoods in metropolitan areas like Los Angeles, San Jose, and Houston. Social-ist policies failed to revitalize the economy and the reunification of the country proved harsh. "The General Retires," a short story by former soldier Nguyen Huy Thiep published in Hanoi in 1987, caused a sensa-tion by depicting the despair of an old soldier contemplating the empti-ness of the society around him.

Vietnam's political life under communist rule has remained au-thoritarian, with little democracy in a one-party state. Although they fought a brief border war with China in 1978, the Vietnamese have also pragmatically pursued warmer relations with their northern neigh-bor and traditional enemy. Unlike politics, restrictions on cultural ex-pression loosened. Several former soldiers became rock and disco stars and many writers like Thiep addressed contemporary problems and the war's legacy in fiction. In the 1980s the Vietnamese government rec-ognized its economic failures and introduced market-oriented reforms similar to those in China favoring private enterprise and foreign invest-ment. These policies gradually increased productivity as well as foster-ing some prosperity, especially in the cities, and a life expectancy of 70 by 2000. The flow of refugees ended. Emphasis on education more than doubled literacy rates to 85 percent of adults.

But the shift from rigid socialism widened inequality as well, espe-cially between urban and rural areas. With most farmers still living just above the poverty line, Vietnamese debate about the appropriate bal-ance between socialist and free market policies to resolve rural poverty. Nguyen Huy Thiep described rural life in the 1980s in a short story, "Re-membrances of the Countryside": "I grew up in a village. [At] harvest time, my mother, my brother's wife, Ngu, Uncle Phung, and I are out in the fields by dawn. Those three cut, and I haul the rice home, following the edge of the path by the ditch. It's very bright outside, probably over 100 degrees. I haul ten loads of rice, which fill the courtyard."[17]

By the late 1990s, the United States and Vietnam had established diplomatic relations, with a former prisoner of war, Pete Peterson, serving as the first U.S. ambassador to Hanoi and the U.S. economic embargo lifted. Bustling Saigon, renamed Ho Chi Minh City, has enjoyed the most dynamic economic growth and prosperity in Vietnam. Vietnam as a whole has enjoyed spectacular economic growth since the late 1990s and is posed, many observers believe, to become another of the "tiger" economies. Many foreign companies have set up operations in industrial zones located in the suburbs of Hanoi and Saigon. Consumers in the United States now buy shrimp and underwear imported from Vietnam while many Americans, including former soldiers and Vietnamese refugees, visit Vietnam as tourists or to do business. Hundreds of American veterans of the Vietnam War operate businesses or social service agencies in Vietnam, sometimes in partnership with former communist soldiers. The process of healing the wounds of war has begun. But Vietnamese leaders have not yet been able to satisfy all the people's expectations for prosperity in a country devastated by decades of war, and the export-driven economy faced a downturn and job losses with the global economic crisis of 2008.

Laos, a poor country of nearly 6 million people, also needed to heal the divisions and destruction caused by war. For years after 1975 thousands of Lao, Mien, and Hmong fled into exile to escape potential retribution from Communist governments or hard times. Nearly

A statue of Ho Chi Minh, garlanded with flowers, sits in front of the Ho Chi Minh City (formerly Saigon) city hall. Contemporary Vietnamese still honor Ho as the revolutionary hero who led the forces that defeated the French and then the U.S. forces. Photo by Craig A. Lockard

300,000 Hmong now live in the United States. The war is still a reality, as every year several hundred people die from unexploded bombs and landmines that litter the countryside. Some of the policies followed by the Laotian regime since 1975 improved life, but others failed. While remaining allies of Vietnam, Laotian leaders have sought warmer relations with neighboring Thailand and China as well as the United States since the 1980s, but these relations have not fostered a more open society or energized the economy. The same group of rigid and reclusive communists who came to power in 1975 still dominates the one-party state. The modest prosperity generated by economic reforms including some economic liberalization, was found mainly in the Mekong valley cities. Increasing numbers of Western tourists also brought in money. Nonetheless, most Laotians have remained poor, living largely from subsistence agriculture, and life expectancy in 2000 was only 53 years. Small town schools often have dirt floors, few books, and no electricity. Watching much freer Thai television or looking across the Mekong at the busy freeways, neon lights, and high-rise buildings on the Thailand side, many Laotians may have concluded that prosperous but politically volatile Thailand and even China offered more successful models of development, but so far few opposition movements have surfaced.

Cambodia faced an even more difficult challenge of reconstruction than Laos, as war was followed there by fierce repression and genocide. Agriculture had been badly damaged by the brutal fighting and U.S. bombing, raising the specter of widespread starvation. When the communist Khmer Rouge, hardened by years of brutal war, achieved power in 1975, they turned on the urban population with a fury, deporting nearly everyone to the rural areas in an attempt to revive agriculture and punish their urban enemies. The Khmer Rouge's impractical, radical vision of a landless, classless peasant society, combined with violence toward those who were believed to dissent or resist, soon led to thousands of refugees and what survivors called the "killing fields." Ultimately the Khmer Rouge and their brutal leader, Pol Pot, were responsible, directly or indirectly, for the death of between 1.5 and 2 million Cambodians in their attempt to create a new communist society and destroy traditional culture. The Khmer Rouge executed perhaps 500,000, many in gruesome death camps, including common people such as peasants and taxi drivers as well as westernized and educated people, such as doctors and artists, sparking comparisons with Nazi Germany. Many more died from illness, hunger, and overwork.

Just surviving was an enormous achievement amidst the terror and poverty under the Khmer Rouge. Among the survivors were children.

One of these, Youkimmy Chan, who now lives in California, reflected on the death and hunger he experienced as a child in a remote village:

> Those who were not murdered by the soldiers were dying a slow death. We traded what little we had been able to hide for food from a government family. An ounce of gold would get us a cup of rice. Soon we had nothing left to trade. We were always hungry. We were always sick. . . . So many of us had been buried around the village that it was impossible to keep track of the burial places. . . . But now my mother was very sick. I was afraid she was dying. She spoke to me quietly. "Son, if you ever get away from the Communists, go to school. They can take away your possessions, but they can't take your education. They can't take what you know." Soon after that, my mother died. I wanted to die, too. . . . Now there was no one to take care of me. I don't know why I didn't die, too. I didn't want to live any more. I was so tired and so hungry. No one had hope.[18]

In 1978 the Vietnamese and an exile army of disaffected former Khmer Rouge invaded Cambodia and rapidly pushed the Khmer Rouge out of Phnom Penh to the Thailand border. The Vietnamese were alarmed at Khmer Rouge claims to Southern Vietnam and appalled by the genocide, which included the murder of thousands of ethnic Vietnamese living in Cambodia. The Vietnamese invasion liberated the Cambodian people from tyranny and installed a more moderate communist government that was closely tied to Vietnam. This government, eventually led by Khmer Rouge defector Hun Sen, introduced some market reforms and rebuilt a Buddhist culture battered by the Khmer Rouge.

But military conflict continued for years as a Khmer Rouge–dominated resistance coalition, subsidized chiefly by a China and United States anxious to weaken Vietnam by forcing it to spend money in Cambodia, controlled some sections of the country. Cambodia proved to be for Vietnam what Vietnam had been for the United States—an endless sinkhole of conflict that drained scarce wealth and complicated Vietnam's relations with the West. In the early 1990s a coalition government was formed under United Nations sponsorship. Eventually the isolated Khmer Rouge splintered, Pol Pot was murdered by colleagues, and most surviving leaders defected to the government side, claiming they had rejected the Khmer Rouge and its policies.

Although peace was welcomed by all, the Vietnam-backed government remained somewhat repressive and corrupt. Sihanouk returned from exile to become king but had little power and served largely as a symbol of Cambodia's link to its past. The ruling party has tolerated some limited opposition but also controlled the electoral system.

Although flawed as a democratic exercise, occasional elections have at least allowed the common people to select local officials. Cambodia's leaders, many of them former Khmer Rouge, have been reluctant to confront the Khmer Rouge legacy of genocide, and the schools teach little about the Khmer Rouge era. A decade of international efforts to bring the surviving top Khmer Rouge leaders to trial finally resulted in trials of a few aging men in 2008. Life for the 13 million Cambodians remains challenging as they face everything from expensive fuel to poor education, problems that have spurred some people to organize in support of more democracy and to call attention to growing social problems such as prostitution. Life in many rural villages remains grim, with no electricity or paved roads and few jobs. The country's life expectancy was around 57 by 2000. Even so, Cambodia, while still haunted by the horrors of the recent past, has been transformed from a traumatized to a functioning society, kept afloat largely by international aid and tourism.

In the twenty-first century the stresses and strains that challenge the unity of each Southeast Asian nation will surely continue to be complicated at times by pressures from the United States, China, and Japan as well as lingering tensions between communist and non-communist nations. With the United States distracted from the region and its prestige damaged by the wars in Afghanistan and Iraq, and the Japanese economy struggling, China has rapidly increased its ties to the region. Many hotels cater largely to businessmen from China. Most of the Southeast Asian nations now view China as the rising world power with which they must cooperate for regional stability. But Southeast Asians have been cooperating among themselves as never before through the Association of Southeast Asian Nations. ASEAN was founded in 1967 by Malaysia, Indonesia, Thailand, Singapore, and the Philippines to foster economic exchange among the noncommunist nations and coordinate opposition to communist Vietnam. However, ASEAN's priorities shifted after the end of the wars in Indochina in 1975. Eventually Vietnam, Cambodia, Laos, Burma, and Brunei became members as well, and ASEAN emerged as the world's fourth largest trading bloc. This regional organization has become a vehicle for military and political as well as economic cooperation, helping broker a Cambodian peace in the 1990s and making efforts (so far unsuccessful) to nudge Burma's government toward more respect for human rights. Despite the region's economic problems and political rivalries, ASEAN provided a structure for the various nations to work out their differences.

Nonetheless, even while working more closely together, the nations of Southeast Asia will most likely retain much of their distinctive characters, the products of rich and complex histories. Traditional rivalries will not disappear anytime soon. Soedjatmoko, an influential Indonesian diplomat and educator, was both a Javanese mystic and confirmed internationalist with a modern, global view. Before his death in 1989, he wrote in an essay, "The transformation of old societies into new nations inevitably leads to ultimate questions about the meaning of life on this earth, the legitimacy of the pursuit of material improvement, the relationship of the individual to other people, and the human relationship to the divine."[19] Most nations are still struggling to answer these questions, in the region's newfound atmosphere of peace and stability. As an old Malay proverb claims, however, "Do not be deceived into thinking that still water holds no crocodiles." But an Indonesian proverb offers an optimistic future: "There is no hill which cannot be climbed; there is no valley which cannot be crossed."

CHAPTER 11

Southeast Asia and the Wider World

The late nineteenth-century Philippine nationalist hero José Rizal claimed that to read the destiny of a people, it is necessary to open the book of their past. The Southeast Asian lands may no longer be as green nor the rivers as blue as they were centuries ago. But with their long, rich connections to the wider world and persistent ability to integrate ideas and institutions from abroad with indigenous traditions, Southeast Asians have made their mark on world history. Although outsiders imposed some influences, Southeast Asians also selected ideas that appealed to them. This process of exchange continues today as the world becomes even more linked through trade, communications, international organizations, migration, and travel. The influential Indonesian thinker Soedjatmoko, summing up the globalizing trends of the later twentieth century, described a world of "collapsing national boundaries and horrifying destructive power, expanding technological capacity and instant communication [in which] we live in imperfect intimacy with all our fellow human beings."[1]

Southeast Asians have contributed to and engaged with the wider world from early in their history. Maritime trade linked the earliest societies to China, India, and beyond. The Golden Age kingdoms and their successors attracted visitors from afar. Many centuries before the first European adventurers sailed into the Straits of Melaka, Southeast Asia was part of a larger Afro-Eurasian economy, and European activity made Southeast Asia an even more crucial part of the developing world economy after 1500. By the early twentieth century, the various Southeast Asian societies had become part of a global system dominated economically and politically by various Western European nations and the United States, connecting these peoples more firmly than ever before to global patterns and networks.

Expanding Western imperial power and the much greater degree of integration of Southeast Asians into the rapidly expanding world economy had profound consequences for political, economic, social, and cultural life, greatly reducing their autonomy and challenging traditional patterns. Colonialism transferred much wealth from Southeast Asia to the West. The exploitation of their colonies in Southeast Asia and elsewhere increased Western wealth and power and, indeed, spurred Western modernization generally. In the past two centuries, millions of people from other regions of Asia, especially China and India, migrated into Southeast Asia temporarily or permanently, to work in plantation agriculture, mining, or trade. The end of colonialism has not dramatically altered the essential structure of the world economy, and Southeast Asians still mostly export natural resources to, and import manufactured goods from, Europe, North America, and Japan, but some nations have seen considerable economic growth and substantial industrialization and now ship their products around the world.

The traffic in ideas and influences has never been entirely one way either, for Southeast Asians have also influenced the wider world. Some of the earliest anticolonial nationalism outside of the Americas emerged in the nineteenth-century Philippines. The Philippine struggle against the Spanish, and later U.S. forces, was an inspiration to many colonized peoples in Asia. The attempt by the United States to crush the Philippine Revolution, while successful, has many parallels to the later ill-fated American experience in Vietnam. The Indonesian Revolution against the Dutch in the 1940s also had electrifying global effects, forcing a major colonial power to abandon its control while giving hope to colonized Africans. Later the Vietnamese communists under Ho Chi Minh, in their ultimately successful 45-year fight against French colonialism, Japanese occupation, and then U.S. intervention, stimulated a wave of revolutionary efforts around the world to overthrow Western domination. The Vietnamese struggle also inspired a surge of student militancy in Europe and North America in the 1960s, with a few of the more radical shouting slogans in praise of Ho Chi Minh while protesting against war and inequality. The fact that the Filipino nationalist José Rizal, partly Chinese in ancestry, had lived for a time in Spain and Germany, and Ho Chi Minh, the son of a mandarin, had lived in London, Paris, and Moscow as a young man, also shows how interconnected the world had become.

Since 1902, in fact, several million Southeast Asians have settled in the United States, Canada, Australia, and Europe, many as refugees from the wars fought by Americans in Indochina. By 2000 there were nearly 5 million people of Southeast Asian origin or ancestry in the United States, including 2.5 million Filipinos, 1.3 million Vietnamese, 400,000

Laotians, 200,000 Cambodians, 63,000 Indonesians, 150,000 Thais, and more than 20,000 immigrants from Malaysia and Singapore.

The Vietnamese communist defeat of the United States and its South Vietnamese ally in 1975 marked the decline, at least for a time, of America's unrivaled economic, political, and military power in the world. It took some years for the United States to recover at home from the social divisions, economic problems, and political uncertainties fostered by the wars in Indochina. In some ways, despite normalization of United States–Vietnamese relations that led to American fast food restaurants in Vietnam and American tourists visiting such wartime sites as the Cu Chi tunnels near Ho Chi Minh City, once used by communist guerrillas, and the "Hanoi Hilton" POW prison, the war has still not ended for many Americans and Indochinese refugees. The Vietnamese American poet Le Thi Diem Thuy complained about narrow American attitudes toward her ancestral country, pleading to let people know that Vietnam is not a war but a country full of people.

Southeast Asia still provides critical resources needed by the world. The gold, pepper, and spices of earlier centuries have been largely replaced by oil, timber, rubber, rice, tin, sugar, and palm oil. Although Southeast Asians export the same natural resources they did in colonial times, some nations have enjoyed dramatic economic growth through industrialization and exploitation of other resources such as oil and timber. The region's role in the world economy has also changed. Beginning in the 1970s Malaysia, Thailand, Singapore, and Indonesia fostered some of the fastest growing economies in the world, interrupted only by the Asian economic meltdown of the late 1990s, and they have recently been joined by Vietnam. They did so by combining their natural resource exports, such as timber and oil, with industrialization aimed at producing products for export. Foreign investors poured money into these emerging economies, while more and more workers produced manufactured goods like shoes, clothing, computer chips, and sports equipment for European and American markets. These "tigers," with their distinctive mix of free-market and state-stimulated economies with semiauthoritarian politics, may offer the best available model for development in the global south. Several countries in Asia, Africa, and Latin America have borrowed ideas from the Southeast Asian "tigers" in their own attempts to spur development. Meanwhile, companies based in Malaysia and Singapore have operations around the world.

In recent decades, rural villages, in addition to the cities, have been more closely tied to the ups and downs of the world economy. Capitalism, with its emphasis on competition, has undermined the traditional values of cooperation and community. More crime, conflict, and alienation have reduced the once powerful sense of community responsibility and cohesion. A much smaller percentage of Southeast Asians remain rural dwellers today than a century ago. Today some 35 to 40 percent of people live in cities and towns. Except for Indonesia and Vietnam, which have several large cities, all the countries in the region are dominated instead by one huge metropolis—such as Bangkok, Manila, Kuala Lumpur, Phnom Penh, or Rangoon (Yangon). The cities are open to global culture and are a multilingual home to a variety of ethnic groups, migrants from all over the country, and foreign residents. Most Southeast Asians live very differently than their ancestors did centuries ago, but there are also ideas and customs that would be familiar to earlier peoples.

Although the continuities with the past are important, engagement with the outside world also shaped modern Southeast Asia. In the cities, global influences and economic development increasingly affect many lives. The resident of an upscale suburb of Kuala Lumpur, Bangkok, or Manila working in a high-rise, air-conditioned office reached by driving a late-model sports car along the crowded freeways clearly has a way of life and outlook vastly different from the few thousand remaining hunters and gatherers living in remote mountains. And the urbanite connected through her home computer or an Internet café to the "information superhighway" has little in common with the peasant villager whose life revolves around traditional social and cultural networks.

To live in Kuala Lumpur, Singapore, or Manila is to potentially experience a lifestyle with many features familiar to most citizens of Western nations, with malls, freeways, supermarkets, boutiques, home computers, color televisions, Hard Rock Cafés, and Planet Hollywoods. Even rural areas, while maintaining many age-old values and traditions, are seeing major changes, as locals can now buy everything from transistor radios, outboard motors, and motor scooters to telephones and sewing machines. Foreign tourists from the West or Japan increasingly visit remote villages in places like Laos, Sulawesi, and Sarawak, inevitably taking Western ideas and products into these traditional cultures. These encounters tie rural peoples more closely to the cities and the rest of the world. In addition, many people growing up in a Southeast Asian city have some familiarity with the local indigenous languages and perhaps several Chinese dialects as well as a Western language such as English or French.

Looking at the modern and westernized neighborhoods of cities can be misleading, however, and change is often mixed with continuity. One can leave a luxury hotel in Bangkok or Jakarta and walk into poor neighborhoods, where restaurants have loudspeakers, microphones, and cold beer but also traditional music and dance as well as fiery hot curries. And many urbanites maintain ties to the villages of their parents or grandparents. On national holidays the highways leading out of Kuala Lumpur or Manila are jammed with city dwellers heading to their native villages or towns for a visit. Middle-class city dwellers often find themselves perched uneasily between the cooperative village values of the past and the competitive, materialistic concerns of the modern world. A lament by the Indonesian poet Intje Hassan reflected the tension between tradition and modernity in Jakarta:

> This is no slum
> Only a village
> Four hundred years old
> Dipped in modernity
> Granted a . . . quantum of kilowatts
> For streetlamps
> To chase shadows
> . . . Prostitutes . . . in darkness waiting
> Nightclubs and casinos opening
> To pass the leisure time
> . . . The frustrated generation, waiting
> Of enormous problems to overcome
> in the developed city.[2]

Older ways of thinking and interacting can often be seen amid the modernity, even in the cities. Most urban youth, despite an affection for blue jeans, video games, and rock music, hold many traditional values including respect for, and deference to, parents as well as to authority generally. They may share the pastimes and fads of North American or European students, but they do not necessarily inhabit the same social, cultural, and intellectual environment. For every youngster who joins the fan club for a Western pop star, another identifies with an Islamic, Buddhist, or Christian organization, possibly a militant one. Sometimes the same person might have both allegiances. This cosmopolitan flavor of the region was apparent many centuries ago to travelers and traders and remains a prominent feature today.

The mixing of old and new, local and imported, is perhaps most obvious in popular music and culture. In the past four decades Southeast Asians have developed a wide variety of popular music styles, all with different audiences. Some styles use traditional songs and instruments while others sound like the music enjoyed by Western audiences. But

Some residents of Ho Chi Minh City have found creative ways to transport an entire family on one motor scooter. The fast-growing cities of Southeast Asia are centers for modernization and industrialization, their streets clogged with traffic. Photo by Craig A. Lockard

whether rooted in local or imported styles, popular music has become a major component of the background of daily life. Today in Indonesia or Thailand or the Philippines, at any hour you can hear pop music in villages, shopping centers, and music stores. Posters of pop stars are displayed in cities and remote villages, in the rooms of teenagers and adults. Shop owners and roadside traders seize any opportunity to sell these posters as well as calendars, exercise book covers, even matchboxes featuring singers. Pop music has planted itself firmly in the local soil, with some musicians offering songs about poverty, corruption, environmental destruction, and the virtues of rural life, themes that appeal to many listeners.

Both imported films—especially from India, Hong Kong, and the United States—and locally made films have also been hugely popular throughout the region, and Indonesia, Thailand, and the Philippines have large filmmaking industries. These countries have produced some cutting-edge films, although most filmmakers have sought a mass audience, churning out entertaining fare criticized by one world-renowned Filipino producer, Lino Brocka, as "kiss-kiss, bang-bang, zoom, boo-hoo, song and dance flickers."[3] Some films, however, deal with historical issues as part of the quest for identity, and in 2007 Thais eagerly watched a spectacular, big-budget, three-part epic on the heroics of sixteenth-century King Naresuan of Ayatthaya, who is believed to have led the Siamese defense against repeated Burmese invasions. Historians debated the historical accuracy of the account but agreed that the series boosted Thai pride and nationalist feeling in the face of rampant globalization.

Even as popular culture reaches across the borders in Southeast Asia, long-established national rivalries continue, as they have for centuries. The Vietnamese still worry about China and compete with Thailand, while the Cambodians and Burmese look at all their neighbors warily. Traditional patterns of political power survive at local levels, with landlords and businessmen controlling rural government in Thailand and the Philippines, for example. Some national leaders also act in traditional ways. Cambodia's Prince Sihanouk could be perceived as resembling an Indianized god-king, Indonesia's President Sukarno as a Javanese symbolic leader, and Vietnamese communist officials as Confucian mandarins.

And yet the nature of government has changed dramatically in all of these countries. Governments have much more contact with citizens and are more bureaucratic than in earlier centuries. People live within fixed borders in countries administered from a large capital city where bureaucrats and the media try to unify diverse populations. These nations each have national myths, flags, anthems, and currencies. And yet, just as premodern states collapsed or were fractured by civil war, new states still appear today. In 2002 newly independent East Timor, a small, impoverished territory that had successfully left Indonesia, held its first presidential election. Perhaps in the future some other restless region of Indonesia such as Acheh will continue the process of reconfiguring the political map by secession. Only two hereditary monarchs remain, the king of Thailand and the Sultan of Brunei, although Malaysia has elected kings with little power. And only Brunei remains an absolute monarchy. The current Thai king, Bhumibol, has a common touch and is an accomplished jazz clarinetist and composer. There are other changes as well. Women have always played an influential role in many societies and women like Corazon Aquino in the Philippines, Megawati Soekarnoputri in Indonesia, and Aung San Suu Kyi in Burma have become political leaders. In most places, government reaches far deeper than it did 300 years ago, and almost all modern leaders have been influenced to some degree by Western ideas, among them the communists who adopted a Western Marxist world view. And yet, as with Vietnamese or

Indonesian communists, Western ideas were often blended with traditional views such as Confucianism or Islam. Given the mix of influences, as well as the challenges facing the region's leaders, Western observers often misunderstand Southeast Asia when they try to impose their notions of how democratic systems or market economies must work, or in assuming that Southeast Asians should necessarily share all their priorities and perspectives.

An old and much loved Indonesian folk song about the Solo River in central Java related the green lands to the blue waters and the local people to the wider world: "Solo River, ancient your histories span. Linking present to past, linking the life of the soil and man. In the summer's heat your streams are sluggish and slow. In the rainy season's height far afield your banks overflow. Now you flow on through fertile rice fields, down to the sea at last. Here are ships of trade, and when your journey's over, sailors brave the ocean wide, seeking some far distant shore."[4] Today, in an increasingly globalized economy and culture, institutions, ideas, ways of life, and traditions are colliding, blending, and even sometimes disappearing. The fried-noodle vendor on the roadside must compete with the nearby flashy fast-food restaurant. The mosque or temple may sit next door to a shopping mall or an Internet café. Action movies, racy novels, and soccer matches compete with *Qu'ran*-reading competitions, shadow plays, and cockfights. But the process of mixing old and new, local and imported, began for Southeast Asians many centuries ago as the region and its peoples were connected, directly or indirectly, to other Asian peoples and to societies all over the Eastern Hemisphere and, after 1500, to the Western Hemisphere as well. The Solo River still flows to the sea, where ships, joined today by airplanes laden with goods from the green lands and travelers, still link Southeast Asians over the waters of blue to other parts of the world.

Chronology

40,000 BCE
Arrival of modern humans

8000–6000 BCE
Earliest agriculture in Southeast Asia (controversial)

4000–2000 BCE
Austronesian migrations into Southeast Asia

2000–1500 BCE
Beginning of Bronze Age in Southeast Asia

1000–800 BCE
First Southeast Asian states

111 BCE–939 CE
Chinese colonization of Vietnam

CA. 60–540 CE
Funan dynasties

192–1460 CE
Champa kingdom or states

802–CA. 1440
Angkor Empire

1044–1287
Pagan kingdom in Burma

1222–1451
Madjapahit kingdom in Java

1238–CA. 1420
Sukhotai kingdom in Siam

1350–1767
Ayutthaya kingdom in Siam

1403–1511
Melaka sultanate

1511–1641
Portuguese conquer and rule Melaka

1565
Spanish conquest of Philippines

1619
Dutch establish a base at Batavia (Jakarta)

1752–1885
Konbaung dynasty in Burma

1767–PRESENT
Chakri dynasty in Bangkok

1786
British establish base at Penang Island

1778–1802
Tayson rebellion in Vietnam

1802–1884
Nguyen dynasty rules Vietnam

1819
British establish base at Singapore

1823–1826
First Anglo-Burman War

1857–1884
French conquer Vietnam

1863
France establishes a protectorate over Cambodia

1868–1910
Kingship of Chulalongkorn in Siam

1886
British conquer Burma

1897
France combines Vietnam, Cambodia, and Laos into Federation of Indochina

1898–1902
United States conquers the Philippines

1932
Nationalists take power in Thailand

1941–1945
Japanese occupation of Southeast Asia

1945–1949
Indonesian Revolution

1946
Philippines gains independence from the United States

1946–1954
First Indochina War

1948
Burma gains independence from Britain

1950
Indonesia gains independence from the Netherlands

1962
Military under General Ne Win seizes power in Burma

1963
Malaya, Singapore, Sabah, and Sarawak form Malaysia

1963–1975
U.S.-Vietnamese War

1965
Singapore secedes from Malaysia

1966–1998
New Order government of General Suharto in Indonesia

1972–1986
Marcos dictatorship in Philippines

1975
Communist victories in Vietnam, Cambodia, and Laos

1975–1979
Khmer Rouge rule Cambodia

1999
East Timorese vote for independence from Indonesia

2005
Tsunami kills 130,000 people, mostly in Indonesia

Notes

INTRODUCTION

1. Quoted in O. W. Wolters, *History, Culture, and Region in Southeast Asian Perspectives*, revised ed. (Ithaca, N.Y.: Southeast Asia Program, Cornell University, 1999), 73.

CHAPTER ONE

1. Amado V. Hernandez, *Rice Grains: Selected Poems* (New York: International Publishers, 1966), 34.
2. Quoted in Barbara Watson Andaya, "Oceans Unbounded: Transversing Asia Across 'Area Studies,' " *Journal of Asian Studies* 65, no. 4 (November 2006): 677.
3. Quoted in Nguyen Ngoc Binh, "The Power and Relevance of Vietnamese Myths," in David Elliott et al., *Vietnam: Essays on History, Culture and Society* (New York: Asia Society, 1985), 62.

CHAPTER TWO

1. Quoted in Paul Wheatley, *The Golden Khersonese: Studies in the Historical Geography of the Malay Peninsula Before A.D. 1500* (Kuala Lumpur: University of Malaya Press, 1966), 177–178.
2. Quoted in ibid., 38.
3. Harry J. Benda and John A. Larkin, eds., *The World of Southeast Asia: Selected Historical Readings* (New York: Harper and Row, 1967), 6.
4. Quoted in Paul Wheatley, *Impressions of the Malay Peninsula in Ancient Times* (Singapore: Eastern Universities Press, 1964), 56.
5. Quoted in Lawrence Palmer Briggs, *The Ancient Khmer Empire* (Philadelphia: American Philosophical Society, 1951), 22, 29.
6. Quoted in Lynda Norene Shaffer, *Maritime Southeast Asia to 1500* (Armonk, N.Y.: M.E. Sharpe, 1996), 23.
7. Quoted in Charles Higham, *The Civilization of Angkor* (Berkeley: University of California Press, 2001), 41.
8. Quoted in Kenneth R. Hall, *Maritime Trade and State Development in Early Southeast Asia* (Honolulu: University of Hawai'i Press, 1985), 179.
9. Quoted in Keith Taylor, "The Rise of Dai Viet and the Establishment of Thang-Long," in Kenneth R. Hall and John K. Whitmore, eds., *Explorations in Early Southeast Asian History: The Origins of Southeast Asian Statecraft* (Ann Arbor, Mich.: Center for South and Southeast Asian Studies, University of Michigan, 1976), 153.
10. Quoted in Thomas Hodgkin, *Vietnam: The Revolutionary Path* (New York: St. Martin's, 1981), 22.
11. Nguyen Ngoc Bich, ed., *A Thousand Years of Vietnamese Poetry* (New York: Alfred A. Knopf, 1975), 89.
12. Quoted in O. W. Wolters, *Early Indonesian Commerce: A Study of the Origins of Srivijaya* (Ithaca, N.Y.: Cornell University Press, 1967), 60, 44.

CHAPTER THREE

1. Quoted in Wheatley, *Impressions of Malay Peninsula*, 70.

2. Quoted in ibid., 71.

3. Quoted in Janet Hoskins, *The Play of Time: Kodi Perspectives on Calendars, History, and Exchange* (Berkeley: University of California Press, 1993), 29.

4. Quoted in Virginia Matheson Hooker, *A Short History of Malaysia: Linking East and West* (Crows Nest, NSW, Australia: Allen and Unwin, 2003), 33.

5. Benda and Larkin, *World of Southeast Asia*, 38.

6. Quoted in W. Robert Moore, "Angkor, Jewel of the Jungle," *National Geographic*, 117, no. 4 (April 1960): 540.

7. Quoted in Christopher Pym, *The Ancient Civilization of Angkor* (New York: Mentor, 1968), 118.

8. Quoted in Higham, *Civilization of Angkor*, 3.

9. Quoted in David Chandler, *A History of Cambodia*, 2nd ed., updated (Boulder, Colo.: Westview, 1996), 74.

10. Quoted in Stephen O. Murray, *Angkor Life* (San Francisco: Bua Luang Books, 1996), 32.

11. Quoted in *Southeast Asia: A Past Regained* (Alexandria, Va.: Time-Life Books, 1995), 106.

12. Quoted in ibid., 105.

13. Quoted in D. G. E. Hall, *A History of South-East Asia*, 4th ed. (New York: St. Martin's, 1981), 169.

14. Quoted in Michael Aung-Thwin, *Pagan: The Origins of Modern Burma* (Honolulu: University of Hawai'i Press, 1985), 41.

15. Benda and Larkin, *World of Southeast Asia*, 45–46.

16. Quoted in D. G. E. Hall, *History of South-East Asia*, 101.

17. Quoted in Helen Creese, *Women of the Kakawin World: Marriage and Sexuality in the Indic Courts of Java and Bali* (Armonk, N.Y.: M. E. Sharpe, 2004), 44.

18. Frederick Hirth and W. W. Rockhill, *Chau Ju-Kua: His Work on the Chinese and Arab Trade in the Twelfth and Thirteenth Centuries*, entitled *Chu-fan-chi*, reprint edition (Taipei: Literature House, 1965), 76–78.

19. Quoted in Jean Gelman Taylor, *Indonesia: Peoples and Histories* (New Haven, Conn.: Yale University Press, 2003), 99.

20. Quoted in Nguyen Ngoc Bich, *Thousand Years*, 11.

CHAPTER FOUR

1. Quoted in Anthony Reid, *Southeast Asia in the Age of Commerce*, Vol. 2: *Expansion and Crisis* (New Haven, Conn.: Yale University Press, 1993), 10.

2. Benda and Larkin, *World of Southeast Asia*, 41.

3. Quoted in G. William Skinner, *Chinese Society in Thailand: An Analytical History* (Ithaca, N.Y.: Cornell University Press, 1957), 8.

4. Klaus Wenk, *Thai Literature: An Introduction* (Bangkok: White Lotus, 1995), 14–16.

5. Quoted in David Wyatt, *Thailand: A Short History*, 2nd ed. (New Haven, Conn.: Yale University Press, 2003), 120.

6. Michael Smithies, *Descriptions of Old Siam* (New York: Oxford University Press, 1995), 91.

7. Benda and Larkin, *World of Southeast Asia*, 93.

8. Smithies, *Descriptions*, 14.

9. Nguyen Ngoc Bich, *Thousand Years*, 46–47.

10. Truong Buu Lam, *Patterns of Vietnamese Response to Foreign Intervention: 1858–1900* (New Haven, Conn.: Southeast Asia Studies, Yale University, 1967), 53.

11. Quoted in Ralph Smith, *Viet-Nam and the West* (Ithaca, N.Y.: Cornell University Press, 1968), 9.

12. M. N. Pearson, "Introduction," in Pearson, ed., *Spices in the Indian Ocean World* (Aldershot, U.K.: Valorium, 1996), xv.

13. Quoted in Wolters, *History, Culture, and Region*, 45.

14. Quoted in Sanjay Subrahmanyam, "And a River Runs Through it: The Mrauk U Kingdom and its Bay of Bengal Context," in *The Maritime Frontier of Burma: Exploring Political, Cultural and Commercial Interaction in the Indian Ocean World, 1200–1800*, ed. Jos Gommans and Jacques Leider (Leiden, the Netherlands: KITLV Press, 2002), 107.

15. Quoted in Wang Gungwu, "The Opening of Relations between China and Malacca, 1403–05," in *Admiral Zheng He and Southeast Asia*, ed. Leo Suryadinata (Singapore: Institute of Southeast Asian Studies, 2005), 16.

16. Quoted in Sarnia Hayes Hoyt, *Old Malacca* (New York: Oxford University Press, 1993), 18.

17. Quoted in Wheatley, *Golden Khersonese*, 313.

18. Quoted in Haji Buyong Adil, *The History of Malacca During the Period of the Malay Sultanate* (Kuala Lumpur: Dewan Bahasa dan Pustaka, 1974), 18.

19. Quoted in K. G. Tregonning, *A History of Modern Malaya* (Singapore: Eastern Universities Press, 1964), 42.

20. Quoted in Richard Winstedt, *The Malays: A Cultural History* (London: Routledge and Kegan Paul, 1961), 159.

21. Quoted in Andaya, "Oceans Unbounded," 682–683.

22. Quoted in Anthony Reid, *Southeast Asia in the Age of Commerce*, Vol. 1: *The Lands Below the Winds* (New Haven, Conn.: Yale University Press, 1988), 1.

23. Quoted in Anthony Reid, *Charting the Shape of Early Modern Southeast Asia* (Bangkok: Silkworm Books, 1999), 218.

24. Quoted in Ian Mabbett and David Chandler, *The Khmers* (Cambridge, U.K.: Blackwell, 1995), 224.

25. Quoted in Hall, *Maritime Trade*, 210.

CHAPTER FIVE

1. Quoted in Anthony Reid, "Early Southeast Asian Categorizations of Europeans," in *Implicit Understandings*, ed. Stuart B. Schwartz (Cambridge, U.K.: Cambridge University Press, 1994), 275.

2. Quoted in Tregonning, *History of Modern Malaya*, 43.

3. John Bastin, ed., *The Emergence of Modern Southeast Asia: 1511–1957* (Englewood Cliffs, N.J.: Prentice -Hall, 1967), 13.

4. Benda and Larkin, *World of Southeast Asia*, 78.

5. Quoted in Nicholas Tarling, "Mercantilism and Missionaries: Impact and Accommodation," in *Eastern Asia: An Introductory History*, ed. Colin Mackerras, 3rd ed. (Frenches Forest, NSW, Australia: Longman, 2000), 115.

6. J. M. Gullick, ed., *Adventures and Encounters: Europeans in South-East Asia* (New York: Oxford University Press, 1995), 11.

7. Quoted in Stanley Karnow, *Southeast Asia* (New York: Time Incorporated, 1962), 42.

8. Gullick, *Adventures*, 235.

9. Quoted in Laura Lee Junker, *Raiding, Trading, and Feasting: The Political Economy of Philippine Chiefdoms* (Honolulu: University of Hawai'i Press, 1999), 31.

10. Quoted in David Joel Steinberg, *The Philippines: A Singular and a Plural Place*, 3rd ed. (Boulder, Colo.: Westview, 1994), 82.

11. Quoted in Christine Dobbin, *Asian Entrepreneurial Minorities: Conjoint Communities in the Making of the World Economy, 1750–1914* (Richmond, U.K.: Curzon, 1996), 23.

12. Quoted in Carolyn Brewer, "From Animist 'Priestess' to Catholic Priest: The Re/gendering of Religious Roles in the Philippines, 1521–1685," in *Other Pasts: Women, Gender and History in Early Modern Southeast Asia*, ed. Barbara Watson Andaya (Center for Southeast Asian Studies, University of Hawai'i at Manoa, 2000), 69.

13. Quoted in Reynaldo Ileto, *Payson and Revolution: Popular Movements in the Philippines, 1840–1910* (Quezon City: Ateneo de Manila University Press, 1979), 16–18.

14. Quoted in Patricia Risso, *Merchants and Faith: Muslim Commerce and Culture in the Indian Ocean* (Boulder, Colo.: Westview, 1995), 81.

15. Quoted in Felipe Fernandez-Armesto, *Millennium: A History of the Last Thousand Years* (New York: Scribner, 1995), 234.

16. Quoted in Alisa Zainu'ddin, *A Short History of Indonesia* (Sydney: Cassell Australia, 1968), 88.

17. Quoted in Reid, *Southeast Asia in Age of Commerce*, 1:164.

18. Benda and Larkin, *World of Southeast Asia*, 127.

19. Quoted in Reid, *Southeast Asia in Age of Commerce*, 2:267.

CHAPTER SIX

1. Quoted in Paul Bennett, *Conference Under the Tamarind Tree: Three Essays in Burmese History* (New Haven, Conn.: Southeast Asia Studies, Yale University, 1971), 129.

2. Quoted in Hooker, *Short History of Malaysia*, 131.

3. Benda and Larkin, *World of Southeast Asia*, 128.

4. Quoted in Benedict O'Gorman Anderson, "A Time of Darkness and a Time of Light: Transpositions in Early Indonesian Nationalist Thought," in *Perceptions of the Past in Southeast Asia*, ed. Anthony Reid and David Marr (Singapore: Heinemann Educational Books, 1979), 219.

5. Quoted in Adrian Vickers, *A History of Modern Indonesia* (New York: Cambridge University Press, 2005), 11.

6. Quoted in Margaret J. Wiener, *Visible and Invisible Realms: Power, Magic, and Colonial Conquest in Bali* (Chicago: University of Chicago Press, 1995), 315.

7. Quoted in Truong Buu Lam, *Resistance, Rebellion, Rebellion: Popular Movements in Vietnamese History* (Singapore: Institute of Southeast Asian Studies, 1984), 11.

8. Huynh Sanh Thong, ed., *An Anthology of Vietnamese Poems: From the Eleventh through the Twentieth Centuries* (New Haven, Conn: Yale University Press, 1996), 214.

9. Quoted in Helen B. Lamb, *Vietnam's Will to Live: Resistance to Foreign Aggression from Early Times through the Nineteenth Century* (New York: Monthly Review Press, 1972), 134.

10. Quoted in Lamb, *Vietnam's Will to Resist*, 152.

11. Huynh Sanh Thong, *Anthology*, 88.

12. Quoted in Truong Buu Lam, *Patterns of Vietnamese Resistance*, 8.

13. Quoted in Lamb, *Vietnam's Will to Live*, 229.

14. Quoted in Jeremy Davidson, "'Good Omens Versus Worth': The Poetic Dialogue Between Ton Tho Tuong and Phan Van Tri," in *Context, Meaning and Power in Southeast Asia*, ed. Mark Hobart and Robert Taylor (Ithaca, N.Y.: Southeast Asia Program, Cornell University, 1986), 72.

15. Quoted in James W. Trullinger, *Village at War: An Account of Conflict in Vietnam* (Stanford, Calif.: Stanford University Press, 1994), 18.

16. Quoted in James C. Scott, *The Moral Economy of the Peasant: Rebellion and Subsistence in Southeast Asia* (New Haven, Conn.: Yale University Press, 1976), 236.

17. Quoted in David Joel Steinberg et al., *In Search of Southeast Asia: A Modern History* (Honolulu: University of Hawai'i Press, 1987), 126.

18. Quoted in ibid., 105.

19. Quoted in Frank N. Trager, *Burma from Kingdom to Republic: A Historical and Political Analysis* (New York: Frederick A. Praeger, 1966), 42.

20. Gullick, *Adventures*, 77.

21. Benda and Larkin, *World of Southeast Asia*, 169.

22. Ibid., 177–179.

23. Quoted in Steinberg, *Philippines*, 64.

24. Quoted in Teodoro A. Agoncillo, *A Short History of the Philippines* (New York: Mentor, 1969), 93.

25. Quoted in Mina Roces, "Reflections on Gender and Kinship in the Philippine Revolution, 1896–1898," in *The Philippine Revolution of 1896: Ordinary Lives in Extraordinary Times*, ed. Florentina Rodao and Felice Noelle Rodriguez (Quezon City: Ateneo de Manila Press, 2001), 34.

26. Quoted in Barbara Watson Andaya, "Gender, Warfare, and Patriotism in Southeast Asia and in the Philippine Revolution," in Radao and Rodriguez, *Philippine Revolution*, 11.

27. Quoted in Craig A. Lockard, "Gunboat Diplomacy, Counterrevolution, and Manifest Destiny: A Century of Asian Preludes to the American War in Vietnam," *Asian Profiles*, 23, no. 1 (February 1995): 39.

28. Quoted in Carl Parrini, "Theories of Imperialism," in *Redefining the Past: Essays in Diplomatic History in Honor of William Appleman Williams*, ed. Lloyd Garner (Corvallis: Oregon State University, 1985), 73.

29. Quoted in Steinberg, *In Search*, 274.

30. Quoted in Sinharaja Tammita-Delgoda, *A Traveler's History of India*, 2nd ed. (New York: Interlink, 1999), 173.

31. Quoted in Daniel B. Schirmer, *Republic or Empire: American Resistance to the Philippine War* (Cambridge, U.K.: Schenkman, 1972), 237.

32. Quoted in Vidda Mayne, "Songs of Dissent and the Music of Agitation," *Far Eastern Economc Review* (February 14, 1985), 67.

33. Quoted in Noam Chomsky, "The United States and Indochina: Far from an Aberration," in *Coming to Terms: Indochina, the United States, and the War*, ed. Douglas Allen and Ngo Vinh Long (Boulder, Colo.: Westview), 165–166.

34. Quoted in David Howard Bain, *Sitting in the Darkness: Americans in the Philippines* (Baltimore, Md.: Penguin, 1986), 2.

35. Quoted in Gary R. Hess, *Vietnam and the United States: Origins and Legacy of War* (Boston: Twayne, 1990), 25.

36. Quoted in Steinberg, *In Search*, 276.

CHAPTER SEVEN

1. Quoted in Ngo Vinh Long, *Before the Revolution: The Vietnamese Peasants Under the French* (New York: Columbia University Press, 1991), v.

2. Quoted in Nicholas Tarling, *Southeast Asia: A Modern History* (New York: Oxford University Press, 2001), 184.

3. Tran Tu Binh, *The Red Earth: A Vietnamese Memoir of Life on a Colonial Rubber Plantation*, trans. John Spragens Jr. (Athens: Center for International Studies, Ohio University, 1985), 26.

4. Quoted in Ian Brown, *Economic Change in South-East Asia, c. 1830–1980* (New York: Oxford University Press, 1997), 130.

5. Quoted in Cheah Boon Kheng, *The Peasant Robbers of Kedah, 1900–1929: Historical and Folk Perceptions* (New York: Oxford University Press, 1988), 60.

6. Quoted in Norman Owen, ed., *The Emergence of Modern Southeast Asia: A New History* (Honolulu: University of Hawai'i Press, 2005), 197.

7. Raden Adjeng Kartini, *Letters of a Javanese Princess*, edited with an introduction by Hildred Geertz (New York: W. W. Norton, 1964), 34, 42, 45, 73.

8. Hajjah Maimunah H. Daud, "Bangsawan Down Memory Lane," *Sarawak Gazette* (September 1993): 14–18.

9. Armijn Pane, *Shackles: A Novel by Armijn Pane*, trans. John H. McGlynn (Athens: Ohio University Center for International Studies, 1985), 102.

CHAPTER EIGHT

1. Quoted in J. D. Legge, *Sukarno: A Political Biography* (New York: Praeger, 1972), 341.

2. Benda and Larkin, *World of Southeast Asia*, 192–193.

3. Quoted in Zainuddin, *Short History*, 202.

4. Robert J. McMahon, ed., *Major Problems in the History of the Vietnam War: Documents and Essays* (Lexington, Mass.: D.C. Heath, 1990), 32.

5. Quoted in Joseph Buttinger, *Vietnam: A Political History* (New York: Praeger, 1968), 180.

6. Quoted in William J. Duiker, *Ho Chi Minh: A Life* (New York: Hyperion, 2000), 45.

7. Quoted in David Marr, "Vietnamese Historical Reassessment, 1900–1944," in Reid and Marr, *Perceptions of Past*, 338.

8. Quoted in Trager, *Burma*, 53–54.

9. Quoted in Chris Baker and Pasuk Phongpaichit, *A History of Thailand* (New York: Cambridge University Press, 2005), 112.

10. Quoted in Soren Ivarsson, "Towards a New Laos: *Lao Nhay* and the Campaign for 'National Awakening' in Laos, 1941–45," in *Laos: Culture and Society*, ed. Grant Evans (Bangkok: Silkworm Books, 1999), 67.

11. Quoted in Vickers, *Modern Indonesia*, 85.

12. Quoted in Paul Kratoska, *The Japanese Occupation of Malaya, 1941–1945* (Honolulu: University of Hawai'i Press, 1997), 115.

13. Quoted in Bob Reece, *Masa Jepun: Sarawak Under the Japanese, 1941–1945* (Kuching: Sarawak Literary Society, 1998), 105.

14. Sitor Simumorang, quoted in *From Surabaya to Armageddon: Indonesian Short Stories*, ed. Harry Aveling (Singapore: Heinemann, 1976), vii.

15. Quoted in Legge, *Sukarno*, 175.

16. Quoted in James S. Olson and Randy Roberts, *Where the Domino Fell: America and Vietnam, 1945–2006*, 5th ed. (New York: Brandywine, 2006), 15.

17. Quoted in Bernhard Dahm, *Sukarno and the Struggle for Indonesian Independence* (Ithaca, N.Y.: Cornell University Press, 1969), 274.

18. Benda and Larkin, *Worlds of Southeast Asia*, 270–273.

19. Quoted in Jean Lacouture, *Ho Chi Minh: A Political Biography* (New York: Vintage, 1968), 119.

20. Quoted in George Donelson Moss, *Vietnam: An American Ordeal*, 4th ed. (Upper Saddle River, N.J.: Prentice-Hall, 2002), 40.

21. Quoted in John Cady, *A History of Modern Burma* (Ithaca, N.Y.: Cornell University Press, 1958), 44.

22. Mochtar Lubis, *Road with No End*, trans. Anthony Johns (Chicago: Henry Regnery, 1968), 9.

23. From Idrus, "Surabaya," in Aveling, *From Surabaya*, 13.

CHAPTER NINE

1. Quoted in Anthony Johns, "Introduction," in Lubis, *Road with No End*, p. 4.

2. Quoted in Stanley Karnow, *Vietnam: A History*, rev. ed. (New York: Penguin, 1991), 146.

3. Quoted in Duiker, *Ho Chi Minh*, 379.

4. Quoted in Lacouture, *Ho Chi Minh*, 170.

5. Quoted in Olson and Roberts, *Where the Domino*, 22.

6. John Foster Dulles, quoted in Olson and Roberts, *Where the Domino*, 27.

7. Quoted in Thomas G. Paterson et al., *American Foreign Policy: A History Since 1900*, 3rd rev. ed. (Lexington, Mass.: D.C. Heath, 1991), 553.

8. Quoted in Arlene Eisen Bergman, *Women of Vietnam*, rev. ed. (San Francisco: Peoples Press, 1975), 123.

9. Quoted in Neil L. Jamieson, *Understanding Vietnam* (Berkeley: University of California Press, 1993), 290.

10. Quoted in Hugh Higgins, *Vietnam*, 2nd ed. (London: Heinemann, 1982), 80.

11. "A Relative Thing," in *Vietnam Voices: Perspectives on the War Years, 1941–1982*, comp. John Clark Pratt (New York: Penguin, 1984), 647–648.

12. Quoted in Legge, *Sukarno*, 342.

13. Aveling, *From Surabaya*, 72.

14. Doreen Fernandez, "Mass Culture and Cultural Policy: The Philippine Experience," *Philippine Studies* 37 (4th Quarter, 1980): 492.

15. Hernandez, *Rice Grains*, 31.

16. Quoted in Kevin Hewison, "The Monarchy and Democratization," in *Political Change in Thailand: Democracy and Participation,* ed. Kevin Hewison (New York: Routledge, 1997), 64.

17. Quoted in Robert S. Griffin, "Notes on the Thai Student Revolution," *Southeast Asia: An International Quarterly* 3, no. 4 (Fall 1974): 1037.

18. Quoted in Katherine A. Bowie, ed., *Voices from the Countryside: The Short Stories of Samruam Singh* (Madison: Center for Southeast Asian Studies, University of Wisconsin, 1991), 17.

19. Quoted in Fred R. Von Der Mehden, *South-East Asia, 1930–1970: The Legacy of Colonialism and Nationalism* (New York: W. W. Norton, 1974), 71.

20. Quoted in Richard Butwell, *U Nu of Burma* (Stanford, Calif.: Stanford University Press, 1963), 250.

21. Quoted in Yong Mun Cheong, "The Political Structures of the Independent States," in Nicholas Tarling, *The Cambridge History of Southeast Asia* (New York: Cambridge University Press, 1992), 2:446.

22. Quoted in Virginia Matheson Hooker, *Writing a New Society: Social Change Through the Novel in Malay* (Honolulu: University of Hawai'i Press, 2000), 263.

23. Sri Delima, *As I Was Passing* (Kuala Lumpur: Berita Publishing, 1976), 64–66.

CHAPTER TEN

1. Ian Brown and Joan Davis, eds. and trans., *On the Vernanda: A Bilingual Anthology of Modern Indonesian Poetry* (New York: Cambridge University Press, 1995), 113, 115, 117, 119.

2. David M. E. Roskies, ed., *Black Clouds over the Isle of the Gods and Other Modern Indonesian Short Stories* (Armonk, N.Y.: M. E. Sharpe, 1997), 97.

3. Quoted in Anton Lucas, "Land Disputes in Indonesia: Some Current Perspectives," *Indonesia* 53 (April 1992): 34–35.

4. Quoted in Bill Frederick, "Rhoma Irama and the Dangdut Style: Some Aspects of Contemporary Indonesian Popular Culture," *Indonesia* 34 (October 1982): 119, 121.

5. "Defense of the Student Movement: Documents from Recent Trials," *Indonesia* 27 (April 1979): 12–13.

6. Quoted in Michael R.J. Vatikiotis, *Indonesian Politics Under Suharto: Order, Development and Pressure for Change* (London: Routledge, 1993), 114.

7. Quoted in Sterling Seagrave, *The Marcos Dynasty* (New York: Fawcett Columbine, 1988), 189.

8. Quoted in David G. Timberman, *A Changeless Land: Continuity and Change in Philippine Politics* (New York: M. E. Sharpe, 1991), xi.

9. Quoted in Robin Broad and John Cavenaugh, *Plundering Paradise: The Struggle for the Environment in the Philippines* (Berkeley: University of California Press, 1993), xvii.

10. Quoted in Craig A. Lockard, *Dance of Life: Popular Music and Politics in Southeast Asia* (Honolulu: University of Hawai'i Press, 1998), 146.

11. Quoted in Pasuk Phongoaichit and Chris Baker, *Thailand: Economy and Politics* (Kuala Lumpur: Oxford University Press, 1995), 79.

12. Quoted in ibid., 413–415.

13. Wenk, *Thai Literature*, 95–98.

14. Quoted in Lockard, *Dance of Life*, 251.

15. Quoted in ibid., 255.

16. Quoted in ibid., 254.

17. John Balaban and Nguyen Qui Duc, eds., *Vietnam: A Traveler's Literary Companion* (San Francisco: Whereabout Press, 1996), 152–153.

18. Dith Pran, comp., *Children of Cambodia's Killing Fields: Memoirs by Survivors* (New Haven, Conn.: Yale University Press, 1997), 23–24.

19. Kathleen Newland and Kamala Chandrakirana Soedjatmoko, eds., *Transforming Humanity: The Visionary Writings of Soedjatmoko* (West Hartford, Conn.: Kumarian Press, 1994), 36.

CHAPTER ELEVEN

1. Newland and Soedjatmoko, *Transforming Humanity*, 186–187.

2. Quoted in Norman Owen, "Economic and Social Change," in Tarling, *Cambridge History*, 2:512.

3. Quoted in Aida Rivera Ford, "Southeasterly Views of Popular Culture," in *Rediscovery: Essays in Philippine Life and Culture*, ed. Cynthia Nogales Lumbera and Teresita Gimenez-Maceda (Manila: National Book Store, 1982), 2:225.

4. Alisa Zainu'ddin, *Lagu-Lagu Indonesia/ Songs of Indonesia* (South Yarra, Vic.: Heinemann, 1969), 34–35.

Further Reading

ATLASES

Cribb, Robert. *Historical Atlas of Indonesia*. Honolulu: University of Hawai'i Press, 2000.

GENERAL WORKS AND HISTORIES

Boomgaard, Peter, ed. *A World of Water: Rain, Rivers and Seas in Southeast Asian Histories*. Leiden, the Netherlands: KITLV Press, 2007.

Brown, Ian. *Economic History in South-East Asia, c. 1830–1980*. New York: Oxford University Press, 1997.

Burling, Robbins. *Hill Farms and Padi Fields: Life in Mainland Southeast Asia*. Tempe, Ariz.: Program for Southeast Asian Studies, Arizona State University, 1992.

Federspiel, Howard M. *Sultans, Shamans, and Saints: Islam and Muslims in Southeast Asia*. Honolulu: University of Hawai'i Press, 2007.

Heidhues, Mary Somers. *Southeast Asia: A Concise History*. London: Thames & Hudson, 2000.

Keyes, Charles F. *The Golden Peninsula: Culture and Adaptation in Mainland Southeast Asia*. Honolulu: University of Hawai'i Press, 1995.

Lester, Robert C. *Theravada Buddhism in Southeast Asia*. Ann Arbor, Mich.: University of Michigan Press, 1973.

Lieberman, Victor. *Strange Parallels: Southeast Asia in Global Context, c. 800–1830*. Cambridge, U.K.: Cambridge University Press, 2003.

Neher, Clark D. *Southeast Asia: Crossroads of the World*. DeKalb: Center for Southeast Asian Studies, Northern Illinois University, 2000.

Osborne, Milton. *Southeast Asia: An Illustrated Introductory History*. 8th ed. Sydney: Allen & Unwin, 2000.

Owen, Norman, ed. *The Emergence of Modern Southeast Asia: A New History*. Honolulu: University of Hawai'i Press, 2005.

Piper, Jacqueline M. *Rice in South-East Asia: Cultures and Landscapes*. New York: Oxford University Press, 1993.

SarDesai, D. R. *Southeast Asia: Past and Present*. 5th ed. Boulder, Colo.: Westview, 2003.

SarDesai, D. R., ed. *Southeast Asian History: Essential Readings*. Boulder, Colo.: Westview, 2006.

Steinberg, David J. et. al. *In Search of Southeast Asia: A Modern History*. Revised ed. Honolulu: University of Hawai'i Press, 1987.

Swearer, Donald K. *The Buddhist World of Southeast Asia*. Albany: State University of New York Press, 1995.

Tarling, Nicholas, ed. *The Cambridge History of Southeast Asia*. 2 vols. New York: Cambridge University Press, 1992.

Tarling, Nicholas. *Southeast Asia: A Modern History*. New York: Oxford University Press, 2001.

NATIONAL AND ETHNIC HISTORIES

Abinales, Patricio N., and Donna J. Amoroso. *State and Society in the Philippines*. Lanham, Md.: Rowman and Littlefield, 2005.

Andaya, Barbara Watson, and Leonard Andaya. *A History of Malaysia*. 2nd ed. Honolulu: University of Hawai'i Press, 2001.

Baker, Chris, and Pasuk Phongpaichit. *A History of Thailand*. New York: Cambridge University Press, 2005.

Brown, Colin. *A Short History of Indonesia: The Unlikely Nation?* Crows Nest, N.S.W., Australia: Allen and Unwin, 2003.

Chandler, David P. *A History of Cambodia*. 4th ed. Boulder, Colo.: Westview, 2007.

Hooker, Virginia Matheson. *A Short History of Malaysia*. Crows Nest, N.S.W., Australia: Allen and Unwin, 2003.

Karnow, Stanley. *Vietnam: A History*. Revised ed. New York: Penguin, 1992.

Mabbett, Ian, and David Chandler. *The Khmers*. Malden, Mass.: Blackwell, 1995.

Myint-U, Thant. *The Making of Modern Burma*. New York: Cambridge University Press, 2001.

Quincy, Keith. *Hmong: History of a People*. Cheney: Eastern Washington University Press, 1995.

Ricklefs, M. C. *A History of Modern Indonesia Since c. 1300*. 3rd ed. Stanford, Calif.: Stanford University Press, 2002.

SarDesai, D. R. *Vietnam: Past and Present*. 4th ed. Boulder, Colo.: Westview, 2005.

Steinberg, David J. *The Philippines: A Singular and a Plural Place*. 4th ed. Boulder, Colo.: Westview, 2000.

Stuart-Fox, Martin. *A History of Laos*. New York: Cambridge University Press, 1997.

Taylor, Jean Gelman. *Indonesia: Peoples and Histories*. New Haven: Yale University Press, 2003.

Trocki, Carl A. *Singapore: Wealth, Power and the Culture of Control*. New York: Routledge, 2006.

Vickers, Adrian. *A History of Modern Indonesia*. New York: Cambridge University Press, 2005.

Woodside, Alexander B. *Community and Revolution in Modern Vietnam*. Boston: Houghton Mifflin, 1976.

Wyatt, David K. *Thailand: A Short History*. 2nd ed. New Haven, Conn.: Yale University Press, 2003.

PREMODERN ERAS

Andaya, Barbara Watson. *The Flaming Womb: Repositioning Women in Early Modern Southeast Asia*. Honolulu: University of Hawai'i Press, 2006.

Andaya, Leonard Y. *Leaves of the Same Tree: Trade and Ethnicity in the Straits of Melaka*. Honolulu: University of Hawai'i Press, 2008.

Aung-Thwin, Michael. *Pagan: The Origins of Modern Burma*. Honolulu: University of Hawai'i Press, 1985.

Bellwood, Peter. *Prehistory of the Indo-Malaysian Archipelago*. Revised ed. Honolulu: University of Hawai'i Press, 1997.

Charnvit, Kasetsiri. *The Rise of Ayudhya: A History of Siam in the Fourteenth and Fifteenth Centuries*. New York: Oxford University Press, 1976.

Chaudhuri, K. N. *Trade and Civilisation in the Indian Ocean: An Economic History from the Rise of Islam to 1750*. New York: Cambridge University Press, 1985.

Hall, Kenneth R. *Maritime Trade and State Development in Early Southeast Asia*. Honolulu: University of Hawai'i Press, 1985.

Higham, Charles. *The Archaeology of Mainland Southeast Asia*. Cambridge: Cambridge University Press, 1989.

Higham, Charles. *The Civilization of Angkor*. Berkeley: University of California Press, 2002.

Hoyt, Sarnia Hayes. *Old Malacca*. New York: Oxford University Press, 1993.

Junker, Laura Lee. *Raiding, Trading, and Feasting: The Political Economy of Philippine Chiefdoms*. Honolulu: University of Hawai'i Press, 1999.

O'Reilly, Dougald J. W. *Early Civilizations of Southeast Asia*. Lanham, Md.: AltaMira, 2007.

Reid, Anthony, ed. *Southeast Asia in the Early Modern Era: Trade, Power, and Belief*. Ithaca, N.Y.: Cornell University Press, 1993.

Shaffer, Lynda Norene. *Maritime Southeast Asia to 1500*. Armonk, N.Y.: M. E. Sharpe, 1996.

Simms, Peter, and Sanda Simms. *The Kingdoms of Laos: Six Hundred Years of History*. Richmond, Surrey, U.K.: Curzon, 1999.

Taylor, Keith Weller. *The Birth of Vietnam*. Berkeley: University of California Press, 1983.

Woodside, Alexander B. *Vietnam and the Chinese Model: A Comparative Study of Vietnamese and Chinese Government in the First Half of the Nineteenth Century*. Cambridge, Mass.: Harvard University Press, 1971.

WESTERN EXPANSION AND THE COLONIAL ERA

Adas, Michael. *The Burma Delta: Economic Development and Social Change on an Asian Rice Frontier, 1852–1941*. Madison: University of Wisconsin Press, 1974.

Andaya, Leonard Y. *The World of Maluku: Eastern Indonesia in the Early Modern Period*. Honolulu: University of Hawai'i Press, 1993.

Elson, R. E. *Village Java Under the Cultivation System*. Sydney: Allen and Unwin, 1994.

Gullick, J. M. *Malay Society in the Late Nineteenth Century*. New York: Oxford University Press, 1989.

Karnow, Stanley. *In Our Image: America's Empire in the Philippines*. New York: Ballantine, 1989.

Larkin, John A. *Sugar and the Origins of Modern Philippine Society*. Berkeley: University of California Press, 1993.

Lim Teck Ghee. *Peasants and Their Agricultural Economy in Colonial Malaya, 1874–1941*. New York: Oxford University Press, 1977.

Lockard, Craig A. *From Kampung to City: A Social History of Kuching, Malaysia, 1820–1970*. Athens, Ohio: Center for Southeast Asian Studies, Ohio University, 1987.

McCoy, Alfred W., and Ed. C. De Jesus, eds. *Philippine Social History: Global Trade and Local Transformations*. Honolulu: University of Hawaii Press, 1982.

Ngo Vinh Long. *Before the Revolution: The Vietnamese Peasants under the French*. Cambridge, Mass.: MIT Press, 1973.

Phelan, John Leddy. *The Hispanization of the Philippines: Spanish Aims and Filipino Responses, 1565–1700*. Madison: University of Wisconsin Press, 1967.

Reid, Anthony, *Southeast Asia in the Age of Commerce, 1450–1680*. 2 vols. New Haven, Conn.: Yale University Press, 1988–1993.

Wyatt, David K. *The Politics of Reform in Thailand: Education in the Reign of Chulalongkorn*. New Haven: Yale University Press, 1969.

NATIONALISM AND REVOLUTION

Bradley, Mark P. *Imagining Vietnam and America: The Making of Postcolonial Vietnam, 1919–1950*. Chapel Hill: University of North Carolina Press, 2000.

Duiker, William J. *Ho Chi Minh: A Life*. New York: Hyperion, 2000.

Duiker, William J. *The Rise of Nationalism in Vietnam, 1900–1941*. Ithaca, N.Y.: Cornell University Press, 1976.

Edwards, Penny. *Cambodge: The Cultivation of a Nation, 1860–1945.* Honolulu: University of Hawai'i Press, 2007.

Huynh Kim Khanh. *Vietnamese Communism, 1925–1945.* Ithaca, N.Y.: Cornell University Press, 1982.

Marr, David G. *Vietnamese Anticolonialism, 1885–1925.* Berkeley: University of California Press, 1971.

McHale, Shawn F. *Print and Power: Confucianism, Communism, and Buddhism in the Making of Modern Vietnam.* Honolulu: University of Hawai'i Press, 2004.

Milner, Anthony. *The Invention of Politics in Colonial Malaya: Contesting Nationalism and the Expansion of the Public Sphere.* New York: Cambridge University, 1994.

Roff, William R. *The Origins of Malay Nationalism.* 2nd ed. New York: Oxford University Press, 1994.

SOUTHEAST ASIA SINCE WORLD WAR II

Beeson, Mark, ed. *Contemporary Southeast Asia: Regional Dynamics, National Differences.* New York: Palgrave, 2004.

Bertrand, Jacques. *Nationalism and Ethnic Conflict in Indonesia.* New York: Cambridge University Press, 2004.

Blackburn, Susan. *Women and the State in Modern Indonesia.* New York: Cambridge University Press, 2004.

Boudreau, Vincent. *Resisting Dictatorship: Repression and Protest in Southeast Asia.* New York: Cambridge University Press, 2004.

Bradley, Mark Philip, and Marilyn B. Young. *Making Sense of the Vietnam Wars: Local, National, and Transnational Perspectives.* New York: Oxford University Press, 2008.

Chalmers, Ian. *Indonesia: An Introduction to Contemporary Traditions.* New York: Oxford University Press, 2006.

Chandler, David P. *The Tragedy of Cambodian History: Politics, War, and Revolution Since 1945.* New Haven: Yale University Press, 1991.

Cheah, Boon Kheng. *Malaysia: The Making of a Nation.* Singapore: Institute of Southeast Asian Studies, 2002.

Duiker, William J. *Sacred War: Nationalism and Revolution in a Divided Vietnam.* New York: McGraw-Hill, 1995.

Elliott, David W. P. *The Vietnamese War: Revolution and Social Change in the Mekong Delta, 1930–1975.* Concise ed. Armonk, N.Y.: M. E. Sharpe, 2007.

Elson, Robert. *Suharto: A Political Biography.* Cambridge, U.K.: Cambridge University Press, 2002.

Hefner, Robert W., ed. *The Politics of Multiculturalism: Pluralism and Citizenship in Malaysia, Singapore, and Indonesia.* Honolulu: University of Hawai'i Press, 2001.

Herring, George C. *America's Longest War: The United States and Vietnam, 1950–1975.* 4th ed. New York: McGraw-Hill, 2002.

Hewison, Kevin, ed. *Political Change in Thailand: Democracy and Participation.* New York: Routledge, 1997.

Kingsbury, Damien. *The Politics of Indonesia.* 3rd ed. New York: Oxford University Press, 2005.

Kingsbury, Damien. *South-East Asia: A Political Profile.* 2nd ed. New York: Oxford University Press, 2005.

Lawrence, Mark Atwood. *The Vietnam War: A Concise International History.* New York: Oxford University Press, 2008.

Lockard, Craig A. *Dance of Life: Popular Music and Politics in Southeast Asia.* Honolulu: University of Hawai'i Press, 1998.

McMahon, Robert J. *The Limits of Empire: The United States and Southeast Asia Since World War II.* New York: Columbia University Press, 1999.

Milne, R. S., and Diane Mauzy. *Malaysian Politics Under Mahathir.* New York: Routledge, 1999.

Olson, James S., and Randy Roberts. *Where the Domino Fell: America and Vietnam, 1945–2006.* 5th ed. St. James, N.Y.: Brandywine, 2006.

Reid, Robert H., and Eileen Guerrero. *Corazon Aquino and the Brushfire Revolution.* Baton Rouge: Louisiana State University Press, 1995.

Rodan, Garry, et al., eds. *The Political Economy of South-East Asia: Markets, Power, and Contestation.* 3rd ed. New York: Oxford University Press, 2006.

Stuart-Fox, Martin. *Laos: Politics, Economics and Society.* Boulder, Colo.: Lynne Rienner, 1986.

Van Estrik, Penny, ed. *Women of Southeast Asia.* DeKalb: Center for Southeast Asian Studies, Northern Illinois University, 1996.

Warner, Roger. *Shooting at the Moon: The Story of America's Clandestine War in Laos.* South Royalton, Vt.: Steerforth, 1996.

Young, Marilyn. *The Vietnam Wars, 1945–1990.* New York: HarperCollins, 1991.

Young, Marilyn, John J. Fitzgerald, and A. Tom Grunfeld. *The Vietnam War: A History in Documents.* New York: Oxford University Press, 2002.

Web Sites

East and Southeast Asia: An Annotated Directory of Internet Resources
bulldog2.redlands.edu/Dept/AsianStudies Dept/index.html
> A set of links to sites containing general information, essays, research institutes, and other useful material from Southeast Asia and elsewhere.

InfoTree: Information Gateway
infotree.library.ohiou.edu
> The International Studies section of this Ohio University–based metasite includes links to many archives, organizations, scholarly materials, and data sources, many from Southeast Asian sources.

Southeast Asia Guide
www.library.wisc.edu/guides/seasia
> Maintained by the University of Wisconsin–Madison, this site offers links to newspapers, databases, libraries and collections, and centers for the study of Southeast Asia throughout the world.

Southeast Asian Images and Texts
digital.library.wisc.edu/1711.dl/SEAiT
> Links to collections of primary sources, including images, maintained by the University of Wisconsin–Madison.

Vietnam: Yesterday and Today
servercc.oakton.edu/~wittman/warlinks.htm
> A student-oriented site emphasizing military matters from a U.S. perspective, offering bibliographies and links to both primary and secondary material.

Virtual Religion Index
www.virtualreligion.net/vri
> An index to Web resources for religious studies research. This site contains essays and primary texts about Buddhism, Hinduism, and Islam.

The Wars for Vietnam: 1945 to 1975
vietnam.vassar.edu
> Created for a seminar at Vassar College taught by Robert Brigham, the first U.S. scholar to have access to the Vietnamese archives on the war, this site presents primary sources on the U.S.-Vietnam War from both Vietnamese and U.S. government archives, as well as essays and studies.

WWW Virtual Library: Asian Studies
vlib.org/AsianStudies
> A vast metasite maintained at Australian National University, with links to hundreds of sites containing primary and secondary sources, many of them on Southeast Asia.

Acknowledgments

This book is the result of a career spent studying, teaching, and writing about Southeast Asian and world history. I began seriously thinking about Southeast Asia in the early 1960s while an exchange student at Chung Chi College, now part of the Chinese University of Hong Kong, where I met undergraduates from Malaysia, Singapore, and Thailand. I pursued the academic study of Southeast Asia while a graduate student of the University of Hawaii, where I had the opportunity to work with pioneering scholars such as Walter Vella, Robert Van Niel, and Daniel Kwok. I am grateful to the East-West Center for funding my M.A. studies and my first research sojourn in Southeast Asia, mostly spent in Sarawak under the auspices of the Sarawak Museum. My Ph.D. studies in Southeast Asian and comparative world history at the University of Wisconsin-Madison allowed me to work with another set of outstanding scholars, among them Philip Curtin, Fred Von Der Mehden, Tonggoel Siagian, Dan Doeppers, Jim Scott, and especially John Smail. A grant from Wisconsin enabled me to do Ph.D. research in Sarawak. During my career teaching Asian, African, and world history at the University of Bridgeport, SUNY-Stony Brook, SUNY-Buffalo and, since 1975, at the University of Wisconsin–Green Bay, I have benefited greatly from my colleagues and students. The Fulbright-Hays program sponsored two year-long appointments at the University of Malaya, first in the History Department and then at the Institute of Advanced Study, allowing me to learn much from the Malaysian academic community.

I would also like to acknowledge the inspiration from the Southeast Asian Studies community worldwide, especially my colleagues and friends in the Association for Asian Studies and the Malaysia-Singapore-Brunei Studies Group. I cannot mention everyone who has provided intellectual stimulation, scholarly insight, and personal support, but would single out for special thanks Jack Larkin, Guy Gran, Paul Rodell, Rich O'Connor, Marc Jason Gilbert, Lynda Shaffer, Bill Frederick, Norman Owen, John Whitmore, David Chandler, Michael Aung Thwin, Ed Moise, Barbara and Leonard Andaya, Carl Trocki, Tony Reid, Thongchai Winichakul, Al McCoy, Don Emmerson, Clark Neher, Jean Taylor, Laurie Sears, Jim Rush, Norm Parmer, Ron Provencher, John Lent, Judy Nagata, Sharon Carstens, Don Nonini, Michael Leigh, Edwin Lee, Paul Kratoska, James Chin, Khoo Kay Kim, Steve Milne, Diane Mauzy, Kent and Lian Mulliner, Ben Kirkvliet, Greg Felker, Bridget Walsh, Meredith Weiss,

Loh Wei Leng, Lufti Abas, Sanib Said, and the late Bruce Fenner. This book might not have been possible without my participation in the World History Association, whose members have provided a true community of teacher-scholars. I also want to thank the editors of this series, Anand Yang and Bonnie Smith, and my Oxford University Press editor, Nancy Toff, for their support of this project. Karen Fein of Oxford University Press and several anonymous readers provided valuable suggestions for the manuscript. Finally, my wife, Kathy, has, as always, been my biggest booster and tolerated the ever growing piles of books and other research materials cluttering up our family room.

—Craig A. Lockard

Index

Page numbers in **bold** indicate illustrations.

feudalism, 75
Fiji, 16, 17
films, 203–4
First Indochina War, 153–54, 157
fishing, 13, 18
five pillars of Islam, 50, 136
Flores, 5, 6
forced labor, 119
France
  August Revolution, 148–50
  Ayutthaya kingdom, **56**
  boat people, 192
  and Cambodia, 107, 160
  Can Vuong rebels, 141
  Cao Daiism, 126
  Chakri dynasty, 110
  civilizing mission, 103
  and colonialism, 118, **120**
  colonization, 78
  diplomacy, **58**
  Federation of Indochina, 104–6, **105**
  First Indochina War, 153–54, 157, 199
  French Communist Party, 140
  French Indochina, 131
  French Socialist Party, 140
  king Narai, 90
  and Laos, 107, 144, 159–60
  missionaries, 90
  Paris Peace Conference, 140
  pro-Nazi government, 145
  and Siam, 90
  and Sihanouk, 162
  Viet Minh, 141, 147–48
  and Vietnam, 90–91, 93, 102–6, 139–41
Franks, 37
free speech, 182
free thought, 152
free trade, 188
French Indochina, 131
Fujian, 91, 130
Funan Kingdom, 25–26, **27**, 33, 35

Gajah Mada, 45
galleon trade, 81–82, 92
gambling, 88, 123, 133
gamelan orchestras, **72**, 133
gangster movies, 133
gender equality. *See also* women's place
  Angkor Kingdom, 40–41
  animism, 19
  bilateral kinship, 32
  Buddhism, 23
  Chams, 28
  Java, 71
  lowland/highland cultures, 12
  matrilineal descent, 28, 32, 40–41
  Pagan Kingdom, 43–44
  polygamy, 103
  Siam society, 58

  Southeast Asia, 32
  Thailand, 8
"The General Retires," 192
Geneva, 154
genocide, 194–96
Germany, 112, 145
The Glass Palace Chronicle, 108–9
globalization, 1, 65, 198, 205
Goa, 79
god-kings
  Angkor Kingdom, 40
  Hindu-Javanese, 45
  Java, 37
  Sihanouk, 204
  Theravada Buddhism, 36
gold
  Borneo, 118
  cash crops, 121
  guns, goons, and gold, 164
  Hindu-Javanese Kingdom, 45
  Malaysia, 98
  maritime trade, 18, 31, 63
  Melaka, 69
  Philippine Islands, 79
  Sailendra dynasty, 31
  trade, 119
Golden Age
  end of, 48, 52, 79
  great tradition and little tradition, 37
  Khmers, 39–42
  kingdoms, **38**
  Malaysia, 69
  maritime trade, 198
  Theravada Buddhism, 36
  Vietnam, **38**, 47
golden peninsula, 2, 18
Golkar, 173
Gowa, 64, 88
"Grains," 8
Great Depression
  impact on Java, 94
  impact on Southeast Asia, 123–24
  Indochinese Communist Party (ICP), 141
  Japanese economy, 145
  Saya San Rebellion, 126
  Siamese nationalism, 143
  taxes, 124
great tradition, 37
Greeks, 18
Guangdong, 130
guerrilla warfare
  Hukbalahap rebellion, 164
  under Japanese occupation, 147
  Malayan Communist Party, 167
  Philippines, 116, 147
  Thailand, 165
  Vietnam, 104
guilds, 42
Gujaratis, 68, 70

and the Dutch, 85
Gupta Empire, 21
Indo-European, 17
Islam, 51, 64
Khmer writing system, 54
and Malaysia, 121, 167
maritime trade, 15, 20–21, 31, 33, 63
and Melaka, 68
migrations, 89
nationalism, rise of, 135
Non-Aligned Movement, 163
North Indian Sanskrit, 22
Penang Island, 97–98
Portuguese empire, 77
South Indian Pallava, 22
and Southeast Asia, 2, 21, 34
spice trade, 17
Straits Settlements, 21, 98, 100
Sunnis, 50
Theravada Buddhism, 22–23
trading communities, 129
Vayu Parana, 20
Indian Ocean
and the Dutch, 79
maritime trade, 17, 63–64, **66**, 79
and Melaka, 67
and Portugal, 77, 79
Indianization. *See also* India
Chams, 26
China, 21, 26
Java, 21–22, 45, 71
Khmers, 21
Mon people, 21
Southeast Asia, 21–22, 35
Theravada Buddhism, 49
Indios, 83
indirect rule, 119
Indochinese Communist Party (ICP), 140–41
Indo-European, 17
Indonesia. *See also* Acheh; Batavia
Al Qaeda, 177
alternative schools, 132
ASEAN, 196
Asian economic collapse, 176
Austronesians, 13–15, 17
Batavia, 97
and capitalism, 97
cash crops, 174
and China, 88, 130, 163, 176
Christianity, 176–77
coffee, 87, 119
communism, 163, 205
Congress of Indonesian Women, 137
corruption, 173–75
creation of, 97
cuisine, 88
cultural diversity, 88–89
democracy, 97, 162, 177

direct rule, 119
and the Dutch, 73, 85–86, 148, 151, 199
economic development, 200
environmental damage, 174
Ethical Policy, 97
ethnic diversity, 173
ethnic division, 162, 176–77
film making, 203
geography of, 2
globalization, 198
Hindu-Javanese Kingdom, 45
independence, 148, 162, **172**
indirect rule, 119
"Indonesia, Land of Robbers," 174
Indonesian Archipelago, 62–63
Indonesian Communist Party (PKI), 136–37, 163
Indonesian Nationalist Party (PNI), 135, 137–39
Indonesian Revolution, 151–53
Intje Hassan, 202
Islam, 65, 70, 91, 163, 175
Kartini (ibu), **129**
kroncong music, 133
languages, 88, 97, 136
life expectancy, 73, 174
literacy, 131, 174
literature, 133–34, 151
maritime trade, 15, **16**, 17, 63
massacres, 163
and Melaka, 68
middle class, 174, 176
migrations into, 13
military rule, 169
mining, 174
music, 174–75, 203
nationalism, 135, 138, 147–48, 152
New Order, 173–77
Non-Aligned Movement, 163
PKI (Indonesian Communist Party), 163
poetry, 174, 202, 205
political organization, 163, 173, 176
population, 131, 173, 186
proverbs, 7
rebellion, 137, 140–41, 177
Sasak, **89**
slavery, 73, 86, 88
social structure, 88
Soedjatmoko, 197–98
spice trade, 17–18
Stone Age sites, 6
and Suharto, 163
and Sukarno, 162–63, 204
unity in diversity, 162
in World War II, 146
youth movements, 176
Indradevi, 41
Indravarman, 39–40
Industrial Revolution, 92, 93, 97

Mataram, 70, 86, **87**
mathematics, 21
matrilineal descent, 28, 32, 40–41
Max Havelaar, 94
McKinley, William, 115
McPhee, Colin, 133
Mecca. *See* Islam
medicine, 21
meditation, 23
Mediterranean Sea
    Greeks, 18
    maritime trade, 15, 36, 63
    Phoenicians, 22
    Suez Canal, 98
Megat Iskander Shah, 65
Megawati Soekarnoputri, 176, 204
Mekong River
    civilizing mission, 103
    Funan Kingdom, 25
    Lan Xang Kingdom, 55
    Luang Prabang, 107
    Pathet Lao, 160
    rice cultivation, 7
    settlements along, 6
    Tai people, 48
    and Vietnam, 61–62, 91
    wet-rice cultivation, 13
    Zhenla, 26
Melaka. *See also* Malaysia
    city life, 69
    cultural diversity, 131
    and the Dutch, 79, 85, 88, 97
    Golden Age, 190
    and Islam, 65–70
    languages, 68
    The Malay Annals, 68–69
    maritime trade, 17, 31, 63–64, **66**, 67–68,
        98, 198
    population, 73
    and Portugal, 75, **76**, 77–78
    Roman Catholic influences, 79
    Straits Settlements, 98
    trade, 52, 67
Melanesians, 13–16
Mesopotamia, 7, 10, 17
mestizos, **82**, 83, 112, 114
metalworking, 10–13
Mexico, 92
Micronesians, 16
middle class
    Brunei, 191
    Indonesia, 174, 176
    Malaysia, 187–88
    Siam, 143
    Singapore, 191
    in Southeast Asia, 202
    Thailand, 181–83
Middle East, 34, 36, 64, 178
Mien people, 160, 193–94

migrations
    and agriculture, 13, 18, 64
    Austronesians, **14**, 14–16, 18
    Bali, 88–89
    to Batavia, 88–89
    Burma, 37
    China, 94, 101, 111, 118, 128–29, 171
    and colonialism, 129
    Europe, 37
    Filipinos, 178
    Fujian, 130
    highlanders, 12
    Hmong, 12, 107
    Ice Ages, 5
    India, 89
    Indonesia, 13
    Javanese, 94, 96
    Khmers, 18
    Melanesians, 15–16
    Pagan Kingdom, 42
    Penang Island, 97
    to the Philippines, 82, 178
    Southeast Asia, 3, 18, 37, 169, 199–200
    Straits Settlements, 98, 100
    Tai people, 37, 48
    United States, 199–200
    Vietnam, 12, 18, 61–62
military rule
    Burma, 184–86
    in Southeast Asia, 169
    Thailand, 169, 180, 186
military technology, 75
millet, 15
Mindanao, 7, 79, 80
Mindon, 109
Ming dynasty, 62, 67
Minh Mang, 102
mining
    coolie labor, 130
    environmental damage, 171
    Indonesia, 174
    Malaysia, 34, 98
    maritime trade, 18
    obsidian, 17
    tin, 10, 100
Minister, 168
missionaries
    Burma, 109
    France, 90
    Portuguese explorations, 75
    Siam, 111
    Vietnam, 103
Miyawaddy, 108–9
modernization
    Ho Chi Minh City, **203**
    Malaysia, 187
    Muslims, 136
    Siam, 119
    in Southeast Asia, 199, 202

First Indochina War, 153–54, 157, 199
and France, 90–91, 93, 102–6, 139–41
Funan Kingdom, 25
geography of, 2
Golden Age, **38**, 47
guerrilla warfare, 104
Han dynasty, 21
Hmong migrations, 107
Ho Chi Minh Trail, 157
independence, 153, 157, **172**, 199
Indochinese Communist Party (ICP),
140–41
Interpreters of the Yellow Door, 20
invade Cambodia, 162, 195
Japanese occupation of, 141, 148, 199
Khmers, 21, 60–61, 107
Le dynasty, 62
life expectancy, 192
literacy, 192
literature, 133–34, 192
Mahayana Buddhism, 28, 35, 60
mandarins, 60, 156, 204
maritime trade, 63, **66**, 91
massacres, 104, 139
Mekong River, 61–62, 91
metalworking, 13
migrations, 12, 18, 61–62
Minh Mang, 102
Mongol invasion, 49
music, 60, 106, 157–58, 192
myths/beliefs, 18
nationalism, 29, 47, 135, 139–41, 145
Ngo Dinh Diem, 154
opium trade, 123
poetry, 6, 60–61, 200
political organization, 60
polygamy, 103
population, 28, 73, 173
poverty, 192
proverbs, 60
rebellion, 29–31, 47, 60, 62, 102, 104, 124
Rhade migrations, 12
rice cultivation, 31, 36–37
Roman Catholicism, 105, 156
rubber growing, 122
rural life, 192
self-government, 139
socialism, 192
son of heaven, 60
spice trade, 18
The Tales of Kieu, 102
Tayson Rebellion, 102
tourism, 200
Tran Hung Dao, 62
Trung Sisters, 29–30
and the United States, 114, 165, 192–93
Van Lang, 18
Viet Minh, 141
Vietnamese Nationalist Party (VNQDD), 139

in World War II, 145, 147–48
youth movements, 199
Vietnam War. *See also* Vietnam
breadth of, 1
communism, 154
deforestation, 158
Ho Chi Minh Trail, 157, 160
NLF (National Liberation Front), **158**
search and destroy missions, **158**
Second Indochina War, 156–62
Tet Offensive, **155**
tourism, 200
Vishnu, 18
Visigoths, 37
VNQDD (Vietnamese Nationalist Party), 139
volcanos, 6, 7

Wah Lau Gang, 190
Wahid, Abdurrahman, 176
warfare. See also *individual wars*
Angkor Kingdom, 40
Ayutthaya and Toungoo, 55
First Indochina War, 153
lowland/highland cultures, 13
and slavery, 58
Southeast Asia, 10, 36
Washington, DC, 118
water buffaloes, 8, 10–11, 41, 48
wayang kulit. *See* shadow puppets
(wayang kulit)
weaving, 28, 46
Western Pacific islands, 13
Western world, 135
Westernization, 131–32
wet-rice cultivation
Angkor Kingdom, 41–42
irrigation, **9**, 37
lowland/highland cultures, 12
river valleys, 8, 13
Southeast Asia, 10, 33
White Man's burden, 115
Wild Tiger Corps, 143
women's place. *See also* gender equality
Aisyah, 136
brothels, 165
Burma, 126–28, 142
Cao Daiism, 126
cigar manufacturing, 123, **125**
under colonialism, 126–28
comfort women, 146
Congress of Indonesian Women, 137
feminist movement, 127–29, 142, 189
First Indochina War, 154
and Islam, 71, 177
Javanese society, 71, 86, 94, 127
Malaysia, 188–89
Megawati Soekarnoputri, 176
Muhammadiyah, 136
as nuns, 59

women's place (*continued*)
  Philippines, 80, 83, 114, 204
  prostitutes, 183
  Siam society, 58
  Sisters of Islam, 189
  Thailand, 181–82
  3D culture, 178
  Vietnam, 60–61, 103, 157
world economy, 92, 118, 123–24
World War I, 140
World War II
  atomic bombings, 148
  Borneo, 101–2, 148
  comfort women, 146
  Indonesia, 146, 151
  industrialization, 170–71
  Japan, 102
  Java, 146
  Laos, 159
  nationalism, 144–45
  Pearl Harbor attack, 145
  Philippines, 148
  slavery, 146
  and Southeast Asia, 144–46
  Thailand, 146, 148, 186
  Viet Minh, 141, 147–48
  Vietnam, 145, 147–48
writing systems
  Khmers, 40, 54

North Indian Sanskrit, 22
Philippines, 80
Vietnam, 90–91, 103

Xavier, Francis, 78

yams, 8, 16
Yangon. *See* Rangoon
Yangzi River, 7
Yap Ah Loy, 100
Yasovarman I, 39
Yavadvipa, 20
Yijing, 23–24
yoga, 28
youth movements
  anticolonialism, 151
  Burma, 184–85
  Indonesia, 176
  Malaysia, 189
  Thailand, 165–66
  Vietnam, 199
Yudhoyono, Susilo Bambang, 176
Yugoslavia, 163
Yule, Henry, 109

Zainab Anwar, 189
Zheng He (Cheng Ho), 67
Zhenla, 27
Zhou Daguan, 39–42

The
New
Oxford
World
History

Forthcoming Titles

CHRONOLOGICAL VOLUMES
The World from 4000 to 1000 BCE
The World from 1000 BCE to 300/500 CE
The World from 300 to 1000 CE
The World from 1000 to 1500
The World from 1450 to 1700
The World in the Eighteenth Century
The World in the Nineteenth Century
The World in the Twentieth Century

THEMATIC AND TOPICAL VOLUMES
The City: A World History
Democracy: A World History
Empires: A World History
The Family: A World History
Race: A World History
Technology: A World History

GEOGRAPHICAL VOLUMES
China in World History
Russia in World History
The Silk Road in World History
South Africa in World History
South Asia in World History

LaVergne, TN USA
30 August 2010
195126LV00004B/1/P